MCSE Internet Explorer 5 For Dummies®

KV-648-842

Cheat Sheet

Customization codes

Without a ten-digit customization code issued by Microsoft, you cannot create a custom IE5 package with the IEAK. If you don't enter a valid code, the IEAK Customization wizard runs in demonstration mode only. You cannot save a customized package for distribution.

IEAK Components

Know which components make up the Internet Explorer Administration Kit:

- ✔ IEAK Customization wizard
- ✔ IEAK Profile Manager
- ✔ IEAK Connection Manager Administration Kit
- ✔ IEAK toolkit
- ✔ IEAK online help

Customization Wizard Stages

The five stages of the Customization wizard:

- ✔ Stage 1: Gathering information
- ✔ Stage 2: Specifying setup parameters
- ✔ Stage 3: Customizing setup
- ✔ Stage 4: Customizing the browser
- ✔ Stage 5: Component customization

Security zones

Internet Explorer 5 has four default security zones:

- ✔ Internet zone
- ✔ Local Intranet zone
- ✔ Trusted Sites zone
- ✔ Restricted Sites zone

Selecting the Correct Role

When you run the Internet Explorer Administration Kit (IEAK), you must select from one of three administrative roles:

- ✔ Corporate administrator
- ✔ ISP (Internet Service Provider)
- ✔ ICP/Developer (Internet Content Provider)

The features available in the IEAK vary depending on which administrative role you select.

Default Security Levels

The default security levels for Internet Explorer 5's security zones are:

- ✔ **High:** The safest, but least functional, way to browse. Less secure features are disabled. Cookies are disabled, which means that some Web sites don't work. Appropriate for sites that may have harmful content.
- ✔ **Medium:** Safe browsing and still functional. Prompts before downloading potentially unsafe content. Unsigned ActiveX controls aren't downloaded. Appropriate for most Internet sites.
- ✔ **Medium-low:** Same as Medium but without prompts. Most content is run without prompts. Unsigned ActiveX controls aren't downloaded. Appropriate for sites on your intranet.
- ✔ **Low:** Provides minimal safeguards and warning prompts. Most content downloads and runs without prompts. All active content can run. Appropriate for sites that you absolutely trust.

For Dummies®: Bestselling Book Series for Beginners

MCSE Internet Explorer 5 For Dummies®

Cheat Sheet

Windows Desktop Update

Windows Desktop Update is available in the Corporate Administrator role only. By using the IEAK Customization wizard, you can elect whether or not to install it by simply clicking Yes or No.

Windows Desktop Update isn't included in Internet Explorer 5, but corporate administrators can make it available in a custom browser package in two ways:

- ✔ If you're running Windows 98, the Windows Desktop Update is included as part of the operating system.
- ✔ If you're running Windows 95 or Windows NT 4.0, then you must install the Windows Desktop Update on your build computer *before* upgrading to Internet Explorer 5.

Messaging protocols

POP3 and IMAP are messaging protocols used for incoming e-mail servers. These protocols store e-mail messages on an ISP's (or organization's) mail server before copying or downloading the message to a mailbox when a user logs on. SMTP is a messaging protocol used for outgoing e-mail messages.

Internet Explorer 5 distribution methods

- ✔ Download
- ✔ CD-ROM
- ✔ Multiple floppy disks
- ✔ Single floppy disk
- ✔ Flat
- ✔ Single-disk branding

Upgrading from Netscape

Internet Explorer 5 automatically detects and imports cookies, bookmarks, and proxy settings from installed Netscape browsers.

For Dummies®: Bestselling Book Series for Beginners

MCSE
Internet
Explorer 5

FOR

DUMMIES®

MCSE
Internet
Explorer 5
FOR
DUMMIES®

by Marcia Loughry, MCSE

IDG
BOOKS
WORLDWIDE

IDG Books Worldwide, Inc.
An International Data Group Company

Foster City, CA ◆ Chicago, IL ◆ Indianapolis, IN ◆ New York, NY

MCSE Internet Explorer 5 For Dummies®

Published by
IDG Books Worldwide, Inc.
An International Data Group Company
919 E. Hillsdale Blvd.
Suite 400
Foster City, CA 94404
www.idgbooks.com (IDG Books Worldwide Web site)
www.dummies.com (Dummies Press Web site)

Library of Congress Catalog Card No.: 99-66493

ISBN: 0-7645-0522-X

Printed in the United States of America

10 9 8 7 6 5 4 3 2 1

1O/SQ/QU/QQ/IN

Distributed in the United States by IDG Books Worldwide, Inc.

Distributed by CDG Books Canada Inc. for Canada; by Transworld Publishers Limited in the United Kingdom; by IDG Norge Books for Norway; by IDG Sweden Books for Sweden; by IDG Books Australia Publishing Corporation Pty. Ltd. for Australia and New Zealand; by TransQuest Publishers Pte Ltd. for Singapore, Malaysia, Thailand, Indonesia, and Hong Kong; by Gotop Information Inc. for Taiwan; by ICG Muse, Inc. for Japan; by Intersoft for South Africa; by Eyrolles for France; by International Thomson Publishing for Germany, Austria and Switzerland; by Distribuidora Cuspide for Argentina; by LR International for Brazil; by Galileo Libros for Chile; by Ediciones ZETA S.C.R. Ltda. for Peru; by WS Computer Publishing Corporation, Inc., for the Philippines; by Contemporanea de Ediciones for Venezuela; by Express Computer Distributors for the Caribbean and West Indies; by Micronesia Media Distributor, Inc. for Micronesia; by Chips Computadoras S.A. de C.V. for Mexico; by Editorial Norma de Panama S.A. for Panama; by American Bookshops for Finland.

For general information on IDG Books Worldwide's books in the U.S., please call our Consumer Customer Service department at 800-762-2974. For reseller information, including discounts and premium sales, please call our Reseller Customer Service department at 800-434-3422.

For information on where to purchase IDG Books Worldwide's books outside the U.S., please contact our International Sales department at 317-596-5530 or fax 317-572-4002.

For consumer information on foreign language translations, please contact our Customer Service department at 1-800-434-3422, fax 317-572-4002, or e-mail rights@idgbooks.com.

For information on licensing foreign or domestic rights, please phone +1-650-653-7098.

For sales inquiries and special prices for bulk quantities, please contact our Order Services department at 800-434-3422 or write to the address above.

For information on using IDG Books Worldwide's books in the classroom or for ordering examination copies, please contact our Educational Sales department at 800-434-2086 or fax 317-572-4005.

For press review copies, author interviews, or other publicity information, please contact our Public Relations department at 650-653-7000 or fax 650-653-7500.

For authorization to photocopy items for corporate, personal, or educational use, please contact Copyright Clearance Center, 222 Rosewood Drive, Danvers, MA 01923, or fax 978-750-4470.

 is a registered trademark under exclusive license to IDG Books Worldwide, Inc. from International Data Group, Inc.

About the Author

Marcia Loughry is a Systems Architect with EDS in Dallas, Texas and a member of Women in Technology International. Marcia has been working in the client/server arena for 10 years. She attained NetWare CNA certification in 1995, received her MCSE in Windows NT 3.51 in 1997, and then completed requirements for the NT 4.0 track in 1998. Marcia became Network+ certified in 1999, CIW Foundations certified in January 2000, and plans to complete the CIW E-Commerce Professional certification in early 2000.

When not immersed in technical work, Marcia enjoys a hectic life with her son Chris, his ill-behaved border collie named Sparky, and a talkative parakeet named Peekaboo.

ABOUT IDG BOOKS WORLDWIDE

Welcome to the world of IDG Books Worldwide.

IDG Books Worldwide, Inc., is a subsidiary of International Data Group, the world's largest publisher of computer-related information and the leading global provider of information services on information technology. IDG was founded more than 30 years ago by Patrick J. McGovern and now employs more than 9,000 people worldwide. IDG publishes more than 290 computer publications in over 75 countries. More than 90 million people read one or more IDG publications each month.

Launched in 1990, IDG Books Worldwide is today the #1 publisher of best-selling computer books in the United States. We are proud to have received eight awards from the Computer Press Association in recognition of editorial excellence and three from Computer Currents' First Annual Readers' Choice Awards. Our best-selling ...For Dummies® series has more than 50 million copies in print with translations in 31 languages. IDG Books Worldwide, through a joint venture with IDG's Hi-Tech Beijing, became the first U.S. publisher to publish a computer book in the People's Republic of China. In record time, IDG Books Worldwide has become the first choice for millions of readers around the world who want to learn how to better manage their businesses.

Our mission is simple: Every one of our books is designed to bring extra value and skill-building instructions to the reader. Our books are written by experts who understand and care about our readers. The knowledge base of our editorial staff comes from years of experience in publishing, education, and journalism — experience we use to produce books to carry us into the new millennium. In short, we care about books, so we attract the best people. We devote special attention to details such as audience, interior design, use of icons, and illustrations. And because we use an efficient process of authoring, editing, and desktop publishing our books electronically, we can spend more time ensuring superior content and less time on the technicalities of making books.

You can count on our commitment to deliver high-quality books at competitive prices on topics you want to read about. At IDG Books Worldwide, we continue in the IDG tradition of delivering quality for more than 30 years. You'll find no better book on a subject than one from IDG Books Worldwide.

John Kilcullen
Chairman and CEO
IDG Books Worldwide, Inc.

Eighth Annual Computer Press Awards ≥1992

Ninth Annual Computer Press Awards ≥1993

Tenth Annual Computer Press Awards ≥1994

Eleventh Annual Computer Press Awards ≥1995

Dedication

To my son Chris, with all my love.

Author's Acknowledgments

A very special thanks to Kyle Looper and Joyce Pepple at IDG Books, who must've thought this book was on a five-year plan.

As always, heartfelt thanks to literary agent Lisa Swayne, of the Swayne Agency, for finding me and introducing me to the world of writing technical books.

Finally, thanks to the gang at work for putting up with me. You know who you are!

Publisher's Acknowledgments

We're proud of this book; please register your comments through our IDG Books Worldwide Online Registration Form located at http://my2cents.dummies.com.

Some of the people who helped bring this book to market include the following:

Acquisitions, Editorial, and Media Development

Senior Project Editor: Kyle Looper

Acquisitions Editor: Joyce Pepple

Copy Editor: Jeremy Zucker, Donna Love

Proof Editor: Teresa Artman

Technical Editor: Eric Yergensen, Sento Corporation

Permissions Editor: Carmen Krikorian

Associate Media Development Specialist: Megan Decraene

Editorial Manager: Leah P. Cameron

Media Development Manager: Heather Heath Dismore

Editorial Assistant: Beth Parlon

Production

Project Coordinator: Maridee V. Ennis

Layout and Graphics: Amy Adrian, Tracy K. Oliver, Brent Savage, Brian Torwelle, Dan Whetstine

Proofreaders: Laura Albert, Corey Bowen, Joyce Dolan, John Greenough, Marianne Santy, Charles Spencer

Indexer: Sherry Massey

Special Help
Amanda M. Foxworth

General and Administrative

IDG Books Worldwide, Inc.: John Kilcullen, CEO

IDG Books Technology Publishing Group: Richard Swadley, Senior Vice President and Publisher; Walter R. Bruce III, Vice President and Publisher; Joseph Wikert, Vice President and Publisher; Mary Bednarek, Vice President and Director, Product Development; Andy Cummings, Publishing Director, General User Group; Mary C. Corder, Editorial Director; Barry Pruett, Publishing Director

IDG Books Consumer Publishing Group: Roland Elgey, Senior Vice President and Publisher; Kathleen A. Welton, Vice President and Publisher; Kevin Thornton, Acquisitions Manager; Kristin A. Cocks, Editorial Director

IDG Books Internet Publishing Group: Brenda McLaughlin, Senior Vice President and Publisher; Sofia Marchant, Online Marketing Manager

IDG Books Production for Dummies Press: Debbie Stailey, Director of Production; Cindy L. Phipps, Manager of Project Coordination, Production Proofreading, and Indexing; Tony Augsburger, Manager of Prepress, Reprints, and Systems; Laura Carpenter, Production Control Manager; Shelley Lea, Supervisor of Graphics and Design; Debbie J. Gates, Production Systems Specialist; Robert Springer, Supervisor of Proofreading; Kathie Schutte, Production Supervisor

Dummies Packaging and Book Design: Patty Page, Manager, Promotions Marketing

◆

The publisher would like to give special thanks to Patrick J. McGovern, without whom this book would not have been possible.

◆

Contents at a Glance

Cartoons at a Glance

By Rich Tennant

page 5

page 313

page 27

page 297

page 253

page 327

page 215

page 391

page 401

Fax: 978-546-7747
E-mail: richtennant@the5thwave.com
World Wide Web: www.the5thwave.com

Table of Contents

Introduction

. . . .

*H*i! Welcome to a study guide for the Implementing and Supporting Internet Explorer 5 using the Internet Explorer Administration Kit 5 exam (Exam 70-080). If you can remember the name of the exam, you should get at least ten bonus points!

My goal with this book is to take the anxiety and stress out of preparing for the exam. I know that you're serious about your career and about Microsoft certification. So am I! Taking the exams can be stressful, so I don't think studying for them should be strictly business. Although I'll lead you through the exam objectives in a lighthearted manner, I won't take the intent of this book — passing the exam — lightly!

So please join me on a guided tour through the intricacies of the Internet Explorer Administration Kit, which I affectionately refer to as IEAK (or "eeeeek!").

How This Book Is Organized

I've divided this book into seven parts, organized according to the main topics of the exam objectives. I've also included some extra information in the final two sections of the book (The Part of Tens and the Appendixes). The parts take you through planning, installing and configuring, optimizing, and troubleshooting. I've tried to follow the order of the exam objectives (listed in Chapter 1) as closely as possible. But in some places it just made more sense to include the information elsewhere.

Part I: The Basics

Part I contains some "getting to know you" chapters. In addition to the planning objectives for the exam, you'll also find information about:

- Exam 70-080
- Test-taking tips
- Features of Internet Explorer 5

Part II: Planning

Planning is the most important aspect of the exam. The information you find in this section contains all the fundamentals. Later objectives build on this information.

Part III: Installing and Configuring

After the planning section come the basics of installing and configuring IE5. Information in this section includes:

- ✔ Identifying your organization's role
- ✔ Methods of deploying Internet Explorer 5
- ✔ Creating and maintaining an installation site

Part IV: Configuring and Managing Resource Access

The information in Part IV gets into the complexities of managing resources using the IEAK. In this part, you'll find:

- ✔ Using the IEAK Profile Manager
- ✔ Managing profiles, logon scripts, and system policies
- ✔ Configuring security zones
- ✔ Managing connection settings

Part V: Integration and Interoperability

Part V covers accessing the Internet and intranets using various methods:

- ✔ Dial-up networking
- ✔ Proxy server
- ✔ PPTP (VPN)

This part also explains the various means of installing Internet Explorer 5 using the IEAK.

Part VI: Monitoring and Optimization

Part VI covers optimizing performance settings, updating user profiles, and understanding licensing requirements. It seems that Microsoft licensing gets more and more complex! IEAK licensing has some special considerations because the product is used to deploy IE5. Obviously, who you deploy IE5 to — internal or external users — makes a big difference in how you'll report licensing.

Part VII: Troubleshooting

No Microsoft exam would be complete without a few questions on troubleshooting! Here you'll find out how to troubleshoot:

- ✔ Proxy configuration errors
- ✔ Dial-up access failures
- ✔ Network connectivity failures
- ✔ Internet Explorer 5 deployment failures
- ✔ Component connectivity failures

Part VIII: The Part of Tens

Like all *For Dummies* books, this one includes a Part of Tens. These chapters introduce lists of ten items about a variety of informative topics. Here you find additional resources, hints, and tips, plus other gold nuggets of knowledge. The Part of Tens is a resource you can turn to again and again. And once you reach the Part of Tens, you know you've studied all the objectives for your exam!

Part IX: Appendixes

The Appendix section includes a variety of information. Here you'll find information on the Microsoft certification program, a practice exam, and how to use the CD-ROM. I've also included a Planning Worksheet for use with the IEAK Configuration Wizard (Appendix C).

Study Information

In this book I've provided you a step-by-step method of studying for the IEAK exam. Each chapter follows an identical format:

 ✔ Self-assessment questions

 ✔ Detailed explanations of the objectives and labs

 ✔ Review questions

When you begin a chapter, always note the exam objectives listed on the first page of the chapter. Then run through the self-assessment questions. If you find yourself unfamiliar with more than half of the answers, pay very close attention to the detailed explanations within the chapter.

Once you've read the chapter, answer the review questions. If you're unable to answer many of the questions, go back and study the material again. Highlighting and taking notes may help you retain the information.

Finally, the front of the book contains a "cheat sheet" of critical information to know for the exam. (When I say "cheat sheet," I don't mean it literally!) Use this as your final study tool before entering the testing center to take your exam.

Icons Used in This Book

I use a variety of icons in the margins of the book to indicate particular points of interest.

Time Shaver helps you manage and save time while taking the exam or studying.

Instant Answer icons highlight information to help you determine correct answers on the exam.

Remember points out capabilities and advantages of the technology that may appear on the test.

Warning points out problems and limitations of the technology that may appear on the exam.

Tip paragraphs won't help your score, but they may save your life, like this: *Take some time to meet your family again after you pass the test.*

Part I
The Basics

The 5th Wave   By Rich Tennant

"Trust me. This practice program has proved 100% effective in training our MCSEs."

In This Part...

*P*art I is more than just getting your feet wet. In this part
you dive right on into the water! Chapter 1 gives you
all the scoop on the exam. You'll find out how many questions, what type of questions to expect, and how to prepare
for the exam. Chapter 2 introduces the components of the
Internet Explorer Administration Kit. These components
are the tools you use to customize and deploy Internet
Explorer 5 — and they're also the heart of the exam!

Chapter 1

The IEAK5 Exam

● ●

*E*xam 70-080, commonly referred to as the Internet Explorer exam, causes a lot of confusion among technical professionals. The actual exam name is (Take a deep breath here!): "Implementing and Supporting Microsoft Internet Explorer 5.0 by using the Internet Explorer Administration Kit." Whew! Let's call it the IEAK5 Exam!

I don't suggest the IEAK5 Exam as your first Microsoft Certification test. I recommend that you take it after taking TCP/IP and perhaps even as one of your last certification exams. It's not that the exam is exceptionally hard. Rather, the exam assumes that you are already comfortable with policies, profiles, NT security, resource access, and network troubleshooting.

Whether or not you plan to pursue MCSE+Internet certification, I do suggest that you consider this exam in addition to your other electives. In light of the huge number of Internet Explorer installs worldwide, it's an application that you should know how to administer efficiently. The planning and strategies taught in deploying Internet Explorer carry over when planning deployments of any kind.

Why an Internet Explorer Test?

The basis of the IEAK5 exam is a little different from the other exams in the MCSE and MCSE+Internet series. While the other core exams cover operating systems and server-based application software, the IEAK5 exam is about — you guessed it — Internet Explorer 5 on the *client* computer. In all other ways, taking the IEAK5 exam is similar to the other Microsoft exams.

You're not tested on the Internet Explorer browser alone. The specific purpose of the exam is to ensure that you can efficiently customize, distribute, and administer the Internet Explorer 5 browser in a corporate or Internet Service Provider (ISP) setting. The Internet Explorer Administration Kit (IEAK) is a set of Microsoft tools to help you deploy your custom, preconfigured versions of Internet Explorer to end users.

It's helpful to frequently remind yourself of the purpose of the exam while studying. Write the following sentence on a 3 x 5 note card and use it as your bookmark: "The exam tests you on your ability to use the IEAK to customize, deploy, and administer the Internet Explorer browser to a large number of end users."

How many questions?

You can take one of two versions of exam 70-080: a standard version or an adaptive version. Unfortunately, you don't know whether you get a standard exam or an adaptive exam until you begin. You know that you have an adaptive exam if at the beginning of the exam you see a screen instructing you that the exam doesn't permit reviewing previous questions.

On the standard exam, you have 90 minutes to answer approximately 30 questions. For the adaptive exam, expect anywhere from 30 to 70 questions. The length of the adaptive exam depends on how many of the initial questions you answer correctly, but you have a maximum of 90 minutes. The test starts with questions of moderate difficulty. If you answer them correctly, you move on to harder questions. If you answer the initial questions incorrectly, the questions become easier. Once the scoring system determines that you have mastered each category of questions (planning, installing, troubleshooting, and so on) — or when you answer all 70 questions — the exam ends.

On the adaptive exams, you cannot go back to look at previous questions like you can on the standard exam.

My version of the exam included many scenario questions, and I have heard others say the same. Scenario questions describe a set of circumstances and then ask you to answer questions based on those circumstances. Despite the lengthy questions, I did have time to go back and review marked questions before exiting the exam.

The advantage of the standard exam is that you can go back and review previous questions. The advantage of the adaptive exam is that if you're well prepared for the exam, you could finish sooner because you'll see fewer questions. Because you can't select the type of exam you'll see, just remember that you won't be able to review previous questions if you get an adaptive exam, so you may want to take a tiny bit more time with your answers.

To help maximize your time on a standard exam, answer the simpler questions first. Mark the lengthy questions and those with exhibits. Come back to them after you answer the easier questions. This gives you an opportunity to preview the exam and determine where to spend the majority of your time.

What type of questions do I expect?

A large percentage of the questions — perhaps 75 percent — are the lengthy scenario-type questions. Many of the questions include exhibits. On some questions you click a radio button, which means that you can select only one correct answer. Other questions have check boxes next to the answers, which indicates that you select multiple answers. You can mark questions and then come back to them later. You can skip back to the previous question or forward to the next question.

Microsoft seems to be very fond of scenario questions that ask you to deliver required outcomes and one or more optional outcomes. The question describes a problem and then tells you how the administrator solved the problem. You must analyze this solution and determine whether it meets the required outcome, whether it doesn't meet the required outcome, or whether it meets the required outcome and one or more of the optional outcomes. Be prepared for several of these questions.

Don't leave any questions unanswered! It's okay to mark a question and go back to it later, but always pick the best possible answer even if you're uncertain. You can usually rule out at least two of the four answers — leaving you with a 50/50 chance of choosing correctly.

How do I study for the exam?

The best way to prepare for any certification exam is to make a plan and then systematically work through it. First, examine the study materials. You should know your schedule and how much time you can spend on your studies each day. Determine how much material you plan to cover each week, and write out a schedule on your calendar. The last two days before the exam should be review time. Based on your study calendar, pick the date for your exam and call Sylvan testing (1-800-EXAM) to schedule it.

As you work your way through the study material, take notes on important topics. Some people use an outline form for note-taking. Others use note cards. Pick the format that you feel most comfortable with. I use a somewhat unusual format involving one sheet of paper for each chapter and multi-colored pens. I jot down a word, phrase, or acronym to remember each important topic. I draw pictures, symbols, and write in the margins. It may sound jumbled, but I can often visualize those colorful notes and characters during my exam when I need to recall an important topic.

Study time and study area are also important. I study best in the evening in 45-minute intervals. If I try to go longer than 45 minutes without a break, the words turn into alphabet soup. After a 15-minute break, I go back to the books for another 45 minutes.

It's important to find a setting that's conducive to concentration. If you can study with a radio or TV on, go right ahead! The weekend before my Windows 95 exam I locked myself in the master bathroom with a set of earplugs and sat on the floor surrounded by my notes. It was highly uncomfortable, but I was undistaggbed and had no problem staying awake! (This may be a good time to point out that, at the time, my household included three dogs, three birds, a hamster, and a teenager. Get the picture?)

Early in my Microsoft certification career, I stumbled across a little book that helped me organize my study habits. Look for a copy of *Last Minute Study Tips* by Ron Fry, published by Career Press in 1996. The book isn't specific to Microsoft exams, but offers a series of study plans geared toward the amount of time left before any type of test. Whether you have six weeks or six hours to prepare, you'll find study suggestions in this book. Very helpful!

You won't pass the IEAK5 exam, however, without downloading and using the IEAK. Practice creating several customized Internet Explorer 5 packages so that you're thoroughly familiar with the Configuration wizard. Then use the Profile Manager to update your customized browser packages. Using the product is the best route to test success.

Where do I take the exam?

Sylvan Prometric has testing centers all across the country. Visit their Web site at www.2test.com to find a testing center near you. Visiting a couple of testing centers before you call to schedule the exam is important. The testing center itself may influence the outcome of your exam.

The first center where I tested had three close, crowded exam stations. I was at Seat One, which was next to the printer. As other candidates finished their exams, they came to stand beside the printer and wait for their score report. I felt as though people were peering over my shoulder for most of the exam, and it made me quite tense. For my next exam I scheduled Seat Three, which was as far from the printer as possible.

On another occasion I tested at a center adjacent to an airport. I found it hard to concentrate when planes took off, and the monitor had a very small screen. But what really threw me were the two noisy flight-simulation machines at the back of the room. It seems this center also tested pilot candidates!

By the time I was ready for my "+Internet" exams, I had discovered a new testing center near my home. I dropped in to check it out and found it spacious and quiet. I picked out the two stations in the far corners (with large monitors!) and asked the receptionist what the seat numbers were. I schedule my exams at those stations now.

Take the time to check out the test centers in your area before you schedule an exam. It could mean the difference between failure and success!

Exam Day Tips

I want to tell you that after 13 successful Microsoft exams, I'm no longer anxious on test day. Unfortunately, I always am. But here are some exam-day tips that you may find useful:

- ✔ **Don't stay up all night studying.** Get a good night of sleep, but allow yourself at least an hour to review before you leave for the testing center.
- ✔ **Arrive a few minutes early.** Look over your notes one more time, then leave them in the car. You can't take them into the exam room, and there may not be a place to store them.
- ✔ **Take two forms of identification.** One of these should be a photo ID.
- ✔ **Write down any of the concepts that give you trouble, and any memorized rhymes or acronyms, on the two sheets of scrap paper that the exam administrator gives you when you enter the exam room.** This saves you time during the exam.
- ✔ **Complete the exam tutorial.** Running through the tutorial, I find, gives me some time to calm down.
- ✔ **Mark lengthy or scenario questions and save them for last.** I find that I'm less nervous if I go through the test once and answer the "easy" questions. By knowing exactly how many "tough" questions I've marked, I can plan my remaining time accordingly.

Exam Objectives

Microsoft publishes the objectives for each certification exam on its Web site at www.microsoft.com. The objectives change from time to time, so make certain that you download the latest copy of the test objectives.

The IEAK5 exam covers six broad topics. Each topic is made up of objectives that you must master in order to pass the exam.

✔ Planning

- Identify and evaluate the technical needs of a business unit. Types of business units include

  ISP

  ICP

  Corporate kiosk-based site

  Corporate single-task-based site

  Corporate general business desktop

- Design solutions based on business rules and organizational policies. Types of business units include

  ISP

  ICP

  Corporate kiosk-based site

  Corporate single-task-based site

  Corporate general business desktop

- Given a scenario, evaluate which components to include in a customized Internet Explorer package

- Develop the appropriate security strategies for using Internet Explorer for various sites. Types of sites include

  Public kiosks

  General business sites

  Single-task-based sites

  Intranet-only sites

- Configure offline viewing for various types of users. Types of users include

  General business users

  Single-task-based users

  Mobile workers

- Develop strategies for replacing other Internet browsers. Other browsers include

  Netscape Navigator

  Previous versions of Internet Explorer

- Given a scenario, decide which custom settings to configure for Microsoft Outlook Express. Types of settings include

  Newsgroups

SMTP Mail

POP3 Mail

HotMail

IMAP folders

View settings

Signatures

Custom settings

Custom content

- Given a scenario, identify which custom settings to configure for Microsoft NetMeeting. Custom settings include

Audio and video

Protocols

File sharing

Directory servers

- Given a scenario, identify which custom settings to configure for the IEAK

Identify the type of installation, such as silent, hands-free, or interactive

Add or replace toolbar buttons

Decide whether to use a custom animated logo

Identify which URLs will be customized, such as search, home, or online support

Identify whether to customize favorites and links

Identify whether to customize channels

Identify whether to use a default, a custom, or no welcome page

Import desktop toolbars

Use a user agent string

Use security settings

- Develop strategies for automatic configuration of customized browsers

Evaluate whether to use automatic or manual configuration

Evaluate whether to use the IEAK Profile Manager for managing deployed browsers

Choose the appropriate method for automatically configuring browser settings

Given a user scenario, select the appropriate settings in the IEAK Profile Manager

• Develop a plan for implementing Install on Demand (IOD)

• Develop strategies for using the CMAK

Develop strategies for using the CMAK to configure PPTP

Develop strategies for using the CMAK to configure Dial-Up Networking

Develop strategies for using the CMAK to validate user security

✔ Installation and Configuration

• Given a role, identify the key features of the IEAK that are available for that role. Roles include

Content Provider/Developer

Service Provider

Corporate Administrator

• Download the IEAK

• Given a scenario, choose the appropriate method for deploying a customized version of Internet Explorer. Methods include

Multiple floppy disks

Single floppy disk

Single disk branding

Download

CD-ROM

Flat

• Configure and maintain an installation site to support multiple languages

• Configure and maintain an installation site to support multiple platforms

✔ Configuring and Managing Resource Access

• Maintain user configurations by using profiles, logon scripts, system policies, and the IEAK Profile Manager

• Create and assign various levels of security for security zones. Types of zones include

Internet

Local intranet

Trusted sites

Restricted sites

- Manage automatic configuration of connection settings by using various methods. Methods include

Microsoft JScript autoproxy

.ins files

.adm files

✔ Integration and Interoperability

- Configure Internet Explorer to allow controlled access to an intranet by using the CMAK. Access methods include

Dial-Up Networking

PPTP

- Configure Internet Explorer to allow controlled access to the Internet. Access methods include

Dial-Up Networking

Proxy Server

PPTP

- Deploy a preconfigured version of Internet Explorer by using the IEAK. Deployment options include

Multiple floppy disks

Single floppy disk

Single disk branding

Download

CD-ROM

Flat

✔ Monitoring and Optimization

- Manage the features of a deployed browser by updating user profiles
- Demonstrate an understanding of the quarterly reporting requirements for a licensing agreement
- Optimize a computer's cache settings and performance settings

✔ Troubleshooting

- Diagnose and resolve connectivity problems. Types of connectivity include

PPTP

Dial-Up Networking

Proxy server

TCP/IP

- Use the IEAK Profile Manager to modify the registry settings of a remote client computer

- Diagnose and resolve the deployment failure of a preconfigured version of Internet Explorer

- Diagnose and resolve problems related to using the IEAK wizard

- Diagnose and resolve connection failures of Outlook Express

- Diagnose and resolve connection failures of NetMeeting

- Diagnose and resolve failures of caching

Your Test Results!

After you finish the exam, or run out of time, the testing software grades your answers. Your test score and a "pass" or "fail" result appear on the screen along with a bar graph. That graph can be scary if the requirements bar and the results bar are too closely matched! Look for the word "pass" or "fail" to make sure that you interpret the graph correctly. Exam scores print out immediately on a printer in the testing center. The exam center staff officially stamps the results and you're free to go forth as a newly certified Microsoft professional!

Chapter 2

Come on Down! (Introducing IE5 and the IEAK)

*B*efore I jump right in to exam objectives and exercises, I want to take a moment to talk about some of the features of Internet Explorer 5 (IE5) and the Internet Explorer Administration Kit (IEAK). After all, you need to understand the tools you're using to get the job done, right? It also helps to understand the job you're trying to do with the tools!

Internet Explorer 5: Do Stuff Faster!

In the days leading up to the release of Internet Explorer 5, the press was full of praise:

- ✓ Industry Support for Internet Explorer 5 is unprecedented.
- ✓ Microsoft delivers world's fastest next-generation browser.
- ✓ Businesses using IE5 report cost and productivity gains.
- ✓ Microsoft launches Internet Explorer 5, passport to the global online community.

Then, on launch day, Microsoft introduced Internet Explorer 5 with the simple message: *Do stuff faster*.

The message was perfect. Internet Explorer 5 enables you to take advantage of all the Web's capabilities — IE5 is faster, simpler, and better.

IE5 features

IE5 offers easy-to-use interfaces and enhanced features. Beginning with installation, everything about this browser is simpler than previous versions of Internet Explorer. Yes, you still download from the Microsoft Web site (www.microsoft.com). But now, if something interrupts your download, you can pick up where you left off. (The previous download process required starting over each time a download was interrupted.) You also have the flexibility to download and install only the components that you need. If you don't plan to use Chat or NetMeeting — don't install them!

IE5 is also a much stabler product than its predecessor. Although IE4 introduced active content delivery, users quickly figured out that turning that feature off was easier than dealing with extremely slow browsing and frequent crashes. IE5 doesn't even attempt channel bars and active desktop. Unless you enabled channel bars and active desktop in IE4 and then upgraded to IE5, you won't find them.

The offline pages concept replaces channels and subscriptions. You can still schedule automatic content updates to your favorite pages, but you use the familiar Properties page to do so.

Don't let the emphasis on simplicity fool you — IE5 has many powerful features, including the following:

- **IntelliSense:** AutoComplete (great for forms), AutoSearch, AutoDetect, AutoInstall, AutoCorrect, and AutoConfiguration combine to *really* let you do stuff faster on the Web.

- **Search Assistant:** A new customizable search pane enables you to choose a search category: Web page, name, address, map, or previous searches.

- **Enhanced Favorites:** This feature enables you to make content available offline through Add, Organize, and Save options.

- **Enhanced History bar:** View browsing history by date, site, most visited site, or order visited today.

- **Windows Radio:** This feature delivers streaming audio through your browser.

- **Offline Browsing:** No more confusing subscriptions. Now you simply make the Web page available for offline viewing.

- **Content Advisor:** Controls access to offensive Web content. You choose the ratings system and the exposure to sex, language, violence, and nudity.

- **Web Accessories:** A collection of Web utilities available from Microsoft and other Web tool developers. Choose from a variety of tools to enhance your Web experience.

✔ **Security Zones:** Defines security settings for Internet, intranet, trusted sites, and restricted sites.

✔ **Related Links:** IE5 analyzes the content of your current Web page and creates a list of related links for you to choose from.

IE5 system requirements

Before installing Internet Explorer 5, you need to ensure that the computer meets the system requirements for the product. IE5 requires the following:

✔ **Computer:** 486DX or above

✔ **Processor:** 66 MHz or higher

✔ **Operating systems:** Windows 95, Windows 98, or Windows NT 4.0 with Service Pack 3

✔ **Memory:** 16MB minimum for Windows 95 and Windows 98, 32MB minimum for Windows NT

✔ **Hard drive requirements:** 45MB free for minimal install, 70MB free for typical install, 111MB for full install

Know the IE5 system requirements for the exam! You're likely to see a scenario question requiring you to identify the systems on which you can deploy IE5.

Internet Explorer Administration Kit 5

Internet Explorer 5 contains more enhanced manageability features than IE4. Corporate administrators and ISPs have greater flexibility to configure and deploy a browser that perfectly fits the needs of their users. Microsoft released a new version of the Internet Explorer Administration Kit (IEAK) with IE5.

The IEAK is a group of utilities that enable you to create, deploy, and manage customized versions of Internet Explorer 5. You can use the IEAK to preconfigure components to the specific needs of your user community. You can restrict access to configuration settings to prevent users from changing their settings. You can also configure IE5 to automatically install components if the user attempts to activate those options (Install on Demand).

Downloading the IEAK

The IEAK is available for download from the Microsoft Web site at
`http://www.microsoft.com/windows/ieak` (see Figure 2-1). The download
process for the IEAK is a bit more complicated than most downloads from a
Microsoft site. Before downloading is permitted, you must decide what role
your organization plays in distributing Internet Explorer 5. (Although you can
download the IEAK without filling out a profile and licensing request, the
IEAK will operate in demonstration mode only. You must obtain a license and
customization code to make the IEAK fully operable.)

Licensing requirements

Do you plan to internally distribute IE5 by using the IEAK (meaning only to
employees of your company) or externally (to customers and people outside
of your company)? Most corporate users choose the internal license agreement, while ISPs use the external license agreement (see Figure 2-2).

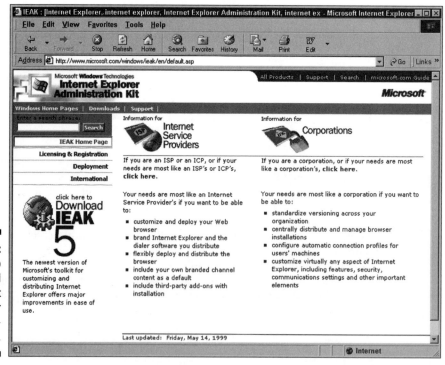

Figure 2-1: Preparing to download the Internet Explorer Administra-tion Kit.

If you choose the external license agreement, you must submit to Microsoft a quarterly count of the number of Internet Explorer 5 browsers you have deployed.

According to the terms of the license agreement, if you receive an e-mail requesting distribution numbers from Microsoft, you have 45 days to respond with the information. Microsoft provides a Web page (see Figure 2-3) where you can submit distribution information.

After you decide which licensing agreement is right for your organization, submit a registration profile by using the online form on the Microsoft Web site. If your licensing request is approved, Microsoft e-mails (within 24 hours) a customization code to you, which allows you to create customized IE5 packages by using the IEAK.

Without a ten-digit customization code issued by Microsoft, you cannot create a custom IE5 package with the IEAK. If you don't enter a valid code, the IEAK Customization wizard runs in demonstration mode only. You cannot save a customized package for distribution.

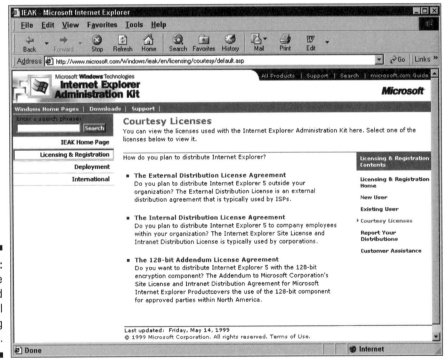

Figure 2-2: Viewing the internal and external licensing options.

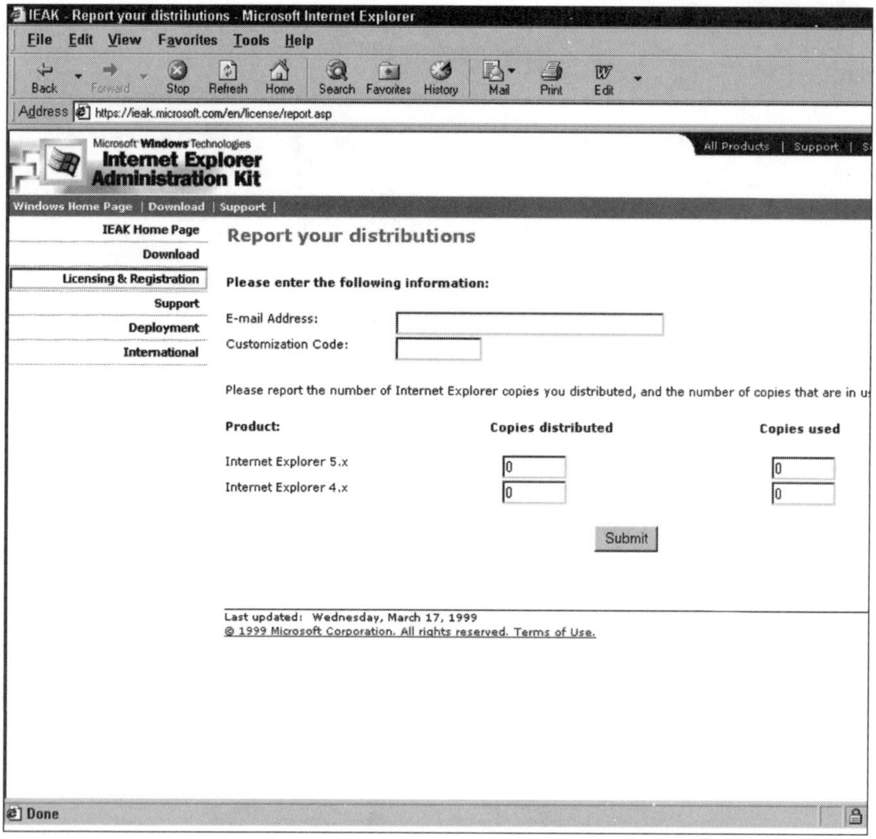

Figure 2-3:
Reporting external licensing distribution information via the Microsoft Web site.

Although I don't know of any exam questions regarding the 128-bit license agreement, it's wise for you to read this document. United States law currently forbids export of 128-bit encryption technology outside the country. Make sure that you understand how this affects IE5 distribution to your employees and customers.

IEAK system requirements

Although the IEAK runs on Intel-based computers only, you can use it to create custom Internet Explorer browser packages for Mac and UNIX computers as well. The system requirements for the IEAK are:

- ✔ **Computer:** 486DX or above

- ✔ **Processor:** 66 MHz or higher

- ✔ **Operating system:** Windows 95, Windows 98, or Windows NT 4.0 with Service Pack 3 or better

- **Memory:** 16MB minimum for Windows 95 and Windows 98 computers, 32MB minimum for Windows NT computers

- **Miscellaneous:** mouse, CD-ROM, VGA or higher graphics card, Internet connection (28.8 Kbps minimum modem speed)

On the exam, you're likely to see a scenario question that asks you to identify the computers that can run IEAK5.

IEAK components

With the IEAK, you can create a customized browser and deploy it on your network or on the Web. IEAK5 includes the following components:

- IEAK Customization wizard

- IEAK Profile Manager

- IEAK Connection Manager Administration Kit

- IEAK toolkit

- IEAK online help

For the exam, know which components make up the Internet Explorer Administration Kit.

Introducing the Customization wizard

You can build customized versions of the Internet Explorer browser by using the Customization wizard. You can include your company logo, additional components (such as NetMeeting, Chat, or FrontPage Express), and customized settings that control how your user community can use the deployed browser. You can create browser packages to download from a server or to install from CD or disk. You can even prevent users from changing their browser settings. Hurray! A few less help desk calls to resolve!

The Customization wizard is a powerful tool that queries you for information and presents numerous choices. The wizard consists of five distinct stages. For the exam, you need to know and understand the purpose of each stage.

The five stages of the Customization wizard:

- Stage 1: Gathering Information

- Stage 2: Specifying Setup parameters

- Stage 3: Customizing setup

- Stage 4: Customizing the browser

- Stage 5: Component customization

In light of all the information that you must provide to run the Customization wizard, it's best that you plan your custom browser in advance. Use the planning worksheet provided in Appendix C to gather information so that you're prepared when you begin the Customization wizard. Enjoy!

You must run the Customization wizard several times to understand the wizard well enough to pass the exam. Use different components and installation options each time so that you see how the wizard creates the custom browser packages. Also, be sure to read the information on each screen of the wizard. Microsoft provides thorough explanations of each stage of the wizard, which can enhance your understanding of the process.

Presenting the Profile Manager

The Profile Manager is the second component of the Internet Explorer Administration Kit. The Profile Manager enables you to manage already deployed installations of Internet Explorer 5. By using the Profile Manager, you can change the settings and component configurations that you specified when you ran the Customization wizard to create the custom package.

The Customization wizard creates a custom package. The Profile Manager lets you change user settings automatically, even after the browser is deployed.

Connection Manager Administration Kit (CMAK)

The IEAK also includes the Connection Manager Administration Kit (CMAK). The CMAK enables you to create preconfigured dial-up and VPN connections to distribute to your users. By using the CMAK, you remove the need to visit each computer to set up those connections. Think of all the help desk calls and trouble tickets you can save!

IEAK toolkit and IEAK online help

The IEAK toolkit is a collection of utilities and samples that enhance your custom browser packages. When IEAK installs itself on your computer, the toolkit files are copied to c:\program files\ieak\toolkit.

The IEAK also installs online help documentation. Take advantage of this information! It's thorough, well organized, and can help you understand how to use the IEAK.

IE5 + IEAK5 = TCO

The combination of Internet Explorer 5 and IEAK5 results in reduced TCO (total cost of ownership) for your corporation. By configuring IE5 before installing it, you avoid visiting each desktop to configure options. Depending on the setup options you choose, you can also simplify IE5 installation so that users don't require support during installation. And by restricting user changes to configuration settings, you further reduce the number of support calls for IE5 and its components. Your boss is gonna love you!

IEAK5 is a powerful deployment tool. Corporate administrators can deploy not only IE5, but also up to ten other applications, including Microsoft Office. And you can tailor IE5 installation packages to a variety of users within the organization. Aside from packaging and installing, you can use IEAK5 to manage IE5 across the enterprise.

Your job, as you prepare for the IEAK5 exam, is figuring out how to properly and effectively configure the browser for a wide range of uses. Then you must understand how to deploy and manage IE5 (by using IEAK, of course) on a network. My job (within the pages of this book) is to help you master the objectives and prepare you for the exam.

Be sure that you're completely familiar with all the features of Internet Explorer 5 and Internet Explorer Administration Kit 5. The test focuses on configuring components in each.

Part II
Planning

"We sort of have our own way of mentally preparing our people to take the MCSE IE5 exam."

In this part . . .

*I*n Part II, the focus is on planning to customize and distribute Internet Explorer 5. In this part, you learn to:

- ✔ Determine the requirements of different IE5 user groups
- ✔ Select the appropriate features to include in a browser package
- ✔ Replace previous browser and e-mail applications
- ✔ Plan security strategies
- ✔ And much more!

Chapter 3

Designing the Right Solution

- -

Exam Objectives

▶ Assessing the technical needs of a business

▶ Determining special needs of ISPs and ICPs

▶ Designing for corporate business users

▶ Designing for single-task sites

▶ Designing for corporate kiosks

- -

*B*efore you can design the correct Internet Explorer 5 solution for a business, you have to understand the business's role and its IE5 needs. Internet Explorer 5 is flexible and full of timesaving features. But not all organizations take advantage of these features. Some organizations use all the components — from Outlook Express to NetMeeting. Others are more concerned with providing a secure and functional Web browser.

In this chapter, I tell you how to determine a business's technical requirements and plan an appropriate IE5 solution. Using the Internet Explorer Administration Kit, you can efficiently and effectively customize IE5, deploy it, manage it in the field, and leap tall buildings in a single bound! (Ahem. I do get carried away on occasion.)

Quick Assessment

Assessing the Technical Needs of a Business

1 The three roles available when running the IEAK are _____, _____, and _____.

2 Users at _____ sites use their IE5 browser for a repetitive task.

Special Needs of ISPs and ICPs

3 A _____ site is located in a public place and is available to anyone.

4 An _____ sells (or provides) Internet access services to its end users.

5 An _____ provides Internet content to its customers.

6 The most common distribution method for an ICP administrator is _____.

Designing for Corporate Business Users

7 The browsers of a company's general business users are usually _____ managed.

8 (True/False). An ISP administrator should not attempt to lock down browser configuration settings to prevent end users from changing them.

Designing for Single-task Sites

9 With free access to a kiosk by the public, it's best to limit additional browser _____.

Designing for Corporate Kiosks

10 Corporate users usually access the Internet through a _____.

Answers

1   *corporate administrator, ISP, and ICP.* See "Matching Technical Needs to Solutions."

2   *single-task sites.* See "Single-task sites."

3   *kiosk.* See "Corporate kiosk sites."

4   *ISP.* See "Designing ISP solutions."

5   *ICP.* See "Designing ICP solutions."

6   *single-disk branding.* See "Designing ICP solutions."

7   *centrally.* See "Solutions for general business users."

8   *True.* See "Designing ICP solutions."

9   *components.* See "Corporate kiosk sites."

10   *firewall.* See "Solutions for general business users."

Matching Technical Needs to Solutions

To effectively customize Internet Explorer 5 for end users — and after all, that's what this whole exam is about — you've got to know more than a little bit about those end users. But tailoring the browser to a large number of individuals is a daunting task unless you classify users into groups with common features. You must consider the needs of the average user in each group.

To determine common features, consider the role of the business. The requirements of end users differ depending on the business role:

- **Corporate administrator:** In a corporation, all the end users have at least one thing in common — they work for the same organization and share the same corporate policies.
- **ISP:** At an Internet Service Provider (ISP), the commonality among end users is that they're all customers who subscribe to your service.
- **ICP:** At an Internet Content Provider (ICP), all the end users are subscribing to (or buying) information from a common source.

Each role (corporate administrator, ISP, and ICP) serves the needs of a different type of user with a different set of Internet Explorer 5 requirements. The job of the system administrator is to ferret out those requirements and appropriately tailor IE5 to satisfy the average user in each of these user groups.

For the exam, you must recognize how each role (corporate administrator, ISP, and ICP) serves a distinct type of user. You must also be able to identify the correct role when given user requirements.

When planning any IE5 browser package, use the planning worksheet in Appendix C to help you determine which features to include in an IE5 package.

Defining corporate requirements

What does the average corporate user need from the IE5 browser? Hmmm. Seems like the users' needs vary according to the work performed, doesn't it? For example, a call center employee taking product orders has a very specific need from a browser. He needs speedy access to a specific intranet page repeatedly throughout the day. His need is vastly different from that of an analyst researching investment information, who accesses a variety of Web sites on the Internet.

Differentiating between the types of IE5 users is necessary to design an appropriate browser package for each type of user. But other factors, such as corporate policies and business rules, also affect the design of a browser package.

For corporate users, it helps to further classify the users into the following categories:

- **General business users:** Perform a variety of tasks. General business users commonly access Internet sites and intranet sites and often use the IE5 browser as the front end to a corporate application.

  General business users frequently use Outlook Express. The same proxy servers, mail servers, security levels, and restrictions usually apply to all users in the company. Otherwise, IE5 settings for general business users are somewhat generic because you have to please a large group performing a variety of functions.

- **Single-task business users:** Perform a single task. Aside from accessing different types of sites, these user groups require different configurations for caching and security. In many cases, single-task users use the IE5 browser as the front end to a corporate browser. The browser is usually customized as a form, so that users can easily capture or retrieve data from a database or application.

  Single-task users generally access one or two sites repeatedly throughout the day. If the site's content is static, the page is cached and updated infrequently. If the content is dynamic (such as stock quotes, interest rates, and so on), then the site updates very frequently.

  Security for single-task users is usually easy to configure. Because you know exactly which site the user accesses, it's easy to determine which security zone and security level are appropriate. In fact, placing the site in the Trusted Sites zone is fairly common for single-task users.

- **Kiosk sites:** Have an altogether different set of requirements. A kiosk site usually performs a single function. It may display a building map, a campus or terminal map, or provide information about a single product.

  Kiosk sites are usually stand-alone systems or are attached to a private network. The kiosk generally has a very restrictive security level, and provides few — if any — components in addition to the browser.

Solutions for general business users

General business users at a single corporation have a lot in common. Despite differing job descriptions, they share many of the same technical requirements. IE5 browser packages distributed by corporate administrators for general business users often include:

- Proxy server configurations
- Multiple connections: one for use on the office LAN, and another for dial-up access when traveling
- Custom favorites and links
- Custom support pages

✔ A corporate home page

✔ Custom search pages

✔ Add-on components, such as Outlook Express and NetMeeting

✔ Automatic configuration URLs

✔ Auto-proxy scripts

This is by no means a complete list. Depending on the company and the nature of its business, users can share many more features, such as icons, support pages, and so on. The point is that you have a group of users whose Internet Explorer 5 requirements are very similar and can be centrally managed, as opposed to ISP end users who tend to have dissimilar requirements and can't be managed.

Corporate administrators can likely distribute one version of a custom browser package that suits the needs of the majority of general business users.

To effectively provide for general business users, corporate administrators create a custom browser package that is full-featured, quick, and geared to accommodate a variety of content. At the same time, corporate administrators make certain that corporate assets remain safe from harmful content. Corporate administrators may also optimize the browsers to minimize network utilization. With the proper planning, corporate administrators can meet all their users' requirements with a single custom browser package.

Browser configuration issues that frequently concern corporate administrators are:

✔ **Security policies:** Corporate security policies dictate whether users can run ActiveX and Java components, whether digital certificates and encryption are required, and whether application sharing is permitted.

✔ **Bandwidth policies:** Other policies governing use of bandwidth may determine whether companies permit audio/video conferencing and site subscriptions.

✔ **Connection settings:** In today's business environment, corporate users frequently use dial-up and VPN connections to access a private corporate network. Corporate administrators must provide and manage these connections as well as configure appropriate security strategies for each type of remote access.

✔ **Proxy servers and firewalls:** Corporate administrators usually have to configure secure access to and from the Internet through a proxy server or firewall. Blocking unauthorized traffic typically isn't enough — corporate administrators must also configure the firewall or proxy server to allow some types of traffic over specific ports. NNTP (news), POP3 (e-mail), and FTP (file transfer) are just some of the protocols a corporate administrator may have to allow through a firewall.

Single-task sites

Single-task users are found in a variety of business settings, from call centers to checkout counters. These workers use their IE5 browser for a repetitive task. An employee at a call center may use the browser to enter product orders throughout the day. This employee needs swift access to a Web page that is very static — usually a form that gathers customer data. And, the customer data is probably stored on the intranet rather than on an Internet site. Similarly, an employee in a corporate mailroom may use the IE5 browser to view postal rates. Again, the Web pages are somewhat static, and the Web sites are probably on the Internet.

In other cases, the IE5 Web browser functions as the front-end to a specialized corporate application. The sole function of the browser is to facilitate user interaction with the application. The application is usually located on the intranet and centralized management of the browser is important.

In the examples I list above, the browser is used for narrowly defined tasks. A corporate administrator faced with this situation must identify the user requirements and match them to IE5 and IEAK features. Administrators must also consider security policies or business rules that affect the use of the browser. The end product is a browser package that best equips this user to complete his task efficiently and effectively.

Browser configuration issues that a corporate administrator faces for single-task users include:

- **Caching:** Single-task users generally perform a repetitive task throughout the day. Due to the nature of the work, rapid access to the Web site used is often a requirement. Depending on whether the site content is dynamic or static, corporate administrators must configure the correct caching strategy for these users.

- **Policies and restrictions:** Single-task users are often found at call centers, order centers, and customer service departments. These users must not be able to alter the configuration of their browser to the point that they cannot complete their work. Corporate administrators, therefore, must effectively lock down the browser settings by selecting appropriate policies and restrictions. Some common restrictions are disabling access to the browser's Internet Options, disabling changes to security zones and security levels, and disabling the user's ability to change e-mail server names and addresses.

- **Security:** Corporate administrators must develop an effective security strategy for single-task users. Because these users could access either intranet or Internet sites, security needs vary widely. The corporate administrator must determine whether sensitive personal or financial data is being sent between the browsers and the Web server. If so, encryption and digital certificates may be needed.

Corporate kiosk sites

Corporate kiosks are the most specialized browser configurations of all. These kiosks are used for very specific functions, such as:

- ✔ Interactive building directories
- ✔ Presentations
- ✔ Product demonstrations and recommendations
- ✔ Maps

Kiosks are most often found in public areas, like lobbies and airport terminals, and are intended for use by the general public.

Sometimes a kiosk is a stand-alone system with all its screen information stored on the local hard drive. In other cases, the kiosk connects to a centralized database where information is gathered and stored. The connection can be to an intranet or Internet site. With free access to the browser by the public, administrators usually limit additional components and lock down the browser's configuration settings. Users shouldn't be able to alter the browser configuration so that the kiosk no longer performs its intended function.

Corporate administrators often configure a kiosk site as follows:

- ✔ No add-on components
- ✔ No user access to browser menus
- ✔ No user access to desktop icons
- ✔ No access to Internet Options
- ✔ Disabled right-click access to object properties
- ✔ Customized splash screens, logos, and title bars

Once again, the corporate administrator faces a very specific set of requirements for the IE5 browser. In this case, the custom browser should support a single, limited purpose.

Designing ISP solutions

The role of a system administrator at an ISP (Internet service provider) is somewhat different from that of a corporate administrator. The ISP administrator creates a custom IE5 browser to distribute to end users. End users are often individuals using the Internet for recreational or personal purposes, but can also include small business users who have signed up for Internet access.

The ISP administrator's primary goal is to make the ISP's services easily accessible to ISP customers. ISP browser packages usually include sign-up solutions so that the ISP can sign up and bill customers.

The end users of an ISP may have very little in common. ISP end users range from children to seniors and from homemakers to office workers. The only thing they may have in common is their subscription to the ISP service. Obviously, a "one-size-fits-all" browser isn't going to suit these users, and you can't create a multitude of packages to suit them all.

Customized ISP browser packages often include:

- ✔ Logos, graphics, and title bars customized to the ISP
- ✔ A custom support page
- ✔ A custom search page
- ✔ Custom help features
- ✔ Customized links and favorites
- ✔ Additional components, such as Outlook Express and Chat
- ✔ A customizable home page
- ✔ A sign-up solution

ISP end users generally want fast page loading and a full range of browser features. Many want Internet e-mail and newsreader applications as well. Most want to take advantage of dynamic Web content — they certainly don't want Java applets and ActiveX controls to be locked down and controlled by the ISP.

Designing ICP solutions

An ICP (Internet content provider) administrator has little control over an end user's browser configuration. At an ICP, the end user is a customer who accesses a site to acquire content — information, applications, and so on. The administrator's primary goal is to enhance the customer's experience at the ICP site. Some of the features the administrator can customize are:

- ✔ Channels
- ✔ Links
- ✔ Favorites
- ✔ Home page

Content providers often provide a custom channel to deliver content to the user's desktop. Frequently, content providers include customizable home pages that users can configure with the content they prefer. Content providers may also supply pertinent links and favorites to their users.

Because an ICP administrator isn't in the business of managing the end user's browser, single-disk branding is usually the preferred distribution method. Single-disk branding allows for customizing limited features of the user's browser (such as logos, graphics, and title bars) without affecting important configuration settings (such as proxy servers, security levels, and so on).

Example

Because this chapter contains a lot of theory, I've included an example of how to put this information to use.

A corporate kiosk scenario

Frank is a corporate administrator tasked with creating an IE5 solution for kiosks located in his company's chain of gourmet coffee stores. The kiosks display product information and a presentation on how coffee beans are harvested, roasted, and blended. The kiosks in all stores are on a private network connected to the corporate office. The only systems on this private network are the kiosks and the Web server that downloads information to the kiosks. Frank will manage all the kiosks from this central location.

Solution: Using his Planning Worksheet (see Appendix C), Frank determines that the IE5 browsers for the kiosks should be configured as follows:

Setting	Value(s)
Role	Corporate administrator
Platform	Windows 9x/NT 4.0
Target Language	English
Installation method (media selection)	Download
Install method	Completely Silent Install
Installation Option	Minimal (Web browser only)
Component Download	Remove the Windows Update option from the Tools menu
Installation Directory	Install in the specified folder within the Windows folder

Corporate Install Options	Internet Explorer is set as the default browser
Advanced Installation Options	Optimize for Web Download
Windows Desktop Update	No
Title Bar Text	Premier Gourmet Coffee
Animated Logo	(Frank includes the corporate logo of a dancing coffee bean)
Static Logo	(see above)
Home page URL	`http://www.pgc.com`
Search part URL	`http://www.pgc.com/search`
Online support page URL	`http://www.pgc.com/support`
Welcome page	Custom at `http://www.pgc.com/welcome`
Automatic Configuration	Enabled, auto configure every 30 minutes
Auto-config URL	`http://www.pgc.com/autoconfig`
Proxy settings	Not enabled
Certification authorities	Do not customize
Authenticode security	Do not customize
Security zones	Do not customize
Content ratings	Do not customize
Programs	Do not customize Program Settings
System Policies and Restrictions	
Offline Pages	Disable all
Corporate Restrictions	
Internet Property Pages	Disable all
Browser Menus	
File Menu	Disable all
View Menu	Disable all
Favorites Menu	Hide
Tools Menu	Disable
Help Menu	Remove all
Context Menu	Disable all
File Download Dialog	Disable Save this program to disk option

Favorites and Search

Favorites Import/Export	Disable
Search	Disable all
Advanced Settings	Launch browser in full screen mode
Security Page	Do not allow users to change policies for any security zone Do not allow users to add/delete sites from a security zone
Software Updates	Disable all
Toolbar Restrictions	Disable all

Web Desktop

Desktop Restrictions	Disable Active Desktop Do not allow changes to Active Desktop Hide Internet Explorer icon Hide Network Neighborhood icon Hide all items on Desktop
Active Desktop Items	Disable all
Desktop Wallpaper Settings	Disable all
Desktop Toolbars Settings	Disable all
Start Menu	Remove all items
Shell	Disable File menu in browser window Hide Drives in My Computer Disable net connections/disconnections
System	Run only specified Windows applications (Internet Explorer 5)

Frank's chosen settings are very restrictive, but appropriate for a kiosk. The only intended function of this browser is to display the coffee bean presentation. Notice that he has disabled access to all the browser menus. He has also hidden all desktop icons and restricted the system so that it only runs the Internet Explorer 5 application. Because all the kiosks are on a private network, and the only browser function is to display a presentation, Frank specified default security settings.

Frank has also configured the browser so that it automatically checks for updated configuration information. This enables Frank to place new configuration files at the automatic configuration URL so that the browsers can update automatically.

Prep Test

1 Sarah is an administrator and plans to distribute a custom IE5 browser to customers who sign up for her company's Internet services. Which administrative role should she select when she runs the IEAK?

A. ○ Corporate administrator

B. ○ ISP

C. ○ ICP

D. ○ Sign-up administrator

2 Fred is a corporate administrator with a network consisting of Windows 98 clients and NT 4.0 servers. He plans to create an IE5 browser package for the corporate call center. What type of users should he create the IE5 package for?

A. ○ End users

B. ○ General business users

C. ○ Single-task users

D. ○ Kiosk users

3 Which of the following items is not appropriate for the browser configuration at a corporate kiosk site?

A. ❑ Outlook Express

B. ❑ Disabled browser menus

C. ❑ A sign-up solution

D. ❑ Customized logos and graphics

4 Which of the following distribution methods is most appropriate for an ICP (Internet Content Provider) distributing a custom IE5 browser package?

A. ○ CD-ROM

B. ○ Single-disk branding

C. ○ Flat

D. ○ Multiple floppy disks

5 Laura is the system administrator at an ISP. She's preparing a custom browser package to distribute to ISP customers. Which IE5 features might Laura customize in this package?

A. ❑ Logos, graphics, and title bars

B. ❑ A custom support page

C. ❑ Customized links and favorites

D. ❑ A sign-up solution

6 Jason is a corporate administrator creating a custom browser package for a large company. Client computers on Jason's network include Windows 98, Windows 95, NT 4.0, and Windows 2000. Jason wants to provide the IE5 browser and Outlook Express in his package. He wants to minimize administrative overhead in maintaining the deployed browser. Given these requirements, which of the following should Jason configure for his browser package?

A. ❑ An automatic configuration URL

B. ❑ Auto-proxy script

C. ❑ Single-disk branding

D. ❑ Sign-up service

Answers

1 *B.* Because Sarah's company provides Internet services, she should select the ISP role rather than the corporate administrator or ICP role. Answer D is not an administrative role for the IEAK. *Review "Matching Technical Needs to Solutions."*

2 *C.* Call center users are usually single-task users. Fred should customize the browser to accommodate the work of these users. Answers A and B aren't the best options because they include more features than necessary for such a narrowly defined task. Answer D isn't appropriate because a call center is not a kiosk site. *Review "Single-task sites."*

3 *A and C.* Kiosk sites should not have additional components, such as Outlook Express, that users could use for a purpose other than what the kiosk is intended for. Sign-up solutions are used by ISPs and aren't appropriate for a corporate kiosk. Answers B and D are highly appropriate for a corporate kiosk site because administrators want to discourage users from using the browser menu to change the kiosk configuration. Customized logs and graphics are one of the key features of a kiosk site. *Review "Corporate kiosk sites."*

4 *B.* Because an ICP administrator isn't in the business of managing the end user's browser, single-disk branding is usually the preferred distribution method. Single-disk branding allows for customizing limited features of the user's browser (such as logos, graphics, and title bars) without affecting important configuration settings (such as proxy servers, security levels, and so on). CD-ROM is another option; however, single-disk branding is most effective for ICPs. Answer C isn't correct because the flat distribution method is meant for downloading the package from a network server. Answer D is incorrect because the single-disk branding method is best for ICPs. *See "Designing ICP Solutions."*

5 *A, B, C, and D.* The ISP administrator's primary goal is to make the ISP's services feature rich and easily accessible to ISP customers. ISP browser packages usually include sign-up solutions so that the ISP can sign up and bill customers. *Review "Designing ISP solutions."*

6 *A and B.* Because Jason is a corporate administrator and one of Jason's requirements is to minimize administrative maintenance of the deployed package, he should consider including an automatic configuration URL and an auto-proxy script and URL. Single-disk branding and sign-up services are not appropriate solutions for these corporate requirements. *Review "Solutions for general business users."*

Designing the Right Solution

Chapter 4

Selecting IE5 Installation Options

● ●

Exam Objectives

▶ Understanding Internet Explorer 5 components

▶ Recognizing components included in minimal, typical, and custom installations of
  Internet Explorer 5

▶ Knowing the hard drive requirements for minimal, typical, and custom installations

▶ Planning for Install on Demand

▶ Using Windows Update

● ●

*I*nternet Explorer 5 contains a multitude of optional components that you
can include in a customized browser package for your users. For the
exam, you're required to know which components are included in each of the
three types of IE5 installations: minimal, typical, and custom.

In addition, you need to know the hard drive requirements for each type of
installation. Hard drive installation requirements vary from a minimum of
45MB to a maximum of 111MB! You certainly don't want to fill valuable disk
space with components that go unused, so it's important that you can evaluate user requirements to determine which components are optional and
which are required.

Finally, you need to know how to plan for Install on Demand and Windows
Update.

Quick Assessment

Under-
standing
Internet
Explorer 5
components

1   For users to be able to download pages for offline viewing, you must include the _____ _____ _____ component in the IE5 package.

2   The _____ _____ _____ _____ Internet Explorer component enables users to run Java applets.

3   The three Internet Explorer installation options are _____, _____, and _____.

Knowing the
hard drive
require-
ments for
minimal,
typical, and
custom
installations

4   You must have at least _____ MB of free disk space to install the minimal version of Internet Explorer 5.

5   You must have at least _____ MB of free disk space to run the minimal version of Internet Explorer 5.

6   You must have at least _____ MB of free disk space to install the full version of Internet Explorer 5.

7   You must have at least _____ MB of free disk space to run the full version of Internet Explorer 5.

Planning for
Install on
Demand

8   When new IE5 components are necessary to properly display a Web page, _____ _____ _____ automatically downloads and installs the components (if they aren't already installed) on users' computers.

Using
Windows
Update

9   _____ _____ enables users to visit the Microsoft update site to add components to their system or to download critical software updates.

10 (True/False). Using the IEAK Customization wizard, you can configure IE5 to use a custom URL to download component updates.

Answers

1 *Offline Browsing Pack.* See "Identifying IE5 Components."

2 *Dynamic HTML Data Binding.* See "Identifying IE5 Components."

3 *minimal, typical, custom.* See "Installation Options."

4 *45.* See "Disk space requirements."

5 *27.* See "Disk space requirements."

6 *111.* See "Disk space requirements."

7 *80.* See "Disk space requirements."

8 *install on demand.* See "Install on Demand."

9 *Windows Update.* See "Windows Update."

10 *True.* See "Windows Update."

Identifying IE5 Components

On the Component Options screen of the Internet Explorer 5 Setup wizard (see Figure 4-1), you see a long list of options that you can install along with the browser. You must know the function of each of these components, particularly Outlook Express, NetMeeting, and FrontPage Express.

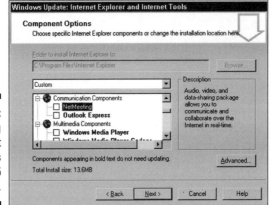

Figure 4-1:
Choosing
component
options
during IE5
setup.

The IEAK exam includes scenario questions that identify the requirements of a particular user community. For example, a question may say that users require offline browsing ability, online collaboration ability, and video viewing ability. You may be asked to identify which Internet Explorer 5 components fulfill those requirements. To help you out, Table 4-1 lists the Internet Explorer 5 component options and describes their function.

Table 4-1	IE5 Components	
Function	*Component Options*	*Description*
Web Browsing	Internet Explorer 5 Web Browser	World Wide Web browser
Web Browsing	Offline Browsing Pack	Enables you to download Web pages for offline viewing with IE5
Web Browsing	Internet Explorer Help	Help files

Function	*Component Options*	*Description*
Web Browsing	Microsoft Virtual Machine	Enables you to display Java applets
Web Browsing	Internet Connection Wizard	Enables you to connect to an Internet Service Provider
Web Browsing	Internet Explorer Core Fonts	True Type fonts optimized for on-screen appearance
Web Browsing	Dynamic HTML Data Binding	Enables IE5 to retrieve and display database information in a Web page
Web Browsing	Internet Explorer Browsing Enhancements	Installs graphical FTP helper and support for font embedding
Communication	NetMeeting	Audio/video/data-sharing application for real-time collaboration over the Internet
Communication	Outlook Express	E-mail and news reader application
Communication	Chat 2.5	Application that enables real-time Internet Relay Chat (IRC) conversations over the Internet
Multimedia	Windows Media Player	Plays multimedia files from the Internet
Multimedia	Windows Media Player Codecs	Support files for Windows Media Player
Multimedia	DirectAnimation	Enables animation and multimedia services on the computer
Multimedia	Vector Graphics Rendering (VML)	Enables viewing of vector graphic images with IE5
Multimedia	AOL ART Image Format Support	Enables viewing AOL ART formatted images with IE5

(continued)

Table 4-1 *(continued)*

Function	Component Options	Description
Multimedia	Macromedia Shockwave	Enables viewing of Shockwave formatted cartoons and games
Multimedia	Macromedia Flash Player	Enables viewing of multimedia, graphics, and animations created using Macromedia Flash
Web authoring	FrontPage Express	Application for creating and editing Web pages
Web authoring	Web Publishing Wizard	Enables uploading content to a Web server
Web authoring	Web Folders	Enables managing Web servers the same way that computer files are managed
Web authoring	Visual Basic Scripting Support	Enables running Visual Basic scripts from Web pages
Web authoring	Additional Web Fonts	Additional True Type Web fonts
Online shopping	Microsoft Wallet	Enables secure storing of credit card data to use for purchases on Web sites
Language selection	Language Auto-Selection	Enables IE5 to auto-detect the language on a Web page
Language selection	Japanese Text Display Support	Enables IE5 to display Japanese text
Language selection	Japanese Text Input Support	Enables inputting Japanese Text in IE5
Language selection	Korean Text Display Support	Enables IE5 to display Korean text
Language selection	Korean Text Input Support	Enables input of Korean text in IE5

Function	Component Options	Description
Language selection	Pan-European Text Display Support	Enables IE5 to display Central European, Cyrillic, Greek, Turkish, and Baltic text
Language selection	Chinese (Traditional) Text Display Support	Enables IE5 to display the traditional Chinese character set
Language selection	Chinese (Traditional) Text Input Support	Enables input of the traditional Chinese character set in IE5
Language selection	Chinese (Simplified) Text Display Support	Enables IE5 to display the simplified Chinese character set
Language selection	Chinese (Simplified) Text Input Support	Enables input of the simplified Chinese character set
Language selection	Vietnamese Text Support	Enables IE5 to display and edit Vietnamese text
Language selection	Hebrew Text Support	Enables IE5 to display and edit Hebrew text
Language selection	Arabic Text Support	Enables IE5 to display and edit Arabic text
Language selection	Thai Text Support	Enables IE5 to display and edit Thai text

On the exam, any requirement that mentions the words "collaborate" or "collaboration" requires NetMeeting as the solution.

Installation Options

Whether you package Internet Explorer 5 for distribution to a user community or you install it on a single client computer (see Figure 4-2), you must choose from one of two installation options:

- ✔ Minimal or Custom
- ✔ Typical

Note that on the minimal or custom option, you select the individual components you want to install. You start with the minimal install and then add other desired components, thus creating a custom installation.

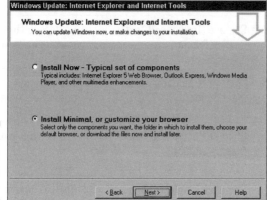

Figure 4-2:
Selecting an
installation
option.

Included components

The exam requires that you can identify when to select each of the three installation options. Table 4-2 shows which components are included in each of the three installation types.

Table 4-2	Components Included with Minimal, Typical, and Custom Installations		
Component	**Minimal**	**Typical**	**Custom**
Internet Explorer 5 Web Browser	x	x	x
Internet Explorer Help	x	x	x
Internet Connection Wizard	x	x	x
Visual Basic Scripting Support	x	x	x
Offline Browsing Pack		x	x
Internet Explorer Browsing Enhancements		x	x
Outlook Express		x	x

Component	Minimal	Typical	Custom
AOL ART Image Format Support		x	x
Language Auto-Selection		x	x
Microsoft Virtual Machine			x
Internet Explorer Core Fonts			x
Dynamic HTML Data Binding			x
NetMeeting			x
Outlook Express			x
Chat 2.5			x
Windows Media Player			x
Windows Media Player Codecs			x
Media Player RealNetwork Support			x
DirectAnimation			x
Vector Graphics Rendering (VML)			x
Macromedia Shockwave			x
Macromedia Flash Player			x
FrontPage Express			x
Web Publishing Wizard			x
Web Folders			x
Additional Web Fonts			x
Wallet			x

You may see an exam question that asks you to identify the components that are included in a minimal or typical installation.

A custom install is indicated whenever a required component is not included in the minimal or typical install. For example, if a system administrator wants to conserve disk space, yet needs to install NetMeeting with the IE5 browser package, he can choose the minimal installation and then manually add the NetMeeting component to the list of included components.

Disk space requirements

Disk space requirements for an Internet Explorer 5 installation vary depending on the components that you install. Requirements for each of the three installation options are as follows:

- Minimal install (browser-only):

    Required for install: 45MB

    Required to run: 27MB after restart

- Typical install:

    Required for install: 70MB

    Required to run: 55MB after restart

- Full install:

    Required for install: 111MB

    Required to run: 80MB after restart

 You're unlikely to see an exam question that simply asks you to identify hard drive requirements for the three installation options. Instead, you may see questions that describe an organization's client computers and user requirements and ask which installation option to select based on these circumstances. You can rule out a full install if the drive is too small for the install.

Post-Deployment Installation Options

After deploying your customized browser package to the user community, you can enable users to selectively install additional components without having a technician visit their desks. Users can add components as their needs change or as new components are developed.

Install on Demand

Internet Explorer 5 includes a new technology called *Install on Demand.* When new components are necessary to properly display a Web page, Install on Demand automatically downloads and installs the components (if they aren't already installed) on users' computers. So even if you select a minimal installation for your custom browser deployment, users can still obtain additional components as they're needed — as long as you haven't disabled Install on

Demand in your browser package. (Install on Demand is enabled in IE5 by default.)

Follow the steps in Lab 4-1 below to enable Install on Demand on your computer.

Lab 4-1   Enabling Install on Demand

1. **In Internet Explorer 5, choose Tools⇨Internet Options to display the Internet Options dialog box.**

2. **Click the Advanced tab.**

3. **Select the Enable Install On Demand check box (see Figure 4-3).**

4. **Click OK to close the Internet Options dialog box.**

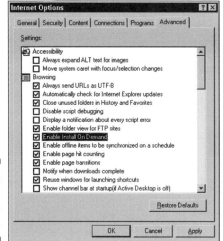

Figure 4-3:
Establishing
Install on
Demand.

Before taking the exam, know the steps you need to take to enable Install on Demand for your users.

As system administrator, you have to determine whether or not you want your user community to use the Install on Demand feature. You can disable the option in your browser package prior to distribution, but users can simply turn it back on. If you really want to exclude the Install on Demand feature on your network, you can disable automatic component installation during Stage 5 of the IEAK Customization wizard.

Figure 4-4 shows the System Policies and Restrictions screen in Stage 5 of the Customization wizard. To prevent the use of Install on Demand on your users' computers, expand the Policies and Restrictions branch and select the Corporate Restrictions folder. Then click the Software Updates policy as shown in the figure and select the Disable Automatic Install of Internet Explorer Components check box in the Automatic Install section. Selecting this option prevents Install on Demand on your users' computers.

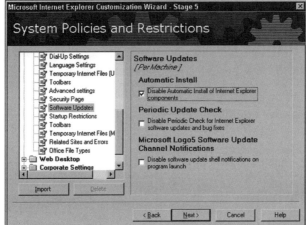

Figure 4-4:
Restricting
use of
Install on
Demand.

Windows Update

Have you always wanted a utility to install upgrades to client computers? With Internet Explorer 5, you have one! Windows Update enables users to visit the Microsoft update site to add components to their system or to download critical software updates. Windows Update examines the system and inventories which components are already installed. Then it returns a list of recommended updates for the system (see Figure 4-5). Users simply check the components that they want to install and then click the Download button.

I recommend using Windows Update because it saves a great deal of effort in updating the browser. Internet security vulnerabilities show up all too often — sometimes daily — and Windows Update is the easiest method to install those updates if IE5 is already deployed in your organization. Also, if you choose not to install components directly from the Microsoft site, you can specify an alternate URL for Windows Update to access additional components. If, for example, you want users to install components from a site maintained by your company, you would specify this site's URL.

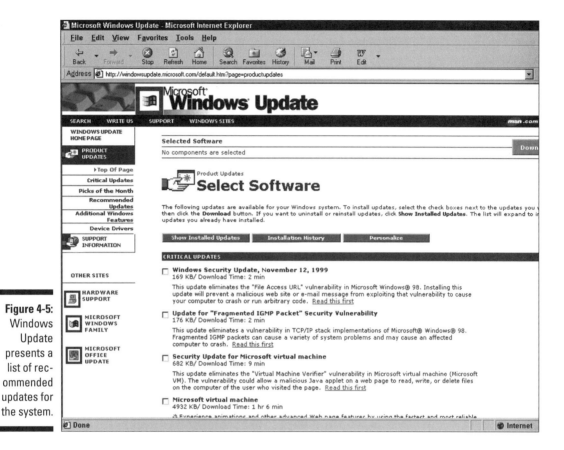

Figure 4-5:
Windows
Update
presents a
list of rec-
ommended
updates for
the system.

Lab 4-2 below shows you how to use Windows Update to add or upgrade components.

Lab 4-2   Using Windows Update

1. **In Internet Explorer 5, choose Tools⇨Windows Update.**

   You temporarily see a dialog box that tells you to wait while Windows Update customizes a product catalog for your computer. Then you see the list of updates that are not yet installed on your computer.

2. **Select the check boxes of the components that you want to install (see Figure 4-5).**

3. **Click the Download button.**

4. **Follow the displayed directions to install the component you selected. (Because the components vary, the on-screen instructions may differ between components.)**

Customizing Windows Update

You can use the IEAK Customization wizard to specify a URL for the Windows Update option on the IE5 Tools menu. On the Component Download screen of the Customization wizard (see Figure 4-6), you can configure the following Windows Update options:

✔ Remove the Windows Update option from the Tools menu

✔ Use the default URL for the Windows Update (windowsupdate.microsoft.com)

✔ Use a custom add-on URL and menu text

✔ Download components from Microsoft after install

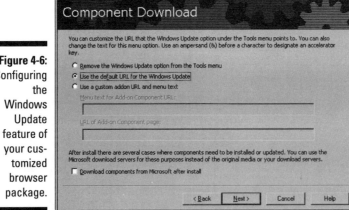

Figure 4-6: Configuring the Windows Update feature of your customized browser package.

By removing the Windows Update option from the Tools menu, users are unable to see that option on the Tools menu in their deployed browser. The Microsoft site for updates to Internet Explorer and for associated components becomes inaccessible. Similarly, you can download updates from your own component server and change the name of the feature on the Tools menu to something more appropriate. For example, if you prefer that users download updates from an internal server, add the URL for that server and change the Tools menu option to read *Browser Update*.

On the exam, you're most likely to encounter Windows Update in a scenario question. For example, the question may describe several user requirements for an organization's proposed custom browser package. One of those requirements may be an ability to update Internet Explorer 5 and its associated components as updates become available. You may be asked to identify which components the administrator must include in the custom browser package.

Prep Test

1 Barbara is a corporate administrator and is preparing a custom IE5 browser package. Knowing that some of the company's client computers have small hard drives, Barbara has selected a minimal installation of IE5. Which components are included in the minimal installation?

A. ○ The IE5 browser

B. ○ Outlook Express 5

C. ○ Web Publishing wizard

D. ○ Offline Browsing Pack

2 Which of the following components are included in a typical IE5 installation? (Choose two.)

A. ❑ Outlook Express

B. ❑ Microsoft Virtual Machine

C. ❑ Microsoft Wallet

D. ❑ Offline Browsing Pack

3 As a corporate administrator, Barbara is using the IEAK Customization wizard to create a customized browser package. She doesn't want to install unnecessary components on her users' computers. At the same time, she doesn't want to restrict users who require additional features and components. How can she meet everyone's browser requirements?

A. ○ Barbara can select a full install and let users delete the components that they don't need.

B. ○ Barbara can select a minimal installation and configure Install on Demand so users can install additional components as needed.

C. ○ Barbara can create a separate custom browser package for each user.

D. ○ Barbara can create a custom installation by selecting only the components that she knows the users will need.

4 Barbara is a corporate administrator creating a custom IE5 browser package. Rather than have users access the Microsoft site to update IE5 components, Barbara wants users to access an intranet site for updated components. What IE5 feature must Barbara modify with the IEAK Customization wizard to achieve this configuration?

A. ○ Windows Update

B. ○ Install on Demand

C. ○ Microsoft Component Update

D. ○ Microsoft Virtual Machine

5 Barbara is a corporate administrator and has deployed IE5 to all the users in her company without customizing the browser. Using SMS, Barbara deploys IE5 security patches and upgrades to each client computer on her network. If Barbara has deployed IE5 with only the default configuration settings, how else could users efficiently receive updates and patches?

A. ○ From the auto-config URL

B. ○ Using the IEAK Profile Manager

C. ○ From Windows Update

D. ○ Through e-mail attachments

6 As a corporate administrator, you have to determine whether you want your user community to use the Install on Demand feature. You can disable the option in your browser package prior to distribution, but users may simply turn it back on. What tool(s) can you use to prevent users from changing the Install on Demand settings? (Choose two.)

A. ❑ IEAK Toolkit

B. ❑ Auto-config URL

C. ❑ IEAK Customization wizard

D. ❑ IEAK Profile Manager

7 Which component should you include in your custom browser package if you want to enable users to collaborate over the Internet?

A. ○ Outlook Express 5

B. ○ NetMeeting

C. ○ Microsoft Chat

D. ○ Internet Explorer 5

8 As a corporate administrator, you don't want users to download upgrades and patches from the Windows Update site. You prefer to distribute necessary patches by using SMS. What can you do to prevent users from using Windows Update?

A. ○ Using the IEAK Customization wizard, remove the Windows Update option from the Internet Explorer Tools menu.

B. ○ Using the IEAK Profile Manager, remove the Windows Update option from the Internet Explorer Options menu.

C. ○ Using the IEAK Toolkit, remove the Windows Update option from the Internet Explorer Tools menu.

D. ○ You can't prevent users from using Windows Update.

Selecting IE5 Installation Options

Answers

1 *A.* A minimal installation of IE5 includes the IE5 browser, Internet Explorer Help, Internet Connection wizard, and Visual Basic Scripting Support. Outlook Express 5, the Offline Browsing Pack, and the Web Publishing wizard are not included in a minimal install. *See "Installation Options."*

2 *A and D.* The Microsoft Virtual Machine and Microsoft Wallet are not part of a typical IE5 installation. Review *"Installation Options."*

3 *B.* Although the other answers work, they're not the most efficient way to meet the requirements. *See "Install on Demand."*

4 *A.* By default, the IE5 browser accesses the Microsoft Windows Update Web site to update IE5 components. But by using the IEAK Customization wizard, Barbara can instead modify the Component Download screen to include a custom URL for updates. The URL can be an Internet or intranet site. *Review "Customizing Windows Update."*

5 *C.* By default, Windows Update is part of Internet Explorer 5 and accesses the Microsoft Web site for upgrades and patches. Barbara is performing unnecessary work by distributing the upgrades and patches via SMS. Although answer A is an efficient means of distributing updates and batches, it isn't a default setting of Internet Explorer — Barbara must first configure an auto-config URL by using the IEAK. Finally, answer D is technically feasible, but it isn't an efficient way of distributing updates and patches. *See "Windows Update."*

6 *C and D.* Both of these tools enable you to make changes to settings and restrictions that prevent users from changing the browser configuration that you deploy. *See "Post-Deployment Installation Options."*

7 *B.* You should have keyed in on the word "collaborate" in this question. On the exam, any time you see the word collaborate, it means that NetMeeting is involved. *Review "Identifying IE5 Components."*

8 *A.* You can also use the IEAK Profile Manager for this task, but answer B is incorrect because the Windows Update is not on the Options menu. *Review "Windows Update."*

Chapter 5

Defend Thyself!

• •

Exam Objectives

▶ Security strategies for public kiosks

▶ Security strategies for general business sites

▶ Security strategies for single-task sites

▶ Security strategies for intranet sites

• •

Configuring secure access to Internet sites is one of the most important jobs of any system administrator. You strive for a careful balance of network security and user freedom. If security controls are too tight, you may deny access to features that your users desire. But if the controls are too weak, you risk endangering valuable systems and data.

In this chapter, I cover strategies for configuring the IE5 browser for the best security at a variety of Web sites. Whether you're accessing an intranet site behind your own firewall or accessing random sites on the Internet, a security strategy enabling safe access exists.

Quick Assessment

1 The four security levels available for configuring security zones are: _____, _____, _____, and _____.

2 The four default security zones in Internet Explorer 5 are: _____, _____, _____, and _____.

3 The _____ zone prevents users from running any content that may be harmful.

4 The _____ zone enables users to run any content with no prior warnings.

5 Businesses that send sensitive data over the Internet should enable _____.

6 Generally, end users demand maximum functionality and minimal _____ on their IE5 browser.

7 The browser configuration for a public kiosk is usually quite _____ compared to the browser configuration of a typical end user.

8 A _____ _____ involves configuring the IE5 browser to perform one specific function.

9 _____ are normally found in public buildings and are used by the general public.

10 Planning security settings for the IE5 browser varies according to how the browser will be _____.

Answers

1   *Low, Medium-low, Medium, High.* See "Security zones."

2   *Internet zone, Local Intranet zone, Trusted Sites zone, Restricted Sites zone.* See "Security zones."

3   *Restricted Sites.* See "Restricted Sites zone."

4   *Trusted Sites.* See "Trusted Sites zone."

5   *encryption.* See "Encryption."

6   *restrictions.* See "Planning for Specific Sites."

7   *restrictive.* See "Planning for Specific Sites."

8   *single-task site.* See "Planning for Specific Sites."

9   *kiosks.* See "Planning for Specific Sites."

10   *used.* See "Planning for Specific Sites."

First Line of Defense

Internet Explorer 5 offers several lines of defense against the malicious activities that occur on the Web. Starting with the four default security zones, system administrators can tweak and tune browser settings to provide the optimum configuration for any type of Web site.

Before I begin discussing specific site scenarios, you should understand the weapons — er, tools — available to defend your environment while accessing the Web. Security zones, certificates, and encryption work together to defend your universe — oops, I mean organization. After you have these settings optimally configured, use the IEAK to lock down any settings that you don't want users to be able to alter.

Who goes where?

Before building a custom browser package, you must determine user requirements to establish how the browser is to be used. The sites that users visit determine the security settings included in a custom browser package.

The exam contains several scenario questions that describe how people use their browsers. From the description, you must identify the appropriate security configuration.

On the exam, you're given the user requirements in scenario questions. While devising security strategies for a custom browser, try to find out the following information to help you determine security requirements:

- From your company's perspective, is it vital that employees be able to access the Internet with your customized browser?
- Should employees be given free access to all sites, or restricted to certain trusted sites?
- Do employees only need access to sites on your own intranet?
- When a user accesses a site, what are they likely to do?
- Will a user download data, scripts, and other information?
- Will a user only read information posted at the site?
- Will a user post files to a Web site?
- What type of information does your user community put on the Internet?
- Are users sending data that shouldn't fall into the wrong hands?
- Are users sending or receiving sensitive financial data?

After you obtain these answers, you can use them to appropriately configure your IE5 browser's security zones, encryption, and digital certificates.

If you're the administrator for an ISP, some of this information doesn't apply to you. Because your users come from a variety of organizations and locations, you probably don't want to track their usage patterns or lock down their browser settings.

Security zones

Internet Explorer 5 has four default security zones:

- ✔ Internet zone
- ✔ Local Intranet zone
- ✔ Trusted Sites zone
- ✔ Restricted Sites zone

Grouping Web sites into one of these zones enables you to control security on the sites as a group. In other words, you can specify any high-risk sites as members of the Restricted zone, set the desired security level for the Restricted zone, and apply that security level to all the sites in the zone.

Table 5-1 shows the four security zones and their default security levels. You can alter the default security levels to more closely align with your needs, but I don't recommend that you weaken them. The default security levels create the appropriate environment for each type of Web site. If none of these zones are quite right for your needs, you can also create your own security zones and customize the settings. (In Chapter 17, I give you instructions on creating and altering security zones.)

Table 5-1	Default Security Levels	
Zone	*Security Levels*	*Effect*
Internet zone	Medium	Warn users before accessing content that could harm the computer.
Local Intranet zone	Medium	Warn users before accessing content that could harm the computer.
Trusted Sites zone	Low	Access all content without any prior warning to the user.
Restricted Sites zone	High	Disable access to any content that could harm the computer.

The definitions for the security levels are as follows:

- ✔ **High:** The safest, but least functional, way to browse. Less secure features are disabled. Cookies are disabled, which means that some Web sites don't work. Appropriate for sites that may have harmful content.

- ✔ **Medium:** Safe browsing and still functional. Prompts before downloading potentially unsafe content. Unsigned ActiveX controls aren't downloaded. Appropriate for most Internet sites.

- ✔ **Medium-low:** Same as Medium but without prompts. Most content is run without prompts. Unsigned ActiveX controls aren't downloaded. Appropriate for sites on your intranet.

- ✔ **Low:** Provides minimal safeguards and warning prompts. Most content downloads and runs without prompts. All active content can run. Appropriate for sites that you absolutely trust.

If, as I suggest in the preceding section of this chapter, you gather information on commonly accessed sites within your organization, you can now assign those sites to the appropriate security zone. To help you determine which zone is most appropriate, refer to the security level definitions earlier in this section and to the configuration settings in Figure 5-1.

Internet zone

For any system administrator, whether in a corporate administrator or ISP/ICP role, most sites outside of your own firewall belong in the Internet zone. The owners of these sites are generally unknown to you, and you don't know whether or not their content can be trusted. The Medium security level is the default setting because it permits access to sites while warning of the potential for hazardous content.

Local Intranet zone

The Local Intranet zone comprises sites and servers that are within your organization's firewall. The default security level is Medium because many of these sites may not be under your direct control.

Trusted Sites zone

The Trusted Sites zone includes sites that you know to be safe. Your own IE5 download site qualifies as a trusted site, as do similar sites that you control. Perhaps you choose to include the Microsoft site and other trusted vendor sites in the Trusted Sites zone. The security level for the Trusted Sites zone is Low, so you should be confident of any sites that you place in this zone.

Figure 5-1: Comparing the settings of the four security zones.

	Internet				Local Intranet				Trusted				Restricted			
	L	ML	M	H	L	ML	M	H	L	ML	M	H	L	ML	M	H
Download signed ActiveX controls	E	P	P	D	E	P	P	D	E	P	P	D	E	P	P	D
Download unsigned ActiveX controls	P	D	D	D	P	D	D	D	P	D	D	D	P	D	D	D
Initialize and script ActiveX controls not marked as safe	P	D	D	D	P	D	D	D	P	D	D	D	P	D	D	D
Run ActiveX controls and plug-ins	E	E	E	D	E	E	E	D	E	E	E	D	E	E	E	D
Script ActiveX controls marked safe for scripting	E	E	E	E	E	E	E	E	E	E	E	E	E	E	E	E
Allow cookies that are stored on your computer	E	E	E	D	E	E	E	D	E	E	E	D	E	E	E	D
Allow per-session cookies (not stored)	E	E	E	D	E	E	E	D	E	E	E	D	E	E	E	D
File download	E	E	E	D	E	E	E	D	E	E	E	D	E	E	E	D
Font download	E	E	E	P	E	E	E	P	E	E	E	P	E	E	E	P
Java permissions	Ls	Ms	Ms	Hs	Ls	Ms	Ms	Hs	Ls	Ms	Ms	Hs	Ls	Ms	Hs	Hs
Access data sources across domains	E	P	D	D	E	P	D	D	E	P	D	D	E	P	D	D
Drag and drop or copy and paste files	E	E	E	P	E	E	E	P	E	E	E	P	E	E	E	P
Installation of desktop items	E	P	P	D	E	P	P	D	E	P	P	D	E	P	P	D
Launching programs and files in an IFRAME	E	P	P	D	E	P	P	D	E	P	P	D	E	P	P	D
Navigate sub-frames across different domains	E	E	E	D	E	E	E	D	E	E	E	D	E	E	E	D
Software channel permissions	Ls	Ms	Ms	Hs	Ls	Ms	Ms	Hs	Ls	Ms	Ms	Hs	Ls	Ms	Ms	Hs
Submit nonencrypted form data	E	E	E	P	E	E	E	P	E	E	E	P	E	E	E	P
Userdata persistence	E	E	E	D	E	E	E	D	E	E	E	D	E	E	E	D
Active scripting	E	E	E	E	E	E	E	E	E	E	E	E	E	E	E	E
Allow paste operations via script	E	E	E	D	E	E	E	D	E	E	E	D	E	E	E	D
Scripting of Java applets	E	E	E	D	E	E	E	D	E	E	E	D	E	E	E	D
User Authentication	AU	AI	AI	P	AU	AI	AI	P	AU	AI	AI	P	AU	AI	AI	P

L = Low, ML = Medium Low, M = Medium, H = High, E = Enable, D = Disable, P = Prompt, Ls = Low safety, Ms = Medium safety, Hs = High safety
AU = Automatic logon with current username and password, AI = Automatic logon only in intranet zone

Restricted Sites zone

The Restricted Sites zone uses the High security level. You include sites in this zone whose content you don't trust. The security settings in this zone prevent users from inadvertently accessing harmful content through Java applets, scripts, or downloaded files. If you encounter a site that contains harmful content, add the site to the Restricted Sites zone. Then lock down IE5 settings by using IEAK policies and restrictions so that users cannot alter the security zone or add and delete sites from a security zone.

If you access a site link that takes you to another site to download a file, the most restrictive security level of the two sites takes effect. For example, a user surfs to Site A, where she clicks a hyperlink to download a file. The hyperlink takes you to Site B to download the file. If Site A is in your Trusted Sites zone, but Site B is in your Restricted Sites zone, then the most restrictive security settings take effect. (In this case, the Restricted Sites zone's security level.)

Certificates

As a system administrator, you may want to configure your IE5 browser to use digital certificates to ensure the authenticity of content. This step is most appropriate for corporate administrators, who bear responsibility for enforcing corporate security policies. Using the IEAK, you install the certificates when you create a customized browser package. Then use the IEAK policies and restrictions to prevent users from changing certificate settings.

Encryption

The data that users transmit via the Internet is also at risk. Sensitive information that users enter into forms or transmit to other users and sites can be hijacked and used inappropriately. Criminals target credit card information, which they sell or use to make fraudulent purchases. Businesses are also vulnerable to intercepted data. Using the IEAK, you can specify that only encrypted data is transmitted on the network.

Planning for Specific Sites

System administrators must prepare the IE5 browser to access a variety of sites. The IEAK exam specifically tests you on the proper browser configurations for:

✔ General business use

✔ Public kiosk use

✔ Single-task use

✔ Intranet-only use

Each of these site types requires a different form of browser configuration. For example, browsers used as the front end to an intranet application can include extremely low security settings compared to browsers that perform a variety of general business uses, such as accessing sites on the Internet. Similarly, the browser configuration for a public kiosk is usually quite restrictive compared to the browser configuration of a typical end user.

On the exam, you see questions that present a scenario involving a public kiosk, a general business site, a single-task site, or an intranet-only site. The exam requires you to identify the correct actions to configure the browser as specified in the question.

General business use

End users generally prefer few restrictions on their IE5 browser but demand maximum functionality. Configuring the IE5 browser for general business users, by comparison, is more complex. Aside from Internet and intranet sites, business users also access *extranet* sites. (An extranet is a network that is shared by two or more organizations. Many companies share an extranet with their vendors to streamline purchasing and order processing.) The IE5 browser is often the front end to customized corporate applications.

As a result of these differing uses, your security planning encompasses a wide range of scenarios. Most businesses have a corporate security policy and/or a corporate resource policy. These policies detail corporate security practices and appropriate use of corporate assets. Business users are usually accustomed to and tolerant of security limitations in the use of their computers.

Depending on corporate policy, you must appropriately configure the browser's four security zones. The Internet zone usually calls for the Medium or High security level. Extranet sites belong in the Trusted Sites zone, where the Medium security level is usually appropriate. The Low security level of the Local Intranet zone is typically appropriate for all intranet sites. Any suspect sites belong in the Restricted Sites zone with High security.

Remember the following guidelines when configuring IE5 for business users:

✔ Prompt before downloading any files or content.

✔ Require username and password authentication.

   ✔ Warn before sending unencrypted data.

   ✔ Restrict users from changing the security zone settings (see Figure 5-2).

   ✔ Install site certificates.

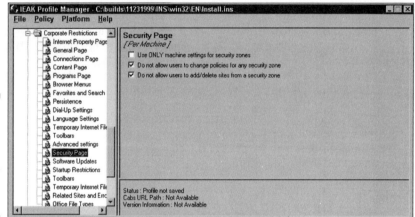

Figure 5-2:
Restricting
users from
changing
security
zone
settings.

Public kiosk use

Public kiosks are computers frequently found in building lobbies and airport terminals, or at trade shows, which perform limited functions, such as presenting a building directory or a presentation. With today's dynamic Web content, using IE5 in public kiosks is a growing trend.

A public kiosk may or may not be connected to a corporate network. Some are maintained as stand-alone computers, while others are networked so that the content can be refreshed from a central location. Because anyone who wanders past the kiosk can use the browser, it should be locked down carefully to prevent users from attempting activity other than what you intend. A good idea is to install only the applications that are needed to run your kiosk application.

Among the security considerations to consider when planning a public kiosk are:

   ✔ **Security zones:** The configuration of the kiosk's security zones depends on whether the PC is networked and whether the browser is used to access other sites. If users access Internet sites from the kiosk, make certain to review the Internet zone settings. If only known sites are accessed, consider placing those sites in the Trusted Sites zone. In short, consider how the browser will be used and what type of sites it will access.

✔ **Scripts and Dynamic Content:** If your kiosk application doesn't use scripts, Java, or ActiveX, you should turn these options off and lock them down so that users cannot perform functions not intended for the kiosk.

✔ **Encryption:** Is your kiosk collecting sensitive information? If so, configure the browser to encrypt data that is gathered at the kiosk. Again, lock down the browser settings so users can't alter them.

✔ **Downloads:** Public kiosks seldom require users to download files or applications. In fact, you probably want to prevent users from doing so by using the IEAK policies and restrictions to restrict downloads and FTP from your kiosk.

You may find it helpful to use the chart in Figure 5-3 when planning your security configurations. Similar to the chart in Figure 5-1, the individual settings are left blank to let you plan your own zone settings.

Single-task use

A single-task site involves configuring the IE5 browser to perform one specific function. The function can be order-entry activity, or any other application that uses the browser to perform one specific task. Security is generally easier to configure for a single-task site. You know exactly where the users are going, and you know precisely what type of information they access from that site. Configuration for security zones, digital certificates, and encryption, therefore, is easily defined.

When thinking about security for single-task sites, consider whether or not the network has access to the Internet. If the network has access to the Internet, follow the guidelines for configuring IE5 for general business users. I also recommend the following:

✔ Place the site that the users are accessing in the Trusted Sites zone.

✔ Install only components necessary to complete the task.

✔ Restrict users from changing the browser configuration.

Intranet-only use

Intranet-only users use the IE5 browser to only access sites on their organization's intranet. Intranet-only users don't access sites on the Internet. In some cases, the Local Intranet zone default settings specify the appropriate security level for this scenario, particularly if there's no Internet connectivity. But other cases, such as an order center that collects credit card information, require that the browser encrypt data that is put on the network. When configuring an intranet-only site, you must lock down the browser so users cannot change the browser configuration.

Figure 5-3:
Planning
security
zone
settings
for your
browser.

	Internet				Local Intranet				Trusted				Restricted			
	L	ML	M	H	L	ML	M	H	L	ML	M	H	L	ML	M	H
Download signed ActiveX controls																
Download unsigned ActiveX controls																
Initialize and script ActiveX controls not marked as safe																
Run ActiveX controls and plug-ins																
Script ActiveX controls marked safe for scripting																
Allow cookies that are stored on your computer																
Allow per-session cookies (not stored)																
File download																
Font download																
Java permissions																
Access data sources across domains																
Drag and drop or copy and paste files																
Installation of desktop items																
Launching programs and files in an IFRAME																
Navigate sub-frames across different domains																
Software channel permissions																
Submit nonencrypted form data																
Userdata persistence																
Active scripting																
Allow paste operations via script																
Scripting of Java applets																
User Authentication																

L = Low, ML = Medium Low, M = Medium, H = High, E = Enable, D = Disable, P = Prompt, Ls = Low safety, Ms = Medium safety, Hs = High safety
AU= Automatic logon with current username and password, AI = Automatic logon only in intranet zone

Figure 5-3:
Planning
security
zone
settings
for your
browser.

Prep Test

Walt is the system administrator for a company that deploys kiosks in airport terminals. Each kiosk contains a single Windows 98 computer with 128MB of RAM and 4GB of disk space. The kiosks are connected to database servers at company headquarters via the Internet. The kiosks use Internet Explorer 5 as the front end to an application that signs users up for magazine subscriptions. Users enter credit card information and other personal information at these kiosks. Walt is using the Internet Explorer Administration Kit to customize the IE5 browser for the kiosks.

Questions 1 through 5 refer to the scenario described above.

1 Which Internet Explorer 5 installation option should Walt specify when creating the custom browser for the kiosks?

A ○ Full installation option

B ○ Typical installation option

C ○ Minimal installation option

D ○ Web Browser installation option

2 Which security zone is most appropriate for the corporate headquarters Web site that the kiosk browsers interact with?

A ○ Internet zone

B ○ Local Intranet zone

C ○ Restricted zone

D ○ Trusted Sites zone

3 How should Walt configure the Submit Nonencrypted Form Data setting?

A ○ Enable

B ○ Disable

C ○ Restrict

D ○ Prompt

4 Which User Authentication Logon setting should Walt select?

A ○ Anonymous logon

B ○ Automatic logon

C ○ Automatic logon only in the Intranet zone

D ○ Guest logon

5 How should Walt configure the File Download setting?

A ○ Disable

B ○ Enable

C ○ Prompt

D ○ Restrict

Elaine is the corporate administrator for a large corporation. She is planning a customized Internet Explorer 5 browser package to be used throughout the corporation. Client computers run Windows 98, Windows 95, and Windows NT. Intranet sites run on Microsoft Internet Information Server. The corporate network is protected from the Internet by a firewall. Users in the purchasing department access extranet sites with customized forms for ordering supplies from partnering vendors.

Questions 6 through 9 refer to the scenario described above.

6 Which description best describes the type of users Elaine will be supporting with the customized IE5 browser?

A ○ General end users

B ○ General business users

C ○ Single-task users

D ○ Public kiosk users

7 In which security zone should Elaine place the extranet sites?

A ○ Internet zone

B ○ Local Intranet zone

C ○ Trusted Sites zone

D ○ Restricted Sites zone

8 What is the best way for Elaine to prevent users from adding or removing sites from the Restricted Sites zone?

A ○ Restrict access to Internet Options on the IE5 Properties menu.

B ○ Use the IEAK Profile Manager to prevent users from changing policies for any security zone.

C ○ Use the IEAK Profile Manager to prevent users from adding or deleting sites from the Restricted Sites zone.

D ○ Use the IEAK Profile Manager to prevent users from adding or deleting sites from the security zones.

9 What is the most appropriate security level for Elaine to configure for the Internet zone?

A ○ Low

B ○ Medium

C ○ Medium high

D ○ High

10 True or False. By default, the Restricted Sites zone uses the High security level, which prompts users before placing cookies on their computers.

A ○ True

B ○ False

Answers

1 *C.* A minimal installation includes only the IE5 browser, and public kiosks should include only the components required to perform the kiosk's specified task. Answers A and B are incorrect because these installation options install more components than the kiosk requires. Answer D is not a valid IE5 installation option. *See "Public kiosk use."*

2 *D.* Answer D is the correct answer because the content of the corporate Web site is known and trusted. Answer A is incorrect because the Internet zone settings may be too restrictive for the kiosk's use. Answer C is incorrect because it's also too restrictive for the kiosk's purpose. Answer B, although a good second choice, isn't correct because answer D is the most appropriate security zone for this purpose. *See "Trusted Sites zone."*

3 *B.* Because users are entering credit card and other personal information, and the data traverses the Internet, data should always be encrypted. Therefore, answers A and D are incorrect. Answer C is not a legitimate option for this setting. *Review "Encryption."*

4 *A.* Answer A is correct because the kiosk is available to the general public, who don't have user names and passwords. Answers B and C are incorrect for the same reason — users don't have user names and passwords. Answer D isn't a legitimate option for this setting. *See "Public kiosk use."*

5 *A.* Users should be unable to download files to a public kiosk. Answer B is incorrect because it enables users to download files. Answers C and D are not legitimate options for this setting. *See "Public kiosk use."*

6 *B.* Elaine is a corporate administrator and has the responsibility of appropriately securing corporate assets. Answer A isn't correct because general end users prefer few restrictions and fully functional browser features. Answers C and D are incorrect because they're too restrictive. *Review "General business use."*

7 *C.* The content on the partner's Web pages is known and trusted. Answers A and D are incorrect because they're too restrictive. Answer B is incorrect because, although less restrictive, the Local Intranet zone isn't as appropriate as the Trusted Sites zone. *Review "Trusted Sites zone."*

8 *D.* Answer A is incorrect because Internet Options is on the IE5 Tools menu. Answer B is incorrect because it only prevents users from altering the security policies — they can still add and delete sites in a zone. Answer C is incorrect because it isn't an option in the IEAK Profile Manager — users can only prevent users from adding and deleting sites for all zones, but not for specific zones. *See "General business use."*

9 *B.* The Medium security level enables users to take advantage of IE5 features while prompting them before completing risky actions. Answer A is incorrect because it doesn't provide adequate security for business users. Answer C is incorrect because it's not a valid setting. Answer D is incorrect because it's too restrictive for general business use. *See "General business use."*

10 *B.* While the default security level for the Restricted Sites zone is High, the High security level does not prompt users before downloading cookies — it prevents users from downloading cookies altogether. So the answer cannot be True. *Review "Security zones."*

Chapter 6

Configuring Offline Viewing

· ·

Exam Objectives

▶ Creating offline Web pages
▶ Scheduling automatic updates
▶ Configuring offline pages for various user groups

· ·

*I*nternet Explorer 5 introduces a new feature — offline Web pages. An offline page is a Web page that you've saved to your hard drive so that you can view it even when you're not connected to the Internet or intranet. This is referred to as *offline viewing*. Several situations exist when offline pages are beneficial to your user community. In particular, offline viewing is useful for mobile workers who need to access data from an offline page while away from the office.

You're likely to see several questions on configuring and updating offline pages on the exam. Be sure that you're familiar with all the offline page configuration options.

Quick Assessment

Configuring Offline Viewing

1 An _____ _____ is a Web page that you've saved to your hard drive so that you can view it even when you're not connected to the Internet or intranet.

Creating a Customized Offline Page

2 The _____ _____ wizard enables you to configure options for an offline page.

Manual Synchronization

3 To save fresh Web content to an offline page on a sporadic basis — without scheduling automatic updates — use the _____ option from the Tools menu.

Single-Task-Based Users

4 Any Web page that is accessed often is a good candidate for an _____ _____.

Managing Offline Pages with the IEAK

5 You can use the IEAK _____ _____ to manage offline pages after your browser has been deployed.

6 If you know that many of your company's computers have small hard drives, you can restrict the amount of Web content that can be _____ to offline pages.

Updating Offline Page Information

7 How you configure offline page _____ is highly dependent on the type of data being accessed.

8 If information is _____ — it doesn't change frequently — you can update the information occasionally or not at all.

Storing Offline Web Pages

9 The _____ _____ _____ folder in the Windows directory stores the offline Web pages.

10 If your operating system is Windows 95 or 98, the default location for offline Web pages is: _____.

Answers

1   *offline page.* See "Configuring Offline Viewing."

2   *Offline Favorites.* See "Creating a customized offline page."

3   *Synchronize.* See "Manual synchronization."

4   *offline page.* See "Single-task-based users."

5   *Profile Manager.* See "Managing offline pages with the IEAK."

6   *downloaded.* See "Managing offline pages with the IEAK."

7   *updates.* See "Updating offline page information."

8   *static.* See "Updating offline page information."

9   *Offline Web Pages. See* "Storing offline Web pages."

10   *C:\windows\Offline Web Pages.* See "Storing offline Web pages."

Creating and Managing Offline Pages

Offline viewing is more than simply saving a page to a hard drive. When information isn't static and changes frequently, users must have access to the fresh data. A system administrator (that's you!) must know when — and how — to schedule automatic page updates that optimize network bandwidth while providing appropriate access to fresh data. You also need to know how to use the IEAK utilities to manage offline pages.

Creating an offline page

Creating offline Web pages is easy. Any user can make a page available offline simply by checking a box as they save a page in their Favorites menu. Because offline pages are covered extensively on the exam, Lab 6-1 takes you through the steps of creating a simple offline Web page in Internet Explorer 5.

Lab 6-1   Creating an Offline Page

1. **While viewing an online Web page in Internet Explorer 5, choose Favorites⇨Add to Favorites.**

   The Add Favorite dialog box appears, as shown in Figure 6-1.

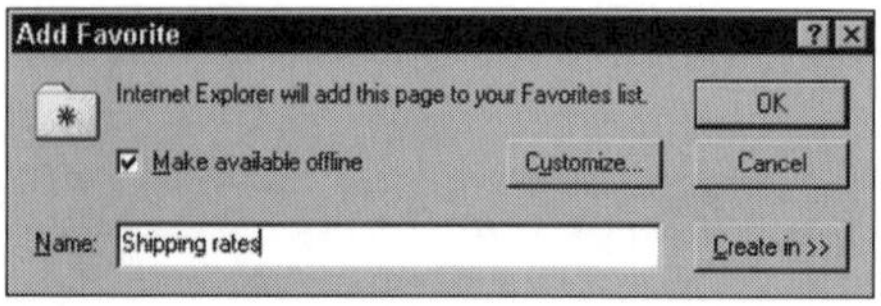

Figure 6-1:
Making a
page avail-
able as an
offline page.

2. **Select the Make Available Offline check box.**

3. **Type a descriptive name for the offline page in the Name box or just use the name that Internet Explorer provides by default.**

4. **If you want to organize this offline page into a folder, click the Create In button to the right of the Name box.**

   Doing so expands the Add Favorite dialog box to include a folder list (see Figure 6-2). Either select a folder in the Create In folder list or click the New Folder button to create a new folder.

5. **Click the OK button to save the offline page and then close the Add Favorite dialog box.**

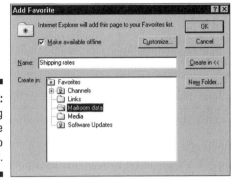

Figure 6-2:
Organizing offline pages into folders.

Creating a customized offline page

On the exam, you're likely to see several questions about offline pages, particularly in regard to customizing offline pages. You can configure some custom settings for an offline page by clicking the Customize button in the Add Favorite dialog box (refer to Figure 6-1). The Customize button starts the Offline Favorite wizard, which you use to further configure an offline page.

The Offline Favorite wizard enables you to configure several options for the offline page:

✔ If the offline page has links to other pages, you can specify to download pages *x* links deep from the original page. In other words, if the original page has a link to a second page, you can specify: *Download pages 1 link deep from this page.* If the second page has a link to a third page that you want to update as well, specify: *Download pages 2 links deep from this page.* Figure 6-3 shows a diagram of a Web site that has links one link deep, and a Web site that has links two links deep.

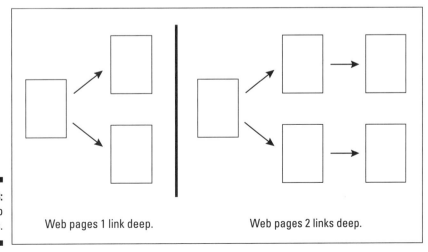

Figure 6-3:
Linked Web pages.

Web pages 1 link deep.   Web pages 2 links deep.

✔ You can specify one of three methods for synchronizing the offline page: by choosing synchronize from the Tools menu, by creating a new schedule, or by using an existing schedule.

✔ You can specify a password to protect the page.

On the exam, you must know when to synchronize manually (choosing Synchronize from the IE5 Tools menu) and when to use scheduled synchronization. Dial-in users should usually synchronize manually because they connect via slow links.

You should also recognize why it's wise to be cautious when choosing to download linked pages. Downloading linked pages can quickly consume several megabytes of space on a hard drive. In addition to consuming valuable disk space, downloading linked pages can tie up the system's resources for a significant amount of time.

Downloading linked pages slows system response time during the download and fills the system's hard drive with many megabytes of information.

In many cases, Web content is updated on a regularly scheduled basis. An employee phone listing on an intranet site, for example, is often updated on a daily basis. In extremely large companies, the phone listing may be updated weekly. Online magazines (sometimes called Webzines or e-zines) are usually updated weekly.

Regularly updated pages are ideal for an automatic update schedule. For example, assume that your corporation updates its intranet phone listing at 6 p.m. on Friday evenings. Friday nights or Saturday mornings are ideal times for a scheduled update to this offline page — times when the data is fresh and when you probably won't inconvenience the user.

Storing offline Web pages

By changing the properties of an offline Web page, you can alter the update schedule. The Offline Web Pages folder in the Windows directory stores the offline Web pages.

If your operating system is Windows 95 or 98, the default location is:

    C:\windows\Offline Web Pages

For a Windows NT 4.0 operating system, the default location is:

    C:\winnt\Offline Web Pages

Select the Offline Web Pages folder, select an offline page, and right-click to access its Properties page. From the Schedule tab, you can change the update schedule.

Updating offline page information

You can update the information in an offline page two ways:

- ✔ Use the Synchronize option from the Internet Explorer 5 Tools menu to synchronize the offline page with the online Web content.
- ✔ Configure an update schedule so that the offline page updates automatically.

On the exam, don't confuse the Refresh button with the Synchronize option. While the Refresh button freshens the information on the screen, it doesn't save new data to an offline Web page. You must use the Synchronize option from the Internet Explorer 5 Tools menu to save new data to an offline page.

Consider the following factors when determining when and how to update offline pages:

- ✔ Frequency of data changes
- ✔ Available network bandwidth
- ✔ Cost of Internet access
- ✔ System hardware of the computer accessing the Web page
- ✔ Work schedule of the user accessing the Web page

Not all of these factors will be pertinent to your situation. Some of the factors vary according to the user's location and job responsibilities. One-size-fits-all may not be the best answer for your user community, and you may be required to assist users in configuring an update method that fits a particular need.

How you configure offline page updates is highly dependent on the type of data being accessed. If the information is static — it doesn't change frequently — you can update the information infrequently or not at all. If the information changes continually — like stock quotes — it's best to access the information online in real time. Most Web sites fall somewhere between these two extremes.

Synchronizing offline pages

To save fresh Web content to an offline page on a sporadic basis — without scheduling automatic updates — use the Synchronize option from the Tools menu. This method of synchronizing gives the user control of offline page updates so that they don't interfere with current work. Synchronizing an offline page that has associated links can tie up system resources and slow browser response time. For this reason, many users prefer to synchronize by using the Tools menu. Dial-up users also frequently use this method to synchronize their offline pages.

Updating Web content can slow a computer system while the computer accesses the Web — especially if the computer is connected via a slow link or a congested network. Page updates are also particularly bothersome for those using older model computers with slow processors or limited memory. Therefore, these users may prefer to update offline pages at an unscheduled time that is convenient to them during the workday.

Manual synchronization

Lab 6-2 shows you how to manually synchronize an offline Web page with the online Web page. Choose manual synchronization when you prefer to randomly select a time to update the offline page content.

Lab 6-2	Synchronizing Offline Pages

1. **In Internet Explorer 5, choose Tools⇨Synchronize.**

2. **On the Items to Synchronize dialog box, select the check box next to the offline page that you want to update (see Figure 6-4).**

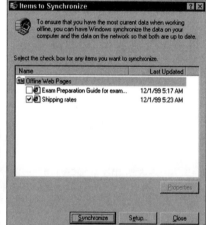

Figure 6-4:
Selecting offline pages to synchronize.

3. **Click the Synchronize button.**

   While the offline page is synchronizing, a Synchronizing dialog box appears that shows the status of the update (see Figure 6-5). When the page synchronization is complete, the Synchronizing dialog box closes automatically.

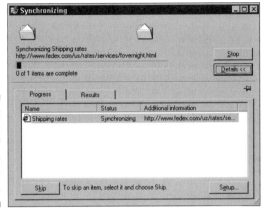

Figure 6-5:
Watching
the status of
a page
synchroni-
zation.

Synchronizing at logon

The Setup button at the bottom of the Items to Synchronize dialog box (refer
to Figure 6-4) takes you to the Synchronization Settings dialog box, as shown
in Figure 6-6. The Synchronization Settings dialog box enables you to set up
convenient times to synchronize your offline pages.

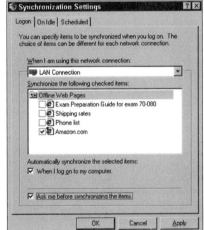

Figure 6-6:
Synchronizing
offline
pages at
logon.

The Logon tab is the first tab in the Synchronization Settings dialog box.
Configure offline page synchronization to occur when you log on to your
computer by selecting the When I Log On to My Computer check box.

Configuring offline pages to synchronize at logon is a common means of preventing stale content.

The following options are available for customizing synchronization when the user logs on to the computer:

- ✔ You can specify whether synchronization occurs when connected via a LAN or also when connected through dial-up access.
- ✔ You can specify which pages to synchronize at logon.
- ✔ You can ask to be prompted before each item is synchronized.

Synchronizing when idle

You can set up synchronization to occur when the computer is idle. Click the On Idle tab in the Synchronization Settings dialog box and select the Synchronize the Selected Items While My Computer Is Idle check box (see Figure 6-7). This synchronization option is often appropriate for general business users and single-task users because it keeps content fresh, while minimizing network accesses. Selecting this option ensures that the updates don't interrupt work.

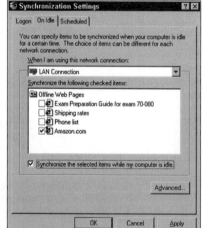

Figure 6-7:
Synchronizing
offline
pages when
system is
idle.

The Advanced button gives users added flexibility when selecting this synchronization method. Notice in Figure 6-8 that users can elect not to synchronize pages when operating on battery power. Users can also specify that synchronization not occur until the system has been idle for a predetermined amount of time.

You must not set this time too short. If you do, a user may briefly turn away to look at notes, and then be stuck waiting for the synchronization to finish because the system is responding slowly.

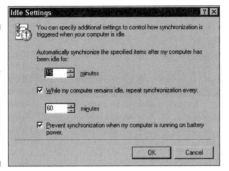

Figure 6-8:
Advanced settings for synchroniz-ing offline pages when system is idle.

Finally, you can configure synchronization to occur every x minutes while the system is idle. I only recommend this option if the page content updates almost continually.

Scheduling synchronization tasks

The Scheduled tab is the last tab in the Synchronization Settings dialog box. Users can set up a schedule to synchronize offline Web pages hourly, daily, or weekly.

To view the schedule, select the Phone list update in the task list and click the Edit button. Figure 6-9 shows the synchronization schedule, which I con-figured to update the page at 7:05 p.m. every Friday (after the corporate Web site is updated at 6:00 p.m. on Friday).

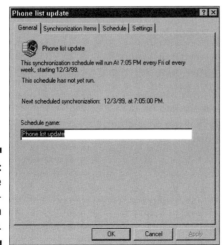

Figure 6-9:
Viewing the synchro-nization schedule.

In Lab 6-3, assume that one of your offline pages is now updated daily at 6 p.m. Create a scheduled task to update this offline page.

Lab 6-3	Creating a Synchronization Schedule

1. **In Internet Explorer 5, choose Tools⇨Synchronize.**

2. **In the Items to Synchronize dialog box, click the Setup button.**

3. **In the Synchronization Settings dialog box, click the Scheduled tab.**

4. **On the Scheduled page, click the Add button to create a new scheduled task. The Scheduled Synchronization wizard starts.**

5. **Click the Next button to advance to the first configuration screen.**

6. **Choose LAN Connection from the Choose a Network Connection For This Synchronization drop-down box and then select the check box of the offline page that you want to update (see Figure 6-10). Click Next to advance to the next screen.**

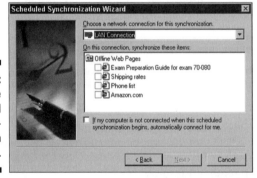

Figure 6-10: Running the Scheduled Synchronization wizard.

7. **Select the time of day for the synchronization to occur (enter 6 p.m.). Under Perform this Task, select Every Day. Enter today's date for the start date. Click Next to advance.**

8. **In the Type a Name for this Scheduled Synchronization text box, type a name (for example, DailySchedule). Click Next to continue.**

9. **Click Finish to add the task to the schedule. The Synchronization Settings dialog box returns, where you see the new task in the task list. Click OK to close the dialog box. Click Close to exit the Items to Synchronize dialog box.**

Managing offline pages with the IEAK

When creating customized Internet Explorer 5 browser packages by using the IEAK Customization wizard, you can include offline Web pages to deploy to your user community. If specific pages are regularly used by many of the employees, it's a nice feature to add to their browser package.

First, you create the offline page on the workstation that you're using to create your custom package. (See Lab 6-1 for assistance with creating an offline page.) Then on the Favorites and Links screen during Stage 4 of the Customization wizard, you add the Web page to the Favorites menu by clicking the Add URL button. Be sure that you appropriately customize the automatic update schedule for this offline page before including it in your browser package.

You can also use the IEAK to manage offline pages after your browser has been deployed. In this circumstance, you use the IEAK Profile Manager to change the Wizard Settings for Favorites and Links.

But you can also configure settings and restrictions for offline pages by using the Profile Manager. (The Profile Manager is most commonly used for this purpose.) Figure 6-11 shows the Policies and Restrictions settings for offline pages. You can use numerous settings to restrict what the user community can do with offline pages.

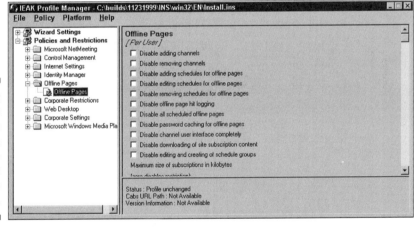

Figure 6-11:
Using the IEAK Profile Manager to set restrictions on offline pages.

If you know that many of your company's computers have small hard drives, you can restrict the amount of Web content that can be downloaded to offline pages. Similarly, if network congestion is a problem for your organization, you may elect to limit offline page updates between 8 a.m. and 5 p.m. You can also eliminate offline pages altogether, depending on the severity of the situation.

The list below shows the available IEAK Profile Manager policies and restrictions that affect offline pages. Be particularly familiar with policies that restrict users from adding or changing schedules, and that limit the amount of content that can be downloaded.

- Disable adding channels
- Disable removing channels
- Disable adding schedules for offline pages
- Disable editing schedules for offline pages
- Disable removing schedules for offline pages
- Disable offline page hit logging
- Disable all scheduled offline pages
- Disable password caching for offline pages
- Disable channel user interface completely
- Disable downloading of site subscription content
- Disable editing and creating of schedule groups
- Maximum size of subscription in kilobytes
- Maximum number of offline pages
- Minimum number of minutes between scheduled updates
- Time to begin preventing scheduled updates
- Time to end preventing scheduled updates
- Maximum offline page crawl depth

Use these settings to create policies and restrictions for creating and updating offline pages as appropriate for your environment.

Using Offline Pages

Aside from their use to mobile employees, offline pages are also valuable to other members of your user community. As a system administrator, you need to know when to recommend offline viewing as well as how to configure updates to these pages.

Scheduling updates to offline pages is always a balance between the urgency of viewing fresh data and the availability of resources, such as connectivity, bandwidth, and disk space.

Single-task-based users

Some workers frequently access a Web page that provides static information. Any Web page that is accessed often is a good candidate for an offline page. For example, mail room employees continually need access to postal rates and shipping rates. Rather than download the information from the Web each time that they access the page, you can save the page for offline viewing so that access is faster and bandwidth utilization is minimized. You can schedule updates for the pages, or show the users how to synchronize from the IE5 Tools menu. If the page content is very static, configuring synchronization at logon is appropriate.

Mobile workers

I've already mentioned some of the needs of mobile users. Mobile users are workers who use their laptops when they travel, but still need access to information from their corporate Web site or from the Internet. A good example is a salesman who wants to show his clients some marketing information that is kept on the corporate Web site. By making this Web page available offline, the salesman has the data on his laptop to show to clients. He can synchronize from the IE5 Tools menu when he returns to the office, or he can use a scheduled update that runs only when connected via the LAN.

Any Web-based information that a user may need to access while away from the office is a good candidate for an offline page.

General Business Users

Users may need to configure offline Web pages for a variety of reasons. Sometimes offline viewing is a solution for users who complain of slow Web page loads. In other situations, offline viewing is a good solution to minimize network utilization on a congested network. General business users don't have a one-size-fits-all formula. Your recommended configurations largely depend on how people use the Web page data and how often the data changes.

Know the needs of the users and the specifics of the environment to create the best offline viewing configurations for your users. Whether you speed up access to pages or minimize network utilization, you have to help users select the best solution for their particular needs. Remember, the formula is freshness of data versus available resources.

Configuring Offline Viewing

1 Ken is the corporate administrator at a company with 1,500 users spread across 20 cities. He's using the IEAK to create a custom IE5 package for these users. Ken plans to configure offline viewing for several frequently used Web pages in the package, including the corporate phone directory that is updated each weekend. How should Ken configure the offline page for the phone directory?

A ○ Ken should configure the offline page for manual synchronization because he doesn't want to interfere with user response time.

B ○ Ken should configure a weekly update for the morning after the phone directory is updated.

C ○ Ken should configure the offline page to synchronize at logon.

D ○ Ken shouldn't worry about making this an offline page because it changes infrequently.

2 Ken has configured schedules for several offline Web pages that he wants to distribute to users within his company. How can Ken include the pages he has configured into an IE5 browser package?

A ❑ Ken can configure the pages on his build computer, and then import them into the IEAK Customization wizard while creating the custom package.

B ❑ Ken can configure the pages on his build computer, and then import them into an IEAK package by using the IEAK Profile Manager.

C ❑ Ken can configure the pages on his build computer, and then distribute them by using the automatic configuration URL.

D ❑ Ken can configure the pages on his build computer, and then import them into an IEAK package by using the IEAK Toolkit.

3 Ken is configuring offline viewing for the sales staff in his company. While traveling, the sales people access several Web pages that contain presentations, pricing, and other marketing materials. How should Ken configure the offline pages for the sales staff?

A ○ Ken should create offline Web pages that synchronize at logon.

B ○ Ken should create offline Web pages that synchronize on a daily schedule.

C ○ Ken should create offline Web pages but let the sales staff synchronize manually.

D ○ Ken should not create offline Web pages because the information could become stale.

4 Ken is configuring offline viewing for the sales staff in his company. While traveling, the salespeople access several Web pages that contain presentations, pricing, and other marketing materials. He feels that the sales staff should manually synchronize these offline pages due to their varying schedules. Ken must train each salesperson on how to use the features of the new IE5 browser. How should he instruct them to synchronize their offline pages?

A ❑ Ken should tell them to click the Refresh button on the browser toolbar to synchronize an offline page.

B ❑ Ken should tell them to choose Synchronize from the browser Tools menu and then check the box for each offline page that they want to synchronize.

C ❑ Ken should tell them to select the Offline Web Pages folder using Explorer and then click the Sync All button on the Explorer toolbar.

D ❑ Ken should tell them to open the Offline Web Pages folder by using Explorer, right-click the offline page that they want to update, and choose Synchronize from the pop-up menu.

5 As corporate administrator for a large firm, Joni is creating a custom IE5 package for general business use. The package includes several offline pages with data that updates often — sometimes several times a day. Joni wants to configure the offline pages to synchronize frequently, but doesn't want to interfere with user productivity. Which synchronization method should Joni select?

A ○ Synchronize when idle.

B ○ Synchronize at startup.

C ○ Synchronize hourly.

D ○ Synchronize manually.

6 Brenda is a corporate administrator creating a custom IE5 package for distribution to her entire user community. She configures several offline pages with preset update schedules. Which of the following options are valid settings and restrictions that Brenda can use to prevent users from altering the scheduled offline page updates?

A ❑ Disable adding schedules for offline pages.

B ❑ Disable editing schedules for offline pages.

C ❑ Disable removing schedules for offline pages.

D ❑ Disable all scheduled offline pages.

7 As corporate administrator for a large corporation, Brenda has created and deployed a custom IE5 package. Brenda notices a marked increase in network usage at certain times of the day. She attributes the increase to update schedules for offline pages. Worried that the network may suffer increasing congestion from these scheduled downloads, Brenda wants to use the IEAK Profile Manager to place limits on scheduled offline page updates. Which of the following settings will help Brenda to accomplish this goal?

A ❑ Disable all scheduled offline pages.

B ❑ Maximum number of offline pages.

C ❑ Time to begin preventing scheduled updates.

D ❑ Disable editing and creating of schedule groups.

E ❑ Maximum offline page crawl depth.

8 Mark is a corporate administrator and includes offline Web pages in the custom IE5 package that he creates and deploys. The offline pages update every hour, beginning at 8 a.m. Mark now faces excessive network utilization between 7:30 and 8:30 each morning. How can Mark reduce some of the traffic without removing the offline pages or changing the scheduled updates?

A ○ Mark can use the IEAK Profile Manager to prevent scheduled updates between 7:30 and 8:30 a.m. each day.

B ○ Mark can use the IEAK Profile Manager to limit the offline page crawl depth.

C ○ Mark can use the IEAK Profile Manager to disable all scheduled offline pages.

D ○ Mark can use the IEAK Profile Manager to increase the minimum number of minutes between scheduled updates.

Answers

1 *B.* To keep the phone directory data from becoming stale, scheduling a weekly update is the best option. Synchronizing at logon is excessive because the page only changes once a week. *See "Updating offline page information."*

2 *A and B.* Ken cannot distribute offline pages via an automatic configuration URL until he has first included them in an .INS file by using the IEAK. *See "Managing offline pages with the IEAK."*

3 *C.* Answer C is the best option for the sales staff because it gives each sales-person the opportunity to control when offline synchronization occurs. Answer A is also a good choice, but not the best choice in this situation. Answer B is not correct because setting a correct schedule is impossible without knowing when each salesperson will log on. *See "Updating offline page information."*

4 *B, C, and D.* Answer B lets the salesperson select one or more specific offline pages to synchronize, answer C synchronizes all offline pages, and answer D synchronizes one specific offline page. Answer A is incorrect because the Refresh button updates the information that is currently being viewed (not necessarily an offline page) in the IE5 browser from the online Web site. *Review "Updating offline page information."*

5 *A.* Joni should configure the offline pages to synchronize when the client computers are idle. This method allows frequent refreshes without disrupting the user's work. Synchronize at startup doesn't synchronize frequently enough because the user may restart the browser only once per day. Synchronizing hourly could interfere with the user's productivity. Synchronize manually may be another good option but could result in stale data if the user doesn't synchronize regularly. *Review "Synchronizing when idle."*

6 *A, B, and C.* Although answer D is a valid setting, it doesn't prevent users from altering the scheduled updates. Instead, it prevents scheduled offline page updates from occurring. *See "Managing offline pages with the IEAK."*

7 *A, B, C, and E.* All these choices will help Brenda to limit the amount of con-tent downloaded during scheduled updates. Answer A prevents scheduled updates altogether. Answer B places a limit on the number of offline pages. Answer C lets Brenda specify specific times of day that scheduled updates are prohibited. Answer E enables Brenda to limit the depth of information that is downloaded from linked Web pages. Answer D is not a good choice because it only prohibits users from altering schedule groups — it doesn't limit the amount of data downloaded in any way. *See "Managing offline pages with the IEAK."*

8 *A.* Answer A is the only option that enables Mark to leave the current update schedules in place, yet still deal with the network congestion. Updates will continue on an hourly basis, with the exception of the time between 7:30 and 8:30 a.m. each day. *See "Managing offline pages with the IEAK."*

Chapter 7

Replacing Other Browsers

· ·

Exam Objectives

▶ Developing a strategy to replace Netscape Navigator

▶ Replacing prior versions of Internet Explorer

· ·

*A*lthough Bill Gates doesn't like to admit it, some folks aren't using Internet Explorer, yet. That's okay, though, because you can help him out by replacing those other browsers with Internet Explorer 5.

When you prepare to deploy your customized browser package, you're likely to be replacing an existing browser. Whether the browser you need to replace is Netscape Navigator or an earlier version of Internet Explorer, you may want to install the new browser while leaving the user's bookmarks, cookies, and important URLs in place. In this chapter, I help you figure out how to correctly replace other browsers with Internet Explorer 5.

Quick Assessment

Replacing Netscape Navigator

1 The choices that you make when replacing a previous browser take place while running the _____ _____ _____.

2 (True/False). If you install Internet Explorer and Netscape Navigator on the same machine, only the default browser will work.

3 After upgrading from Netscape Navigator to IE5, bookmarks from Netscape Navigator become Internet Explorer 5 _____.

4 (True/False). When upgrading from Netscape Navigator to IE5, cookies do not migrate to IE5.

5 A _____ _____ deploying IE5 to an organization is likely to specify IE5 as the default browser.

Replacing Other Versions of Internet Explorer

6 _____ mode allows Internet Explorer 5 to perform as though it were a previous version of Internet Explorer.

7 (True/False). Two versions of Internet Explorer cannot exist on the same bootable partition.

8 Windows Desktop Update is available in the _____ role only.

9 If you're running Windows 98, the Windows Desktop Update is _____ as part of the operating system.

10 (True/False). If you're not running Windows 98 or Windows 2000, the Windows Desktop Update cannot be installed using Internet Explorer 5.

Answers

1   *IEAK Customization wizard.* See "Replacing Netscape Navigator."

2   *False.* See "Replacing Netscape Navigator."

3   *favorites.* See "Replacing Netscape Navigator."

4   *False.* See "Replacing Netscape Navigator."

5   *corporate administrator.* See "Replacing Netscape Navigator."

6   *Compatibility.* See "Replacing Other Versions of Internet Explorer."

7   *True.* See "Replacing Other Versions of Internet Explorer."

8   *corporate administrator.* See "Replacing Other Versions of Internet Explorer."

9   *included.* See "Replacing Other Versions of Internet Explorer."

10   *False.* See "Replacing Other Versions of Internet Explorer."

Replacing Netscape Navigator

When you take the IEAK5 (Internet Explorer Administration Kit 5) exam, you're being tested on deploying IE5 by using the IEAK5. (Sounds like alphabet soup, doesn't it?) So as I talk about replacing Netscape Navigator with IE5, I concentrate on doing so by using the IEAK.

Selecting a default browser

The choices that you make when replacing a previous browser take place while running the IEAK Customization wizard. First, on the Corporate Install Options screen during Stage 3 of the Customization wizard, you must determine whether to install IE5 as the default browser (see Figure 7-1).

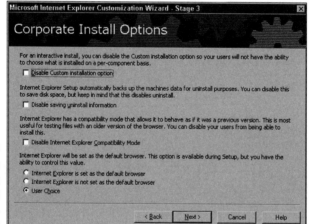

Figure 7-1:
Specifying a default browser.

You have three choices in specifying a default browser, as you see at the bottom of the Corporate Install Options screen:

- ✔ Internet Explorer is set as the default browser
- ✔ Internet Explorer is not set as the default browser
- ✔ User Choice

A corporate administrator deploying IE5 to an organization is likely to specify IE5 as the default browser. ISPs, on the other hand, may not want to make that decision for a user. ISPs usually let the user choose their browser. Because the IE and Netscape browsers can peacefully coexist on the same machine, this isn't a problem.

If you specify a silent installation for your organization, the users don't see any installation messages and are unable to make this selection!

Migrating cookies, bookmarks, and proxy settings

The IEAK doesn't overwrite or delete Netscape just because you specify Internet Explorer 5 as the default browser. Your users can still use their Netscape browser, should they decide to do so.

Internet Explorer 5 automatically detects and imports cookies, bookmarks, and proxy settings from installed Netscape browsers.

You can determine whether the users' existing favorites (called bookmarks in Netscape) are kept or deleted during Stage 4 of the IEAK Customization wizard (as shown in Figure 7-2). As a corporate administrator, you may choose to overwrite the users' favorites — but consider your users' reactions carefully before doing so.

ISPs seldom select the Delete Existing Favorites and Links If Present check box. Doing so may annoy a paying customer by removing the customer's personal settings.

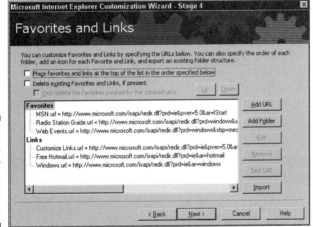

Figure 7-2: Choosing to keep or delete favorite Web pages.

IE5 doesn't automatically specify additional default components, such as e-mail or chat applications. You still have to specify whether Outlook Express is the default e-mail and news reader application (see Figure 7-3).

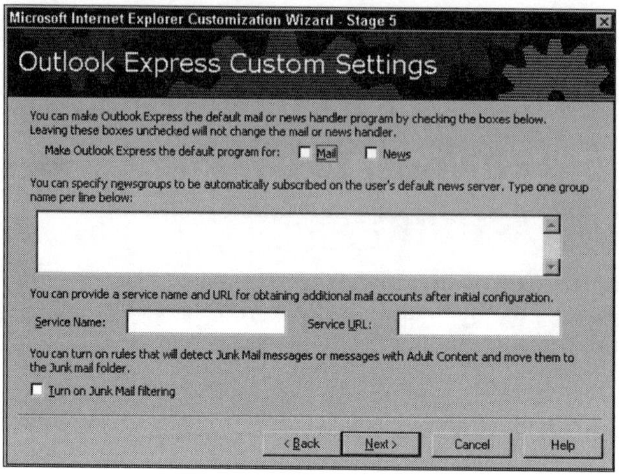

Figure 7-3:
Specifying
Outlook
Express as
the default
mail and
news
application.

On the exam, you can expect to see scenario questions in which you are asked to determine how to replace the user's Netscape browser while retaining certain existing settings. You may be asked to identify the correct steps and IEAK components to accomplish the task.

Replacing Other Versions of Internet Explorer

Upgrading from earlier versions of Internet Explorer is pretty straightforward. You cannot, however, have two versions of Internet Explorer on the same computer unless they are on separate bootable partitions. Upgrading to IE5 replaces existing files with the newer IE5 files. Cookies, favorites, links, and proxy settings, however, are retained and automatically migrated.

Similar to replacing a Netscape browser, you must be careful of removing the user's existing browser settings. Be sure to consider whether or not to remove existing favorites, links, and cookies. (Users tend to get a bit irritable when all their personal settings disappear!)

When you upgrade to Internet Explorer 5, be sure to upgrade other components (such as Outlook Express and NetMeeting) as well. The older versions of these components may not be compatible with Internet Explorer 5.

Issues exist that you must prepare for when upgrading from earlier versions of Internet Explorer. The first involves the use compatibility mode to make IE5 compatible with Internet Explorer 4. Another involves the Windows Desktop Update, which first became available in Internet Explorer 4.

Using compatibility mode

Compatibility mode allows Internet Explorer 5 to perform as though it were a previous version of Internet Explorer. Compatibility mode is provided primarily so that developers can test applications with previous versions of the browser. On the Corporate Install Options screen (refer to Figure 7-1) of the Customization wizard, you can specify whether or not your users can enable compatibility mode.

On the exam, you may see a scenario question that describes several requirements for a customized browser package. If users require compatibility with a previous version of Internet Explorer, do not disable compatibility mode.

Planning for Windows Desktop Update

The Windows Desktop Update was introduced in Internet Explorer 4 and included Active Desktop, Web views, and a Web-type taskbar. Windows Desktop Update was Microsoft's early attempt to mute the distinction between the local computer and the Internet. Windows Desktop Update, particularly the Active Desktop, was not initially well received. Due to early installation problems and slow system response, many users elected not to install it.

Windows Desktop Update is available in the Corporate Administrator role only. During the IEAK Customization wizard, you can elect whether or not to install it by simply clicking Yes or No (see Figure 7-4).

Windows Desktop Update isn't included in Internet Explorer 5, but corporate administrators can make it available in their custom browser package in two ways:

- ✔ If you're running Windows 98, the Windows Desktop Update is included as part of the operating system.

- ✔ If you're running Windows 95 or Windows NT 4.0, then you must install the Windows Desktop Update on your build computer *before* upgrading to Internet Explorer 5.

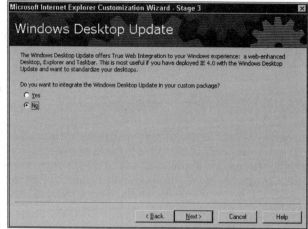

Figure 7-4:
Integrating
Windows
Desktop
Update into
a custom
browser
package.

If you're not running Windows 98 or Windows 2000 and if you don't install Windows Desktop Update prior to upgrading, then you must remove Internet Explorer 5, install the Windows Desktop Update in Internet Explorer 4, and then reinstall Internet Explorer 5.

Prep Test

1 Daniel is a corporate administrator charged with deploying Internet Explorer 5 to Windows 98 and Windows NT clients throughout the company. All the clients are currently using the Netscape Navigator browser. He wants to use the Internet Explorer Administration Kit (IEAK) to customize and deploy IE5. Using the IEAK, what options will Daniel have in regard to making IE5 the default browser on the client machines?

A ❏ Internet Explorer is set as the default browser.

B ❏ Internet Explorer is not set as the default browser.

C ❏ The IEAK doesn't include this option but rather automatically specifies Internet Explorer as the default browser.

D ❏ The user can choose whether IE5 is the default browser.

2 Daniel is a corporate administrator charged with deploying Internet Explorer 5 to Windows 98 and Windows NT 4.0 clients throughout the company. All the clients are currently running Internet Explorer 4 and all are configured to use the Active Desktop. Daniel wants to use the Internet Explorer Administration Kit (IEAK) to customize and deploy IE5. Which users will be able to use the Active Desktop after IE5 is deployed?

A ○ All of them.

B ○ None of them.

C ○ The Windows NT clients will be able to run the Active Desktop, but the Windows 98 clients will not.

D ○ The Windows 98 clients will be able to run the Active Desktop, but the Windows NT clients will not.

3 Daniel is a corporate administrator charged with deploying Internet Explorer 5 to Windows 98 and Windows NT 4.0 clients throughout the company. All the clients are currently running Internet Explorer 4 and some have installed the Active Desktop. Daniel wants to use the Internet Explorer Administration Kit (IEAK) to customize and deploy IE5. Which users will be able to use the Active Desktop after IE5 is deployed?

A ❏ All of them.

B ❏ The Windows NT clients.

C ❏ The Windows 98 clients.

D ❏ The Windows NT clients who had Active Desktop installed prior to the upgrade.

4 You install IE5 on your workstation, which was running Windows 95 and Internet Explorer 4. After the IE5 installation, you cannot use the Active Desktop. What must you do if you want to use the Active Desktop with IE5?

A ○ Nothing. If you didn't install the Active Desktop prior to the upgrade, there's nothing you can do.

B ○ Uninstall IE5. Reinstall IE4 with the Active Desktop. Then install IE5 again.

C ○ Install a Service Pack for Windows 95.

D ○ Download and install the Active Desktop component from the Microsoft Web site.

5 John is the system administrator at an ISP. He's preparing a custom IE5 browser package to upgrade his IE4 customers. He doesn't see an option for the Windows Desktop Update while using the IEAK on his build computer. Why?

A ○ He didn't install Windows Desktop Update prior to upgrading to IE5 on his build computer.

B ○ He must upgrade the build computer to Windows 98 or Windows 2000 to be able to include Windows Desktop Update in his custom browser package.

C ○ Windows Desktop Update doesn't run on Windows 95 computers.

D ○ Windows Desktop Update doesn't appear in the IEAK unless the administrator is in the corporate administrator role.

6 When replacing Netscape Navigator with Internet Explorer 5, which personal user settings can migrate to Internet Explorer 5?

A ❏ Bookmarks

B ❏ Links

C ❏ Cookies

D ❏ Graphics

7 Daniel is creating a new IE5 browser package for distribution throughout his company. He supports a variety of Windows 98, Windows 2000, and Windows NT client computers. All the client computers are currently using Internet Explorer 4, Outlook Express, and NetMeeting. Should Daniel add the Outlook Express and NetMeeting applications to the new custom browser package?

A ○ Yes.

B ○ No.

C ○ It doesn't matter.

Answers

1 *A, B, and D.* Daniel can choose to set IE5 as the default browser, to not set IE5 as the default browser, or to let each user choose whether or not to make IE5 the default browser. *See "Replacing Netscape Navigator."*

2 *A.* Because Windows Desktop Update was installed on the clients' computer prior to upgrading, all the clients are able to run the Active Desktop. *See "Planning for Windows Desktop Update."*

3 *C and D.* The Active Desktop is included with Windows 98 and Windows 2000 clients. Answer C is correct because the Active Desktop is still available. Answer D is correct because any of the NT clients who installed Active Desktop prior to the upgrade can still use Active Desktop. Answers A and B are incorrect because on Windows 95 and Windows NT clients' computers, you must install the Active Desktop prior to upgrading or the Active Desktop becomes unavailable. *Review "Planning for Windows Desktop Update."*

4 *B.* Answer A is incorrect because you can uninstall IE5 and reinstall IE4 with the Active Desktop before installing IE5 again. Answers C and D are incorrect because you cannot run the Active Desktop on Windows 95 and IE5 unless it was installed prior to the installation of IE5. *Review "Planning for Windows Desktop Update."*

5 *D.* Answers A, B, and C are incorrect because John can't include Windows Desktop Update in an IEAK package while in the ISP role. Windows Desktop update is only available in the corporate administrator IEAK role. *Review "Planning for Windows Desktop Update."*

6 *A, B, and C.* Bookmarks, links and cookies are still available in Internet Explorer 5. In Internet Explorer 5, however, the bookmarks are called favorites. *See "Replacing Netscape Navigator."*

7 *A.* Daniel should include the Outlook Express and NetMeeting applications in the custom browser package. The older versions of these components may not be compatible with Internet Explorer 5. *See "Replacing Other Versions of Internet Explorer."*

Chapter 8

Planning for Outlook Express

• •

Exam Objectives

▶ Identifying Outlook Express components

▶ Configuring settings

▶ Including Outlook Express in a custom browser package

• •

*F*or a free messaging application provided with Internet Explorer 5, Outlook Express is pretty impressive! Outlook Express 5 provides Web-integrated messaging (e-mail) and news reader capabilities, and enables you to receive mail from multiple e-mail accounts into a single Outlook Express mailbox. Outlook Express includes many additional features, such as HotMail integration, offline synchronization, multiple identities, and more.

In this chapter, you figure out how to plan an Outlook Express configuration to include with your custom browser package. I identify the key features of Outlook Express and show you how to configure them and include them in your custom package.

Quick Assessment

Identifying
Outlook
Express
Components

1 To download newsgroup messages to your Outlook Express inbox, you must configure access to a _____ server.

2 Outlook Express is commonly used to retrieve mail from _____ or _____ servers.

3 An _____ server is used to send outgoing e-mail messages.

4 Outlook Express users can sign up for free e-mail services through _____.

Configuring
Settings

5 You can use the _____ _____ _____ to import Outlook Express settings from your build computer into a custom browser package.

6 _____ files are used to append frequently used text to outgoing mail messages.

Including
Outlook
Express in a
Custom
Browser
Package

7 The _____ _____ _____ enables you to prevent users from modifying their Outlook Express accounts.

8 The _____ pane lets you view the content of messages before actually opening them.

Answers

1   *NNTP.* See "Reading and posting newsgroup messages."

2   *POP3, IMAP.* See "Messaging protocols."

3   *SMTP.* See "Messaging protocols."

4   *HotMail.* Review "HotMail."

5   *IEAK Customization wizard.* See "Configuring Outlook Express Features."

6   *Signature.* See "Signature files."

7   *IEAK Profile Manager.* Review "Reading and posting newsgroup messages."

8   *preview.* See "Enjoying the view!"

Pieces and Parts: Outlook Express Components

Outlook Express has a number of key features that make it versatile and convenient. One of the most valuable features is the ability to connect to multiple types of mail servers, such as POP3, SMTP, and IMAP. As a frequent traveler, I find Outlook Express convenient for accessing all my mailboxes while I'm on the road.

For the exam, you must know which features are available in Outlook Express. You're likely to see a scenario question that describes the requirements of a group of users. You will need to identify the appropriate components to meet the specified requirements. Among the many features of Outlook Express are:

- ✔ Integration with HotMail accounts
- ✔ Synchronization between online and offline mailboxes
- ✔ Multiple accounts available on the same computer
- ✔ Customized signature files that can be added to any mail message
- ✔ Contact information that can be shared among multiple identities
- ✔ Customizable stationery for e-mail messages
- ✔ Tip of the Day messages for beginners
- ✔ Internet newsgroup messaging support
- ✔ Signature files that can include text and HTML content
- ✔ Access to SMTP, IMAP, and POP3 servers
- ✔ Digital signature securing and the ability to encrypt e-mail messages

Before you begin creating a custom browser package, you must identify the needs of your organization's user community. Based on these needs, you then determine which Outlook Express features to configure and include in your package.

For example, some users work from multiple computers. For these users, you want to configure the option to store messages on the server so that they can be accessed from any computer. Other users travel with a laptop, and you need to configure the option that makes their mail available to download for later reading. Still other users need to sign all outgoing messages with a legal disclaimer that you must configure for them.

I can write an entire book on Outlook Express alone, but that won't help you pass the exam. Instead, I briefly concentrate on each of the features that you must be familiar with in order to pass the exam.

Messaging protocols

POP3 and IMAP are messaging protocols used for incoming e-mail servers. These protocols store e-mail messages on an ISP's (or organization's) mail server before copying or downloading the message to a mailbox when a user logs on. SMTP is a messaging protocol used for outgoing e-mail messages.

If users regularly log on from different computers (roaming or roving users), you should configure the mail so that it's stored on the server. (Note that mail builds up quickly and users must be warned to delete outdated messages frequently.) If users travel with a laptop or dial in to an ISP for mail service, you may want to configure their mail so that it downloads from the server and is stored on their laptop. Users can then read their mail despite not being connected to the ISP or mail server. Both POP3 and IMAP can be configured for either of these scenarios by checking the box labeled `Leave a copy of messages on server` on the Advanced tab of the mail account's Properties window (see Figure 8-1).

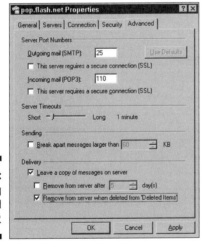

Figure 8-1: Configuring POP3 and IMAP.

HotMail

Some time ago, Microsoft purchased the popular HotMail service, which provides free Internet e-mail to subscribers. You can configure Outlook Express 5 to receive and send messages through your HotMail account. You can synchronize your online and offline folders, and you can even acquire a new HotMail account by using Outlook Express 5.

Signature files

Another handy feature of Outlook Express is the ability to store signature files that are automatically appended to the end of your messages. Most people type their name, company, and contact information into a signature file and attach it to the end of each outgoing message. Others use signature files to attach popular quotes, advertising information, graphics, or legal disclaimers to their outgoing messages.

Signature files can be entered directly through the Outlook Express Signature option or can be file attachments. You can see in Figure 8-2 that I've added several lines of information in the Edit Signature option for Signature #1. By selecting the Add Signatures to All Outgoing Messages check box and the Don't Add Signatures to Replies or Forwards check box, you tell Outlook Express to append the signature to all outgoing messages except those that are replies or forwarded messages.

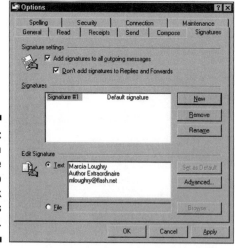

Figure 8-2:
Adding a signature file to Outlook Express messages.

You can configure multiple signature files in Outlook Express and associate a different signature with each account. Or, you can configure multiple signature files for a single account. For "official" or work related messages, I use a formal signature listing my company name and contact information. For casual messages to friends, I use my name and a silly quotation.

Lab 8-1 below takes you through the steps of configuring a signature for your account.

Lab 8-1   Adding an Outlook Express Auto Signature

1. **In Outlook Express, choose Tools⇨Options.**

2. **In the Options window, click the Signatures tab.**

3. **Click the New button to the right of the Signatures box.**

4. **Near the bottom of the screen, under Edit Signature, type the information below into the box labeled Text:**

```
<your name>
<your phone number>
```

5. **Click OK to close the Options window.**

6. **In Outlook Express, click the New Mail button.**

   Notice that the resulting blank mail message already contains the signature information that you just configured. Cancel the mail message to end the lab exercise.

Reading and posting newsgroup messages

Outlook Express 5 is also a fully functional newsreader application. You can use Outlook Express to view and post messages to newsgroups quickly and easily. Similar to downloading mail messages, you can download newsgroup messages for reading later when you're offline. Or, you can download only the message headers (their subject, sender, and date information, but not the text of the message itself), marking messages that interest you for download and reading at a later time.

Newsgroup access is configured similarly to message server access. Your corporation or ISP must specify an NNTP server (a news server), and you configure your account for access to this server (see Figure 8-3).

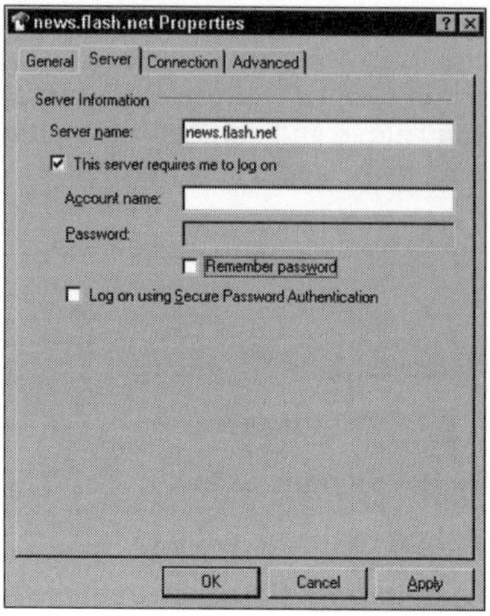

Figure 8-3:
Configuring
access to
a news
server.

In some cases, users may find it helpful to be preconfigured for access to newsgroups. If many of your users access certain newsgroups, you can configure the newsgroups on your build computer and then import that setting into a custom package by using the IEAK Configuration wizard. You can also use the IEAK Profile Manager to add newsgroups at a later time.

But remember, newsgroups can contain thousands of messages. Downloading messages is quite time consuming, and they can take up a great deal of hard drive space. As an administrator, knowing how to restrict access to newsgroups is as important as knowing how to configure access. In most cases, only those operating in the corporate administrator role will want to restrict newsgroup access.

If you decide to restrict access to newsgroups, you can use the IEAK Profile Manager to prevent users from adding, removing, or changing account settings. Figure 8-4 shows how to restrict access by selecting the check box labeled `Disable access to accounts (accounts cannot be added, removed, or modified)`.

Customizing the InfoPane and Welcome message

Outlook Express has a customizable InfoPane that runs across the bottom of the application window. You add content to this pane by specifying an HTML file, a graphic file, or a URL (see Figure 8-5). You can also configure a custom welcome message that users receive in their inboxes.

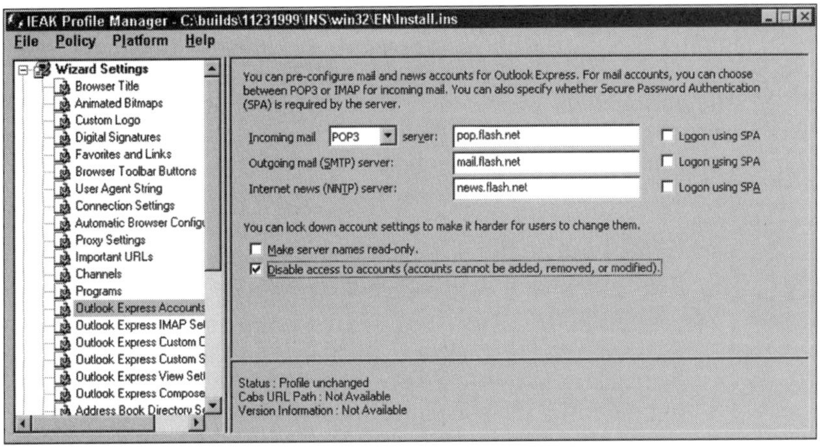

Figure 8-4: Restricting access to Outlook Express accounts.

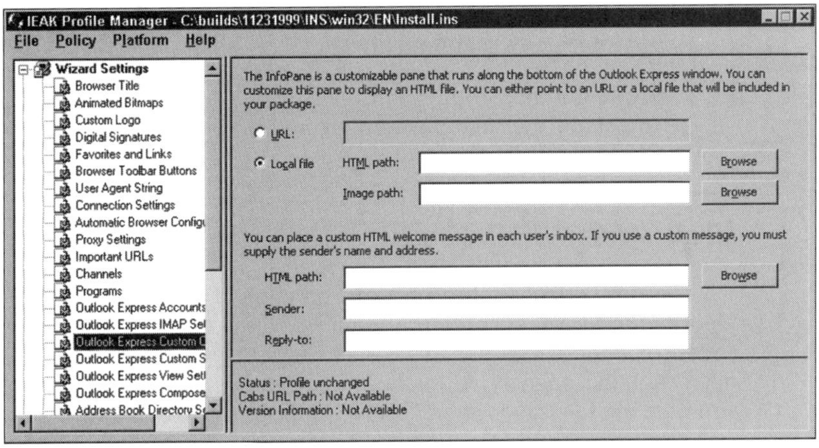

Figure 8-5: Customizing the Outlook Express InfoPane.

Take a look at Figure 8-5. The top of the screen includes the following settings for adding a file to the InfoPane:

- **URL:** To select the URL option, click the URL radio button; then type the URL in the adjacent text box. The content that the URL points to then appears in the Outlook Express InfoPane of the custom browser package.

- **Local File:** To select the Local File option, click the Local File radio button. To add a file from your local computer, type the file name in the HTML Path text box. To add an image from your local computer, type the image file name in the Image Path text box.

If you don't want to configure the InfoPane, then don't enter any information in the URL or Local File text boxes.

The bottom of Figure 8-5 includes settings for adding a welcome message to each user's Inbox. Users opening Outlook Express for the first time see the welcome message in their Inbox as you configure it by using these settings. You can configure the welcome message by using the following options:

- ✔ **HTML Path:** In the HTML Path text box, type the name of the HTML file that is to appear in the welcome message.

- ✔ **Sender:** In the Sender text box, type the name of the person who is to be viewed as the originator of the message. Some organizations enter Postmaster in the Sender text box. The welcome message then appears to be sent by the e-mail postmaster. You could also enter the company president's name so that each new employee receives a welcome message from the company president.

- ✔ **Reply-To:** In the Reply-To text box, type the mailbox to which you wish to direct replies to the welcome message. If you enter the CEO's name in the Sender text box, for example, you don't want users to send him a reply, telling him about their e-mail woes. Instead, you would enter the name of another mailbox — a group box perhaps — for users to reply to.

Enjoying the view!

You can dramatically alter the look and feel of Outlook Express by using the View menu. The best configuration is very much a matter of personal preference. For example, rather than using the preview pane, I prefer instead to open each message individually. In addition, I prefer to view not only the date and time my messages were received, but also the date and time that they were sent. You want to configure Outlook Express for maximum ease of use and efficiency.

You can configure the view of Outlook Express in many ways. Don't familiarize yourself with each of the View menu options for the exam. You're not likely to be tested on configuring these options, but you should be familiar with them for assisting users.

Configuring Outlook Express Features

After you know the features of Outlook Express, you must be able to associate those features with a given set of user requirements. If, for example, users need to leave mail on their server, you must plan for and include this feature. If users need to append standard information to every outgoing message, you must plan to include this feature as well.

The IEAK exam requires you to interpret requirements and appropriately plan your Internet Explorer package to meet the requirements.

Before you distribute your custom browser package to the user community, you should configure the Outlook Express settings so that you don't need to visit every desktop to individually configure mail accounts and other settings.

You can configure Outlook Express settings in two ways:

✔ Configure Outlook Express on your build computer and import those settings by using the IEAK Customization wizard (see Figure 8-6).

✔ Configure the Outlook Express settings by using the IEAK Profile Manager (refer to Figure 8-4).

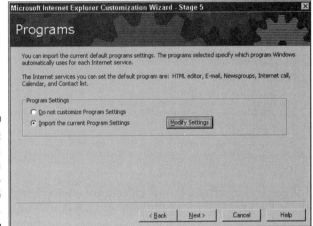

Figure 8-6: Importing program settings into the IE5 package.

Use a planning form similar to the one in Appendix C when you are preparing to create an IE5 custom package. Because so many components and configurable options exist, you're unlikely to remember all the settings that you need for your package.

1 Which of the following is a messaging protocol used by outgoing mail servers?

A ○ OLAP

B ○ SMTP

C ○ POP3

D ○ ODBC

2 Joe is a corporate administrator creating a custom browser package, and he wants to include Outlook Express 5. The package must be deployed at a call center where three shifts of employees use the same set of computers each day. Joe wants to distribute one contact list to be shared among all users on a computer. Can Joe configure Outlook Express 5 for use by differing employees on a single computer and still let them access a common contact list?

A ○ No

B ○ Yes

3 Joe is the corporate administrator at a financial services company. He's creating a custom browser package that includes Outlook Express. The corporate call center employees use Outlook Express and must add a legal disclaimer to each outgoing e-mail message. How can Joe best configure this disclaimer so that it's added to each outgoing mail message?

A ○ Joe should configure an InfoPane for the call center users. The message appearing in the InfoPane will be appended to outgoing messages.

B ○ Joe should configure a signature file for the call center users, and configure Outlook Express to append the signature file to all outgoing messages.

C ○ Joe should use the IEAK Profile Manager to configure an .inf file for the call center users. The .inf file will be appended to each outgoing e-mail message.

D ○ Joe should configure an NNTP message to append the disclaimer to each outgoing e-mail message.

4 What kind of server must Joe configure to provide newsgroup messages to users of his custom browser package?

A ○ An SMTP server

B ○ An ILS server

C ○ A POP3 server

D ○ An NNTP server

5 Nancy is a corporate administrator at a corporation with 500 Windows 98 clients, 25 Windows 2000 clients, and 350 Windows NT 4.0 clients. She created and deployed a custom browser package that included Outlook Express 5. Although Nancy configured the correct mail servers in the package, users keep altering their e-mail configurations. The resulting help desk tickets are causing Nancy to work long hours. What else can Nancy configure to reduce the number of tickets due to altered e-mail configurations?

A ○ Nancy is out of luck. After the browser is deployed, she cannot make configuration changes.

B ○ Nancy can use the IEAK Profile Manager to restrict users from changing their e-mail configuration. She can then update the browsers from the automatic configuration URL.

C ○ Nancy should ask her boss to hire another administrator.

D ○ Nancy can use the IEAK Customization wizard to create and deploy a new custom browser package that restricts users from altering their e-mail configuration.

Answers

1 *B.* SMTP is a messaging protocol used by outgoing mail servers. POP3 is a messaging protocol used by incoming mail servers. ODBC and OLAP aren't messaging protocols at all. *Review "Messaging protocols."*

2 *B.* One of the features of Outlook Express 5 is that it allows multiple e-mail accounts on a single computer. Each user simply selects their own account when they start Outlook Express. In addition, Outlook Express users can share common items, such as phone directories or contact lists. *Review "Pieces and Parts: Outlook Express Components."*

3 *B.* Answer A is incorrect because the InfoPane displays information in the user's Outlook Express application. Answers C and D were made up just to throw you off track. If you chose one of them, you're either very tired or you didn't read the chapter! *Review "Signature files."*

4 *D.* Joe must provide access to an NNTP server (also called a news server) and configure the accounts to access this server. An SMTP server is an outgoing mail server, a POP3 server is an incoming mail server, and an ILS server is a NetMeeting directory server. *Review "Reading and posting newsgroup messages."*

5 *B.* Answer D is an alternative that would work, but it's not the best solution to Nancy's problem. Users shouldn't have to download a new browser package when they only need to update the configuration of the existing package. *Review "Configuring Outlook Express Features."*

Chapter 9

Planning for NetMeeting

● ●

Exam Objectives

▶ Identify features of Microsoft NetMeeting

▶ Configure NetMeeting custom settings

▶ Use the IEAK Customization wizard to include NetMeeting in a custom package

▶ Use the IEAK Profile Manager to modify NetMeeting settings and restrictions

● ●

*M*icrosoft NetMeeting is an Internet collaboration tool that enables sharing audio, video, whiteboards, files, and applications. You can install NetMeeting as an optional component in your IE5 custom package. If you choose to include NetMeeting in your package, you should preconfigure it for your users. Because NetMeeting is bandwidth-intensive, you should configure and manage it carefully. In cases where bandwidth is inadequate, you may choose to limit NetMeeting installs to a select group of users.

Microsoft is understandably proud of NetMeeting, and you will see several NetMeeting questions on the exam. The key to doing well on these questions is to recognize user requirements for NetMeeting and to understand the configuration options. In this chapter, I explain NetMeeting features and discuss the configuration options that you're likely to see on the test.

Quick Assessment

Customizing NetMeeting Features

1 The NetMeeting _____ _____ _____ helps you configure the audio features on your computer.

2 _____ improves audio performance by shortening the time span between when audio is sent and when it's received.

3 A _____ sound card enables the user to listen and talk at the same time.

4 The NetMeeting features that you can use depend on the _____ _____.

Determining System Requirements

5 On Windows 95/98 and Windows NT 4.0, NetMeeting requires at least a _____ processor.

6 NetMeeting requires _____ of available disk space for installation.

NetMeeting Protocols

7 By implementing an _____ _____ _____, you can contact NetMeeting users by accessing them through their directory listing.

8 _____ is an Internet standard that enables Web browsers to find and access information in a directory service database.

9 Basic PC-to-PC Internet communication occurs between _____ _____.

Using the IEAK with NetMeeting

10 After creating a custom browser package that includes NetMeeting, you can manage NetMeeting from a central location by using the _____ _____ _____.

Answers

1   *Audio Tuning wizard.* See "Customizing NetMeeting Features."

2   *DirectSound.* See "Customizing NetMeeting Features."

3   *full-duplex.* See "Customizing NetMeeting Features."

4   *computer's components.* See "Customizing NetMeeting Features."

5   *Pentium 90.* See "Determining System Requirements."

6   *10MB.* See "Determining System Requirements."

7   *ILS directory server.* See "NetMeeting protocols."

8   *LDAP.* See "NetMeeting protocols."

9   *IP addresses.* See "NetMeeting protocols."

10   *IEAK Profile Manager.* See "Using the IEAK with NetMeeting."

Determining System Requirements

Because some of NetMeeting's features are bandwidth-intensive or require special configuration, the administrator must plan the organization's configuration and deployment of NetMeeting very carefully. In planning for NetMeeting, the administrator should ask the following questions:

- ✔ Do all users need NetMeeting?
- ✔ Which specific features are needed?
- ✔ Do all users need all features?
- ✔ Does the current desktop hardware support the required NetMeeting features?

The answers to these questions determine whether you include NetMeeting in a single IE5 package deployed to all users or create multiple packages configured for specific NetMeeting features. You may also need to plan hardware upgrades at the desktop before you deploy the package.

If the user requirements dictate multiple browser packages, work with one package at a time. First create the package with the most features and then create subsequent packages from this initial build.

The system requirements for NetMeeting vary according to which features you plan to use. NetMeeting for Windows 95, Windows 98, and Windows NT 4.0 (and for Windows 2000 when it's released) is available as a free download from the Microsoft Web site.

If your custom package includes data sharing, audio conferencing, and video conferencing, the following hardware is required:

- ✔ Windows 95 and Windows 98 require at least a Pentium 90 processor and 16MB of RAM. A Pentium 133 and 16MB RAM, however, are recommended.
- ✔ Windows NT 4.0 requires Service Pack 3 or higher, a Pentium 90 computer, and 24MB RAM. A Pentium 133 and 32MB RAM are recommended.
- ✔ Installation requires 10MB of additional disk space. NetMeeting itself requires 5MB of disk space.
- ✔ LAN connectivity, ISDN connectivity, or a 28.8Kbps modem and dial-up line.
- ✔ Sound card that includes a microphone and speakers.
- ✔ Camera with a video-capture card, USB camera, or a parallel-port camera with a Video for Windows driver.

NetMeeting protocols

Microsoft NetMeeting is based on open standards and is an H.323 and T.120 compatible program. This means that NetMeeting communicates with other vendor's H.323 and T.120 compliant applications. H.323 is an audio/video conferencing standard that is governed by the International Telecommunications Union (ITU). T.120 is a data conferencing standard. Together, these standards enable a NetMeeting PC to place calls through an H.323 gateway to public telephone lines to communicate with other PCs and telephones.

NetMeeting also uses the LDAP standard. LDAP (Lightweight Directory Access Protocol) is an Internet standard that enables Web browsers to find and access information in a directory service database. LDAP is based on the X.500 Directory Access Protocol (DAP) but is more

efficient and more widely used. Microsoft's Active Directory and Internet Locator Service (ILS) products are both LDAP compliant directory services.

Many organizations, and some service providers, use Microsoft ILS directory servers to provide contact information for NetMeeting users. Basic PC-to-PC Internet communication occurs between IP addresses. But when users dial-in or use DHCP for IP addressing, their IP addresses often change. By implementing an ILS directory server, you can always contact the user by accessing them through their ILS directory server listing. (It's just like looking them up in a phone book.) When an ILS server is in place, each time the user starts NetMeeting their IP address and e-mail address register with the ILS server, keeping their listing up-to-date.

If your custom package includes only data and audio conferencing, the following hardware is required:

- ✔ Windows 95 and Windows 98 require at least a Pentium 90 processor and 16MB of RAM. A Pentium 133 and 16MB RAM, however, are recommended.

- ✔ Windows NT 4.0 requires Service Pack 3 or higher, a Pentium 90 computer, and 24MB RAM. A Pentium 133 and 32MB RAM are recommended.

- ✔ Installation requires 10MB of additional disk space. NetMeeting itself requires 5MB of disk space.

- ✔ LAN connectivity, ISDN connectivity, or a 14.4Kbps modem and dial-up line.

- ✔ Sound card that includes a microphone and speakers.

Customizing NetMeeting Features

Many organizations rely heavily on NetMeeting as a conferencing tool — a NetMeeting conference saves thousands of dollars on travel expenses. NetMeeting has a lot of features that can change the way you work. (Yes, with NetMeeting you can do things faster!) You can:

- ✔ Audio conference
- ✔ Video conference
- ✔ Share whiteboards
- ✔ Share applications.
- ✔ Transfer files
- ✔ Chat

On the exam, you're likely to see scenarios that list a user requirement to collaborate with other team members or customers. This usually means sharing a whiteboard or an application so that several users can work together on the same document or file.

When you determine which of the features your organization requires, configure the NetMeeting settings to customize the features for your users.

Configuring a directory server

Before using NetMeeting for the first time, you must configure a directory server, as shown in Figure 9-1. When NetMeeting starts for the first time, a Setup wizard helps you configure user information, tune audio settings, and configure a NetMeeting directory server. If your organization has its own directory server, enter the server name in the Server Name box of the wizard. If you're using a public server, as I am in the example in Figure 9-1, select it from the drop-down list of the Server Name box. (The sidebar titled NetMeeting protocols gives you additional information about directory servers.)

Figure 9-1:
Using the NetMeeting Setup wizard to configure a directory server.

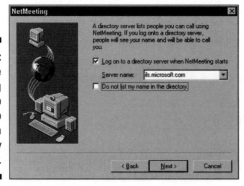

If you've run NetMeeting before, you can configure a directory server from within NetMeeting by choosing Tools⇨Options (see Figure 9-2). On the General page of the Options window, notice the Directory Settings box near the middle of the window. Enter your directory server name (or select one from the drop-down list) in the Directory box.

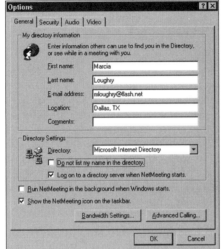

Figure 9-2:
Configuring
a
NetMeeting
directory
server.

If you know the IP address of the person that you want to collaborate with, you don't need to use a directory server to contact them. Simply call them by using their IP address as a "phone number."

To place a call by using the ILS directory server, simply click the directory icon and select the person that you want to contact from the directory listing. Or, to place a call by using an IP address, simply click the call icon and enter the IP address in the To text box of the Place A Call dialog box (see Figure 9-3).

Figure 9-3:
Placing a
network call
by using an
IP address.

Configuring audio and video

Planning for NetMeeting audio and video configuration depends on how your client computers are configured and which system administrator role you hold. As a corporate administrator, if you're preparing a customized browser package that includes NetMeeting, you need to know precisely what components are included with the client computers. As an administrator at an ISP, you don't have that luxury. You must be certain that you don't lock down the NetMeeting settings and prevent users from altering their configuration.

Audio configuration

When configuring NetMeeting audio settings, knowing what type of sound card is installed in the PC is important. Full-duplex sound cards produce the best audio results. With a full-duplex sound card, you can listen and talk simultaneously. With a half-duplex card, the system functions similarly to a speaker phone — when you're speaking, you can't hear the caller. As a corporate administrator, you probably know the system components on your client computers and you can plan accordingly. ISP administrators should probably plan for full-duplex sound cards — but remember not to lock down the audio settings as users may need to make adjustments.

NetMeeting provides an Audio Tuning wizard to help properly configure audio settings. To launch the wizard, choose Tools⇨Audio Tuning wizard. The Audio Tuning wizard enables you to adjust the playback volume on your computer and also adjusts recording volume as you read a short script from the wizard screen, as shown in Figure 9-4.

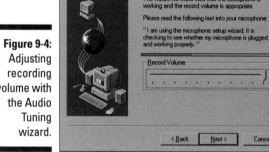

Figure 9-4:
Adjusting
recording
volume with
the Audio
Tuning
wizard.

You can also manually configure NetMeeting audio settings by choosing Tools⇨Options and then clicking the Audio tab (shown in Figure 9-5). On the Audio page, you can:

✔ **Enable full-duplex:** As discussed earlier in this section, if you have a full-duplex sound card, this setting provides the best sound. Selecting this option lets you speak and listen at the same time.

✔ **Enable auto-gain control:** Auto-gain automatically adjusts microphone volume if your sound card and driver support this feature.

✔ **Automatically adjust microphone volume while in a call:** This setting also automatically adjusts microphone volume during a call. Use this setting if your sound card doesn't support auto-gain.

✔ **Enable DirectSound:** DirectSound shortens the time span between when audio is sent and received, thus improving audio performance.

✔ **Adjust silence detection automatically:** This refers to the microphone detecting silence during a NetMeeting call. Automatic detection is recommended.

✔ **Manually adjust silence detection:** Rather than use automatic silence detection, you can adjust the setting yourself. Doing so isn't recommended, however, because it is difficult to adjust correctly.

✔ **Launch the Audio Tuning wizard:** Click the Tuning wizard button to run the wizard.

✔ **Manually configure compression settings:** You find this option by clicking the Advanced button on the Audio page. Using the automatic configuration setting, however, is recommended.

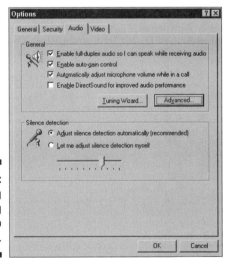

Figure 9-5:
Configuring
NetMeeting
audio
settings.

Remember that the audio options that you configure depend on the components that are installed on the computer. If you don't have a sound card, you won't see the Audio tab in the Options dialog box. If you don't have a full-duplex sound card, the Enable Full-duplex option on the Audio page will be grayed out.

Video configuration

Video conferencing consumes a great deal of network bandwidth. Most corporate administrators limit video conferencing to a select group of users. Others limit the amount of bandwidth available for video conferencing. Administrators at ISPs seldom limit video capabilities in their browser packages because the users they support are customers and not corporate employees.

If you plan to include NetMeeting video capability in your custom browser package, the client computers must have video cameras. If you don't have a camera, you can't send video pictures to the person on the other end of the call. You can, however, view video if the other caller has a video camera.

Just as with audio components, your configuration options depend on the components that you have installed. If you don't have a video camera installed, you can view the Video page in the Options dialog box, but some of the settings will be grayed out (see Figure 9-6).

If you plan to include NetMeeting video in your custom browser package, you should have a video camera installed on the build computer.

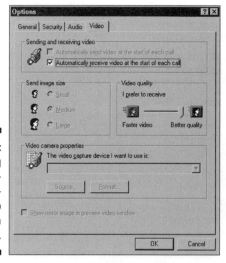

Figure 9-6:
Configuring
video set-
tings with-
out a video
camera
installed.

Sharing and collaborating

NetMeeting is a great tool for collaborating on a project with a group of coworkers. Suppose you're working on a project team of people who work in many geographic locations. Using NetMeeting, the entire team can share a whiteboard or an application to work on a document or design together. You can all share a whiteboard space — whatever anyone draws or writes on the whiteboard is visible to everyone on the call.

Similarly, you can open an application, such as Microsoft Word, and everyone on the call can share the document while discussing it. You can also choose to collaborate on the document, enabling all users to view and make changes to the document. Then when you save the document, you can send the file to everyone on the call.

Application sharing and collaborating are slightly different activities. With application sharing, users on the call can view the applications and files you open in real-time on their workstations. With collaboration, other callers can not only see the document in real-time, they can work on the document or file with you. NetMeeting sharing and collaboration features include:

- ✔ Whiteboard sharing
- ✔ Application sharing
- ✔ File transfer

As part of planning your custom browser package, you must decide whether to enable users to share applications or to collaborate by using NetMeeting. Some companies view NetMeeting application sharing as a security threat, and their system administrators use the IEAK to restrict users' abilities to share applications or transfer files. In other cases, administrators are concerned about bandwidth and choose to limit availability of NetMeeting features.

For the exam, know the purpose of NetMeeting collaboration and how you can provide audio/video capability while allowing or disallowing shared whiteboards and applications.

Using the IEAK with NetMeeting

All this talk about NetMeeting features is leading up to creating a custom IE5 package that includes NetMeeting. Now that you know which features are available, you can decide how to best configure NetMeeting for your organization. But before you begin creating the package, take a few moments to plan which features you will include.

Planning a NetMeeting package

First, a few of those pesky questions I'm so fond of:

✔ Do you want all the NetMeeting features to be available to every user in your organization?

✔ Do you have available network bandwidth to provide video conferencing to all employees?

✔ Does your organization deal with sensitive data that should not be shared via collaboration?

Answering these three questions should give you a pretty clear picture of how to proceed with your NetMeeting configuration. Before you begin to build your browser package, you should determine whether "one size fits all" or whether you need multiple packages. You also need to determine how to configure the individual NetMeeting settings and restrictions in each package.

For each package that you create, decide in advance whether the package will enable NetMeeting users to:

✔ Send and receive files

✔ Use audio features

✔ Send and receive video

✔ Share applications

✔ Collaborate

✔ Use NetMeeting between two computers via a null modem cable

✔ Adjust their NetMeeting configuration

✔ Limit bandwidth available to NetMeeting

Creating the package

After you determine which NetMeeting features your user community requires and configure the desired features on your build computer, you're ready to use the IEAK Customization wizard to create your custom browser package.

You can do much more than just configure NetMeeting by using the IEAK. You can use the Customization wizard and the Profile Manager to preconfigure settings for all users in your organization. You can restrict users from using NetMeeting features that you don't want them to use on your network. Finally, you can lock down your choices so users can't alter their NetMeeting configurations.

In order to include NetMeeting with your IE5 browser, make sure to select it on the Installation Options screen of the IEAK Customization wizard. The Minimal and Typical IE5 installation options don't include NetMeeting by default. If you choose either of these installation options, you must click NetMeeting in the Components Available list box on the left side of the screen. Then click the right arrow button to move NetMeeting to the Components To Install list box on the right side of the screen (see Figure 9-7).

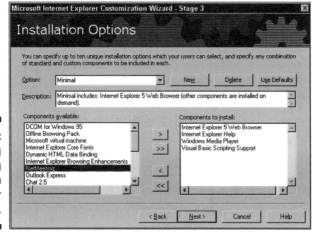

Figure 9-7:
Including
NetMeeting
in a custom
browser
package.

You can further customize the NetMeeting settings in your custom package in Stage 5 of the Customization wizard. The System Policies and Restrictions screen (see Figure 9-8) includes options for NetMeeting Settings and NetMeeting Protocols. The settings that you configure here override the Registry settings on user workstations, enabling you to standardize and manage NetMeeting settings across your organization.

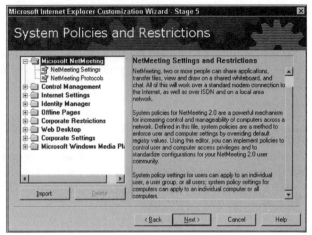

Figure 9-8:
Configuring
NetMeeting
policies and
restrictions.

The per-user NetMeeting settings that you can configure on the System
Policies and Restrictions screen of the Customization wizard are

- ✔ Prevent the user from sending files

- ✔ Prevent the user from receiving files

- ✔ Disable all application sharing features

- ✔ Prevent the user from sharing the clipboard

- ✔ Prevent the user from sharing MS-DOS windows

- ✔ Prevent the user from sharing explorer windows

- ✔ Prevent the user from collaborating

- ✔ Disable the General options page

- ✔ Disable the My Information options page

- ✔ Disable the Calling options page

- ✔ Disable the Audio options page

- ✔ Disable the Video options page

- ✔ Disable the Protocols options page

- ✔ Prevent the user from answering calls

- ✔ Prevent the user from using audio features

- ✔ Prevent the user from sending video

- ✔ Prevent the user from receiving video

✔ Prevent the user from using directory services

✔ Set the default Directory Server

✔ Set Exchange Server Properties for NetMeeting Address

✔ Preset User Information Category (only applicable for silent installs)

✔ Set the NetMeeting home page URL

✔ Set average audio/video throughput limit (in bps)

The per-machine NetMeeting protocol configuration options are

✔ Disable TCP/IP

✔ Disable null modem

Audio/video conferencing and collaboration are bandwidth intensive and many corporate administrators elect to restrict use of these features within their organizations. A corporate administrator who is worried about bandwidth may prohibit sending or receiving video, prohibit sharing applications and files, prohibit collaborating, and then, perhaps, prohibit the user from accessing these options so that they cannot be changed. If a select number of users will be using the full set of NetMeeting features, a corporate administrator may limit the bandwidth available for audio/video. Administrators at ISP/ICPs seldom restrict NetMeeting settings because their end users are customers with a wide variety of browser needs.

Modifying the package

After you create a custom browser package that includes NetMeeting, you can manage NetMeeting from a central location by using the IEAK Profile Manager. The Profile Manager includes the same NetMeeting settings and restrictions that are available in the Customization wizard. If you need to modify the original NetMeeting configuration, use the IEAK Profile Manager to alter the settings and then distribute the new profile by using the automatic browser configuration URL. (Chapter 11 provides instruction on setting up automatic browser configuration.)

If you plan to limit NetMeeting collaboration or video to a select group of users, you must create two browser packages. One package is for the users who use the NetMeeting features, and a second package is for those who don't use them. Using the IEAK Customization wizard, create the first package with the NetMeeting features enabled. Then use the IEAK Profile Manager to edit the .ins file and create a second package with the NetMeeting features restricted.

Prep Test

1 Mary is a corporate administrator and is planning a custom IE5 package. Client computers in her organization include Windows 98, Windows 95, and Windows NT 4.0. Network services run on Windows NT Server 4.0 and include WINS, DHCP, and DNS. The company wants to provide video conferencing for its globally dispersed employees. What additional servers, if any, must Mary install to support video conferencing?

A ○ Mary doesn't need to add any servers.

B ○ Mary must add an audio/video conferencing server.

C ○ Mary must add an ILS directory server.

D ○ Mary must add a Microsoft NetMeeting server.

2 Mary is a corporate administrator and is creating a custom IE5 package. She has planned her NetMeeting features and is ready to use the IEAK to create her browser package. What tool(s) can Mary use to configure NetMeeting settings and restrictions? (Choose all that apply.)

A ❑ The NetMeeting Tuning wizard

B ❑ The IEAK Customization wizard

C ❑ The IEAK Profile Manager

D ❑ The NetMeeting Administration Kit

3 What type of sound card do client computers require in order for users to listen and talk simultaneously?

A ○ Half-duplex sound card

B ○ Audio/video sound card

C ○ Full-duplex sound card

D ○ Auto-gain card

4 Mary is a corporate administrator and is creating a custom IE5 package. Mary is concerned that the use of NetMeeting video will saturate the company network. What steps can Mary take to prevent this? (Choose all that apply.)

A ❑ Use the IEAK Customization wizard to prevent users from sending and receiving video.

B ❑ Use the IEAK Profile Manager to prevent users from sending and receiving video.

C ❑ Use the IEAK Customization wizard to limit audio/video throughput.

D ❑ Use the IEAK Profile Manager to limit audio/video throughput.

5 Mary is a corporate administrator at a financial services firm and is creating a custom IE5 package. Mary is concerned that NetMeeting users will jeopardize sensitive financial information during NetMeeting calls. What IEAK settings and restrictions can Mary use to prevent this from happening? (Choose all that apply.)

A ❑ Disable all application sharing features.

B ❑ Prevent users from collaborating.

C ❑ Disable null modem connections.

D ❑ Disable the ILS directory server.

6 (True/False). In order to run NetMeeting, client computers must have at least a Pentium 133 processor.

A ○ True

B ○ False

7 Which NetMeeting feature enables all users on a NetMeeting call to write or draw on the same whiteboard?

A ○ Audio/video conferencing

B ○ Application sharing

C ○ Collaboration

D ○ Chat

8 Mary is a corporate administrator and is planning a custom IE5 package. Client computers in her organization include Windows 98, Windows 95, and Windows NT 4.0. Mary wants to enable NetMeeting video conferencing among corporate officers only. How many times must Mary run the IEAK Customization wizard to accomplish this objective?

A ○ Twice.

B ○ Three times.

C ○ Only once.

D ○ Mary doesn't need to run the Customization wizard at all.

9 Mary is a corporate administrator and is preparing to create a custom IE5 package that includes NetMeeting. Mary doesn't want users to be able to use video conferencing. She also doesn't want them to be able to alter their video configuration. What can Mary do while creating the custom package that will prevent users from altering their NetMeeting video configuration?

A ○ Use the IEAK Customization wizard to disable the Video options page.

B ○ Use the IEAK Profile Manager to disable the Video options page.

C ○ Use the IEAK Customization wizard to prevent the user from sending video.

D ○ Use the IEAK Profile Manager wizard to prevent the user from sending video.

10 Microsoft NetMeeting is based on which open standards? (Choose all that apply.)

A ❑ T.120

B ❑ LDAP

C ❑ H.323

D ❑ ILS

Answers

1 *C.* Because Mary's network uses DHCP for IP addressing, answer A is incorrect. Mary must add an ILS (Internet Locator Service) server to enable callers to access other NetMeeting users through the directory server. Answers B and C aren't legitimate options. *Review "NetMeeting protocols."*

2 *B and C.* Answers A and D aren't legitimate options, although NetMeeting does have an Audio Tuning wizard. *See "Using the IEAK with NetMeeting."*

3 *C.* A full-duplex sound card is required for users to talk and listen at the same time. Answer A is incorrect because a half-duplex card enables users to listen or speak, but not do both simultaneously. Answer B is not a correct answer because the card must be a full-duplex card to enable listening and talking simultaneously. Answer D isn't a legitimate answer because auto-gain is a feature used to adjust microphone volume. *Review "Audio configuration."*

4 *A, B, C, and D.* Mary can use either the IEAK Customization wizard or the IEAK Profile Manager to prevent users from sending and receiving video and to limit audio/video throughput. By using the Customization wizard, Mary can access these settings while creating the custom package. By using the Profile Manager, Mary can access these features by editing the .ins file after the package is created. *Review "Using the IEAK with NetMeeting."*

5 *A and B.* By preventing collaboration and application sharing, users cannot accidentally reveal sensitive financial information by displaying files stored on their computers. *See "Using the IEAK with NetMeeting."*

6 *B.* Computers running NetMeeting require a Pentium 90 processor, although a Pentium 133 is recommended for better performance. *See "Determining System Requirements."*

7 *C.* Collaboration enables all participants in a NetMeeting call to write and draw on the whiteboard. Answer A is incorrect because audio/video conferencing merely enables participants to talk and view each other over the network. Answer B is incorrect because application sharing enables a single user to display an application that all participants can view. Answer D is incorrect because the chat features enable users to converse in real-time, but not to share a whiteboard. *See "Customizing NetMeeting Features."*

8 *C.* Mary needs to run the IEAK Customization wizard once to create the package for the corporate officers. Then she can use the IEAK Profile Manager to edit the .ins file and create a second package for all the other users. Answers A, B, and D are incorrect because Mary needs to run the IEAK Customization wizard just one time. *Review "Using the IEAK with NetMeeting."*

9 *A.* Answer B isn't correct because the question asks what Mary can do while creating the package, not while editing the package. Answers C and D are incorrect because they do not prevent users from altering their video configurations. *See "Using the IEAK with NetMeeting."*

10 *A, B, and C.* NetMeeting is based on the LDAP directory access protocol, the T.120 data conferencing standard, and the H.323 gateway access standard. Answer D is incorrect because ILS is the Microsoft Internet Locator Service and is not an open standard. *Review "NetMeeting protocols."*

Chapter 10

Using the IEAK
Customization Wizard

● ●

Exam Objectives

▶ Customizing setup with the IEAK Customization wizard

▶ Stage 1: Gathering Information

▶ Stage 2: Specifying Setup parameters

▶ Stage 3: Customizing setup

▶ Stage 4: Customizing the browser

▶ Stage 5: Component customization

● ●

*1*n this chapter, I explain how to use the IEAK to customize the individual components of the setup program and the browser package. I cover each stage of the IE Customization wizard in sequence. You soon understand why I continually emphasize planning — you have a lot of information to configure!

The screens in Stage 3 of the wizard determine how the user experiences Internet Explorer 5 setup when they install your custom package. Stage 4 deals with customizing individual components of the browser. For the exam, make certain that you can distinguish between the different installation options. Also, concentrate on how the various browser settings can be customized.

Quick Assessment

Gathering
Information

1 Microsoft provides the _____ as the tool to help you customize and deploy Internet Explorer.

2 The IEAK Customization wizard contains _____ stages.

3 Without a _____ from Microsoft, you cannot run the IEAK Customization wizard.

4 The features available in Internet Explorer 5 are dependent on the _____ type.

5 _____ compares the components already on your system with current versions of the files on the Internet.

6 (True/False). You can't incorporate several languages within one package.

Specifying
Setup
Parameters

7 A _____ is a code that distinguishes one program from another.

8 Up to _____ additional applications can be included in your custom package.

Customizing
Setup

9 A _____ install does not prompt users for installation information, but they do see error messages and progress indicators in the screen as installation takes place.

10 The _____ is a wizard that guides you through customizing and configuring the Microsoft Connection Manager dialer.

Answers

1 *IEAK Customization.* See "Using the Customization wizard."

2 *five (5).* See "Stage 1: Gathering Information."

3 *customization code.* Review "Stage 1: Gathering Information."

4 *platform.* See "Stage 1: Gathering Information."

5 *Automatic Version Synchronization.* Review "Stage 1: Gathering Information."

6 *True.* Review "Stage 1: Gathering Information."

7 *Globally Unique Identifier (GUID).* See "Stage 2: Specifying Setup parameters."

8 *ten (10).* Review "Stage 2: Specifying Setup parameters."

9 *hands-free.* See "Stage 3: Customizing setup."

10 *Connection Manager Administration Kit (CMAK).* Review "Stage 3: Customizing Setup."

Using the Customization Wizard

Microsoft provides the IE Customization wizard as the tool to help you customize and deploy Internet Explorer. The first three stages of the Customization wizard deal with customizing Active Setup, the installation utility for Internet Explorer.

Detailed screen information fully explains each stage of the Customization wizard. If you're still not clear on what information each stage of installation is requesting after reading the screen, turn to the Help feature for additional support.

The IEAK Help utility also provides complete detail about the five stages of the Customization wizard. Read through the information in the Help utility before running the Customization wizard for the first time.

Start the IE Customization wizard from the Microsoft IEAK folder or from the Start menu.

Stage 1: Gathering Information

Stage 1 of the Customization wizard requests basic information about configuring the package that you're about to build. The information requested includes the name of your company, the platform you want to build the package for, the language in which you want to distribute the package, and the distribution medium of the package. The following sections tell you about the screens you meet in Stage 1 of the IEAK Customization wizard.

The Company Name and Customization Code screen

This is where you enter your organization name and customization code as well as choose your customization role.

Before you can run the IEAK Customization wizard, you must register with Microsoft and obtain a customization code. Without a code that matches your licensing agreement, you can't build a custom package.

Chapter 3 explains how to gather the planning information you need to figure out which role is appropriate for each deployment. If you don't have the planning information, the Help button provides detailed assistance.

The Platform Options screen

In this screen, you choose the platforms for which you want to build the custom package. You can build a package for

- **A 32-bit browser:** Supported by Windows 95, Windows 98, Windows 2000, or Windows NT 4.0

- **A 16-bit browser:** Supported by Windows 3.1, Windows for Workgroups 3.11, or Windows NT 3.51

- **A UNIX-based browser:** Supported by Solaris 2.5.1 or Solaris 2.6, and HP-UX

Internet Explorer 5 does not support the Macintosh platform.

The features available in Internet Explorer 5 are dependent on the platform type. For example, features that are available in the browser on the Windows 98 operating system may not be available for the Windows 3.1 or UNIX-based browser. In short, the features available in each customized package you create vary according to the target operating system.

You can't create a single package that runs on all platform types. Rather, you run the Customization wizard a separate time for each platform type you must support to build a custom package for each. You can then store packages for multiple platforms within the same directory.

The File Locations screen

This is where you specify the location of the destination folder that will contain the finished package. Clicking the Advanced Options button leads to more complex configuration information (see Figure 10-1):

Figure 10-1: The Advanced Options dialog box.

Advanced Options

☑ Check for latest components via Automatic Version Synchronization (if you installed the IEAK from the Internet, AVS must be run at least once to download the components)

Path of .INS file to import settings from:

[   ] [Browse]

Component Download folder:

[C:\PROGRAM FILES\IEAK\Download] [Browse]

[OK] [Cancel]

✔ **Check for latest versions using AVS:** *Automatic Version Synchronization* (AVS) compares the components already on your system with current versions of the files on the Internet. Note that during Stage 1 of the Customization wizard, you are merely enabling (checking the box) or disabling (not checking the box) AVS; you don't actually compare or download files until Stage 2.

✔ **Specify existing .INS file:** You can specify the name of an existing .INS file from which to import settings. The Customization wizard doesn't modify the existing .INS file; it imports the settings from that file and creates a new .INS file for the package that you're currently building by using the Customization wizard.

✔ **Specify component download folder:** You can enter the path and name of a folder to hold the components that you download for your custom package. When AVS compares downloaded components to those available on the Internet, it compares the Internet components with components in this folder. Synchronizing components overwrites existing files in this folder. If you must keep the older versions for a specific package, remember to change the name of this folder before you synchronize.

The Language Selection screen

This screen allows you to choose the target language for the package (such as English, German, Japanese, and so on). You have to run the Customization wizard a separate time for each language that you want to distribute the package in.

You can't incorporate more than one language into a single package. You must run the Customization wizard once for each language version that you create. But you can store all the packages in the same destination folder.

The Media Selection screen

The options available to you in this screen are dependent on the licensing role that you select when you register your IEAK package and on the licensing role you chose earlier in Stage 1 of the Customization wizard. Notice in Figure 10-2 that some of the options are deactivated.

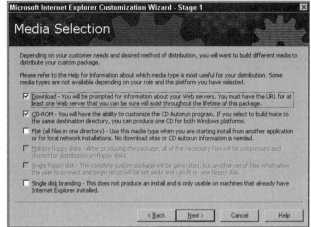

Media Selection

Depending on your customer needs and desired method of distribution, you will want to build different media to distribute your custom package.

Please refer to the Help for information about which media type is most useful for your distribution. Some media types are not available depending on your role and the platform you have selected.

☑ Download - You will be prompted for information about your Web servers. You must have the URL for at least one Web server that you can be sure will exist throughout the lifetime of this package.

☑ CD-ROM - You will have the ability to customize the CD Autorun program. If you select to build twice to the same destination directory, you can produce one CD for both Windows platforms.

☐ Flat (all files in one directory) - Use this media type when you are starting install from another application or for local network installations. No download sites or CD autorun information is needed.

☐ Multiple floppy disks - After producing the package, all of the necessary files will be compressed and divided for distribution on floppy disks.

☐ Single floppy disk - The complete custom package will be generated, but another set of files which allow the user to connect and begin setup will be set aside and can fit on one floppy disk.

☐ Single disk branding - This does not produce an install and is only usable on machines that already have Internet Explorer installed.

< Back   Next >   Cancel   Help

Figure 10-2:
The Media Selection screen of the Customization wizard.

The choices available in this screen are:

- ✔ **CD-ROM:** If you select a CD-ROM installation, you have the opportunity to customize the Autorun feature with your own bitmaps and text. A set of folders on the CD-ROM stores the files that comprise your package.

  You can include packages for different Windows platforms on one CD by building additional packages to the same destination folder. (Review the "Platform Options" section in this chapter.)

- ✔ **Download:** If you plan to deploy the custom browser from an Internet or intranet site, choose the Download option. The Customization wizard requires you to supply the URL of at least one Web server from which your users may download the browser.

- ✔ **Flat (for network installs):** You use the flat media selection when you plan to deploy the package from a network server. You place all the files into a single (or flat) destination folder.

- ✔ **Multiple Floppy Disks:** If CD-ROM or network downloads aren't available, you can also create an installation package on multiple floppy disks. This media option places the files for the custom package into the \Mfloppy folder within the destination directory. This option also groups the files into folders named Disk 1, Disk 2, and so on.

  The Automatic Installation option isn't available with the Multiple Floppy Disk media selection.

- ✔ **Single-Disk Branding (for ISP role only):** Single-disk branding customizes an existing Internet Explorer install if it is version 4.01, Service Pack 1 or higher. This media option creates a SETUP.EXE within the BrndOnly folder in your destination location. The setup file customizes some features in the existing browser. Despite the name of this media option, you can distribute the branding file via server or download as well as on a single floppy disk.

✔ **Single Floppy Disk (for ISP role only):** For administrators working in the ISP role, the single floppy disk media option is available. This option copies a set of initialization files to a floppy disk. The ISP provides this disk to its customers, who execute a file on the floppy disk to begin the setup and download process.

The single floppy disk media option isn't available on the Media Selection screen if you specify the No-Sign-Up method in the Customization wizard when creating the custom package.

The Feature Selection screen

The Feature Selection screen enables you to select the features that you want to customize. You may choose to alter a number of features when creating a custom browser package. If you select a feature within the list on the Feature Selection screen, you see the customization screens for the feature during the Customization wizard.

The Customization wizard uses the default configuration — you don't see its customization screens if you don't choose a feature in the list. Be sure to deselect the check boxes for features that you don't want to customize. Otherwise, you may go through many unnecessary configuration screens while building your package!

By deselecting the check box adjacent to a feature in the Feature Selection screen, you prevent the customization screens for that feature from appearing while running the Customization wizard.

Stage 2: Specifying Setup Parameters

In Stage 2 of the IEAK Customization wizard, you identify the download sites that you want to obtain components from. If you didn't disable it during Stage 1, Automatic Version Synchronization (AVS) runs during Stage 2 as well. The initial screen in Stage 2 details the information that this stage requires.

The Microsoft Download Site screen

In the Download Site screen, you find a drop-down list of Microsoft download sites. Select a site from which to download Internet Explorer files and related optional components.

The Automatic Version Synchronization screen

Provided that you haven't disabled AVS in Stage 1 and that you have run the Customization wizard at least once before, you see the Automatic Version Synchronization screen, as shown in Figure 10-3. If you're uncertain about the content of the components in the list, select the component and click the Help button to see a description of the component.

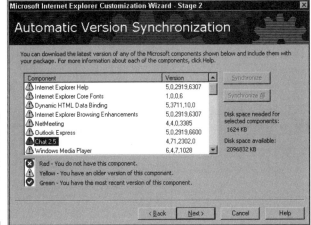

Figure 10-3:
AVS
ensures that
your compo-
nents are
up-to-date.

AVS uses a color code to signify whether or not your component is up-to-date. You can choose to download the newer components, or simply choose to use the existing version. As you see from the legend in Figure 10-3, a green symbol means that your version is current. Yellow signifies an out-of-date version on your computer. Red means that you do not have the component at all. You can update a component by selecting it and clicking the Synchronize button. Or you can click the Synchronize All button to update all components.

For AVS to run a comparison, you must run the Customization wizard at least once. Obviously, AVS can't compare newer files to existing files if you don't run the Customization wizard and download files beforehand. Expect a question on this topic on your exam!

After AVS compares all components, it also reports

   ✔ The amount of disk space required to store all the downloaded components

   ✔ The amount of disk space available on your system

The Add Custom Components screen

Figure 10-4 shows the Add Custom Components screen. In this screen, you can specify additional applications that you want to include in your custom package. The applications can be other popular desktop applications, such as Microsoft Office, or they can be organization-specific applications within your company.

You can include up to ten additional applications in your custom package.

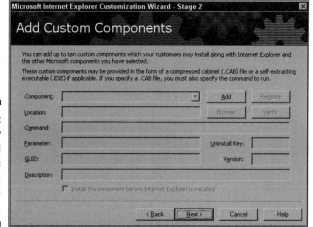

Figure 10-4:
Specify
additional
applications
to include in
the package
here.

You can install additional components from self-extracting executable files or from .cab files. If you install components from .cab files, you must specify the command file that runs the application. Other requested information on this screen includes:

✔ **Location of the application files:** The path to the application files.

✔ **Parameters:** This field contains startup parameters for the application.

✔ **Uninstall Key:** Specifying an uninstall file here allows users to uninstall the application by using the Add/Remove Programs feature in Control Panel. The file must contain the uninstall subkey for the component. Syntax for the subkey looks like this:

```
HKEY_LOCAL_MACHINE\Software\Microsoft\Windows\Current
        Version\Uninstall\<Application
        Name>\<UninstallString>
```

Substitute the application name for <Application Name>. Substitute the command for the uninstall application for <UninstallString>.

✔ **GUID:** A *globally unique identifier* is a code that distinguishes one program from another. The Customization wizard randomly generates a GUID in this field if your application does not come with a GUID for you to enter.

✔ **Version:** This field enables you to track down the installed version of an application.

✔ **Description:** This field enables a 511-character description of the application.

The last option in this screen enables you to specify that the application be installed prior to the installation of Internet Explorer. If, for example, you need to run a Registry cleaning application prior to installing IE5, you can specify this here.

Stage 3: Customizing Setup

During Stage 3, you provide information that customizes the Internet Explorer Setup wizard. You can specify the bitmaps and titles that appear on setup screens, the download sites for your package, the installation options, and more.

The Customize Setup screen

In the Customize Setup screen, you enter the path to your bitmap images, the text for your Setup wizard title bar, and a name for your Custom Components installation group.

The Silent Install screen

The Silent Install screen presents three options for customizing user interaction during setup. For the exam, be sure you understand the implications of each type of installation:

✔ **Interactive Install** is not a silent installation at all. The user is prompted to enter installation information.

✔ **Hands-Free Install** does not prompt users for installation information. Users do, however, see error messages and progress indicators in the screen as installation takes place.

✔ **Completely Silent Install** functions with no user interaction and no error or progress indicators. If the installation is not successful, the user receives no error messages. This installation is equivalent to installing from the command line by using the /Q:A switch.

Completely Silent Install and Hands-Free Install both use parameters you enter through the Customization wizard to complete the installation. The parameters accept the license agreement and bypass all prompts that usually require user intervention. The first specified download site in the Customization wizard downloads files. Remember as you make selections in the following screens that the users don't see any of these choices. You make the selections for the user.

The Installation Options screen

The Installation Options screen (see Figure 10-5) offers a great deal of flexibility. Suppose that you're a corporate administrator at an organization with 2,000 users. Some of those users need only basic browse access to the company intranet. Others need full Internet access and a handful need NetMeeting. You can satisfy all these installation needs by specifying uniquely named installation options in this screen.

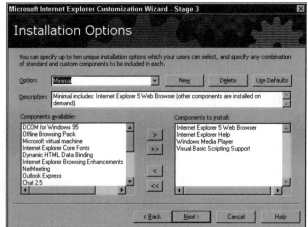

Figure 10-5: Creating unique installation options.

You can create your own options if the standard Minimal, Typical, and Full installation options do not meet the needs of your user community. You can choose the components from the available components list that you want to make available to your users through the custom install.

For example, for the users needing only intranet access, create a Basic Install option that includes only the Internet Explorer 5 Web browser component. The second group of users could receive a newly created Internet Install option containing, for example, the Internet Explorer 5 Web browser, the Offline Browsing Pack, and Outlook Express. For the last group, you could create an option that you name NetMeeting Install and include the NetMeeting component along with the other options you add. You can have up to ten unique installation options.

The Completely Silent installation method doesn't prompt users to select an installation option. You must run the Customization wizard once for each type of install you want to create.

The Component Download Site screen

On the Component Download Site screen, you specify the download sites from which you download your package. If you're not doing a silent install, you can specify up to ten sites. By specifying multiple sites, you provide alternatives in case the first listed site is down.

If you choose Completely Silent Installation, you can enter only one download site because the user doesn't receive any installation prompts. If the site is unavailable, the installation fails.

The screen information that each download site requires is a site name, URL, and site region. The site name should be a friendly name that users can recognize. The region should specify the city, state, or country that locates the download site. The URL, of course, is the Web address of the download site.

The download site information is added to a file named IE5SITES.dat.

The Component Download screen

In the Component Download screen of the Customization wizard, you determine how your users receive new versions of Internet Explorer when they use the Windows Update option from the Tools menu. Do you want them to connect to the original download site that they access to download your package? Or do you want to direct them to the Microsoft Download Site?

You have three options in the Component Download screen:

- ✔ **Remove the Windows Update option from the Tools menu:** If you don't want users adding new component versions to their systems, choose this option.

- ✔ **Use the default URL for the Windows Update:** The default URL for the Windows Update is the original download site that you specify in the Customization Wizard screen.

- ✔ **Use a custom add-on URL and menu text:** You can also add a different site for Windows Update to access for component updates. Do this by entering menu choice text and the site's URL.

If you want Windows Update to go to the Microsoft site to download add-on components, such as NetMeeting and Chat, after the initial installation (while still updating files from the site you chose), select the Download Components from Microsoft after Install check box.

The Installation Directory screen

In this screen, you specify the target directory for the installation. If you decide to select the Allow the User to Choose the Installation Directory check box, the directory you specify in this screen becomes the default installation directory.

The screen does not prompt the user for input if you choose a silent install. Instead, the wizard installs the package to the default directory.

You have three options for the root path of the folder for the custom package:

- ✔ The Windows folder
- ✔ The Program Files folder
- ✔ The full path to a custom folder that you specify

If the computer has Internet Explorer on it, the wizard installs the files from your custom package into the existing Internet Explorer folder.

The Corporate Install Options screen

The purpose of this screen is to allow an administrator to disable the ability of users to choose a custom installation. Three check boxes appear in the screen:

- ✔ **The Disable Custom Installation Option check box:** During an interactive installation, users sometimes elect not to install all of the available components. Selecting this option prevents users from choosing which components they want to install.

  If you specify a silent installation instead of an interactive installation, users don't see installation options, so you don't need to select this check box.

- ✔ **The Disable Saving Uninstall Information check box:** In most installations, uninstall information is saved so that users can back out or remove an application that causes problems on the system. Select the Disable Saving Uninstall Information check box to prevent saving this information. (I don't recommend that you select this option. The uninstall method is usually the cleanest way to remove an application.)

✔ **The Disable Internet Explorer Compatibility Mode check box:** In compatibility mode, Internet Explorer 5 is backward compatible with previous versions of Internet Explorer. Select this check box to prevent users from selecting the compatibility mode of operation.

The last options on this page determine whether or not you set Internet Explorer as the default browser. The three choices are very straightforward: Internet Explorer is the default browser, Internet Explorer is not the default browser, or User Choice (of whether or not Internet Explorer is the default browser).

The Advanced Installation Options screen

Setup detects whether or not a component is already present on the system. If the component version is present, it doesn't download again. This saves a great deal of download time. In the Advanced Installation Options screen, you have an option to enable or disable this feature.

Select the Optimize for Web Download check box to enable the ability to check before downloading. If you do not select the check box, Setup downloads all components, whether a compatible version exists on the machine or not.

Also in the Advanced Installation Options screen is a list of all the components available for installation in this package (see Figure 10-6). If you select the check box next to a component, the user sees the item in a list of optional components to install. Leaving the check box blank changes the status to Force Install, meaning that the component automatically installs along with the Internet Explorer browser.

Figure 10-6:
Selecting the check box next to a component allows the user to choose whether to install the component.

The status column to the right of the component list makes it easy to determine which items are visible to the users in their list of optional installation components. The labels for each component are either Show in Custom Mode or Force Install.

Clicking Next in the Advanced Installation Options screen takes you to either the Connection Manager Customization screen or to the Components on Media screen. If you deselect any components in the Advanced Installation Options screen, you see the Components on Media screen next.

The Components on Media screen

The Components on Media screen identifies any components that download during AVS but that aren't in the installation options for this package. The wizard lists these components with a check box to the left of each one and selects the check boxes by default. Any selected components are copied to the distribution media, which makes it available for automatic installation. Unselected components aren't copied to the distribution media.

The Connection Manager Customization screen

The Connection Manager Administration Kit, or CMAK, is a separate wizard that works with the Internet Explorer Administration Kit. The CMAK allows you to create a customized version of Connection Manager that enables users to connect to the Internet. The custom Connection Manager can contain your own graphics, help files, and icons.

When you run the CMAK, you create a profile that the Customization wizard can later import. Enter the path and profile name in the Connection Manager Customization screen. After importing, the wizard includes the profile in your custom package.

You can also launch the CMAK from the Connection Manager Customization screen and create the profile to use in your custom package. Your custom package includes this profile.

CMAK is a timesaving tool for administrators because users often have trouble configuring their Internet connections. Using the CMAK, you can preconfigure the connection and deploy it to the user desktops with your custom packages.

The Windows Desktop Update screen

The Windows Desktop Update screen simply offers you the choice of whether or not to include Windows Desktop Update in your custom browser package. Choose Yes or No.

Windows Desktop Update doesn't come with Internet Explorer 5. This feature is available if you upgrade from Internet Explorer 4.0 and have the Windows Desktop Update on your computer. Windows Desktop Update is also available if you're running Internet Explorer 5 on the Windows 98 platform because Windows 98 includes the Windows Desktop Update.

The Windows Desktop Update allows users to view their computer in the same way that they view the Web. Explorer functions similar to the Internet Explorer browser. The Favorites menu is available when you browse the computer, and you can add active content to the desktop, folders, and toolbar.

The Digital Signatures screen

If you obtain digital certificates to sign your applications, you must enter this information on the Digital Signatures screen (see Figure 10-7).

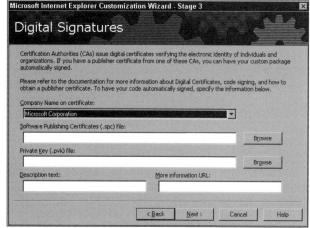

Figure 10-7: Specifying digital signatures.

Information that the Digital Signatures screen requires includes:

✔ **Company providing the certificate:** If you have an installed digital certificate on you computer, the name of the company providing the certificate appears in this drop-down list.

> ✔ **.SPC file (Software Publishing Certificate):** Enter the name of the .SPC file associated with the digital certificate in this text box.
>
> ✔ **.PVK file (Private Key file):** Enter the name of the .PVK file associated with the digital certificate.
>
> ✔ **Description text:** Contains the text that displays in the dialog box when users download files signed with this digital certificate.
>
> ✔ **URL for more information:** Users can click this URL to obtain more details about the digital certificate and the company.

Stage 4: Customizing the Browser

Stage 4 of the Customization wizard deals with customizing the appearance and functions of the browser. Configurable options include favorites, links, bitmaps, and connections. The following sections take you through the screens in Stage 4 of the IEAK Customization wizard.

The Browser Title screen

The Browser Title screen lets you customize the browser title bar. The text that you type in the Title Bar Text field appears at the left side of the title bar of the browser.

The text that you type here is appended to the phrase "Microsoft Internet Explorer provided by." If, for example, you type the words *Deployments 'R Us* in this field, the title bar of the browser in your custom package reads: `Microsoft Internet Explorer provided by Deployments 'R Us.`

If you include Outlook Express in your custom package, the title bar text appears in Outlook Express as: `Outlook Express provided by Deployments 'R Us.`

Another option on this screen lets you specify the bitmap to use as background on the toolbar. Yet another way for you to truly customize the browser to enhance the user experience!

The Browser Toolbar Buttons screen

The Browser Toolbar Buttons screen gives you the opportunity to customize the browser by adding or deleting toolbar buttons.

By clicking the Add button, you advance to the Browser Toolbar Button Information screen where you must specify the following for the new button:

- ✔ Button caption
- ✔ Executable file or script to run when the button is clicked (you can browse to this)
- ✔ The filename of the color icon to appear on the toolbar button (you can browse to this)
- ✔ The filename of the grayscale icon to appear on the button (you can browse to this)

Finally, specify whether or not the new button appears on the toolbar by default. You can add a full toolbar of buttons that are customized for the phrasing and lingo that are familiar to your user community.

The Animated Logo screen

You can replace the animated logo in the Internet Explorer window with the animated logo of your choice.

If you're already familiar with animated graphics, you may find this screen self-explanatory. If you're not an animated graphics buff, however, read the Help file to take advantage of this feature. You have to enter a path and file-name for both a large and small version of the animated bitmap.

Microsoft provides two tools, along with the IEAK, to help you create and view your animated logo. These tools are the animated bitmap creator and the animated bitmap previewer:

- ✔ **Animated Bitmap Creator (makebmp.exe):** This tool is located in the \Toolkit\Graphics\Tools subfolder of the IEAK folder. (Mine is located under Program Files.) Use this tool to combine a *stack* of images in sequence to create an animated logo.
- ✔ **Animated Bitmap Previewer (animbmp.exe):** This tool is also located in the \Toolkit\Graphics\Tools subfolder. With the animated bitmap pre-viewer, you can preview the animated logo that you created by using makebmp.exe.

Know the purpose and location of makebmp.exe and animbmp.exe.

The Static Logo screen

You can specify a static logo to replace the static Internet Explorer logo in the upper-right corner of the browser. In this screen, you can enter a small and large version of the bitmap you want to use. Note that the static bitmap is not in motion at any time.

The Important URLs screen

In the Important URLs screen, you can specify the URLs for

- ✔ **A custom home page:** Enables you to specify the URL of the page that users see when they launch their browsers or click the Home button.

- ✔ **A custom search page:** Enables you to specify the URL of the page that users see when they click the Search button.

- ✔ **A custom online support page:** Enables you to specify the URL of the page that users see when they choose Help➪Online Support. By default, Online Support uses the URL of the Microsoft online support Web site. You can change this to direct users to your organization's online help site.

The Favorites and Links screen

On the Favorites and Links screen of the Customization wizard, you can add useful Web pages for your user community. You can also specify the order and organization of the information listed under Favorites and Links. Figure 10-8 shows the screen.

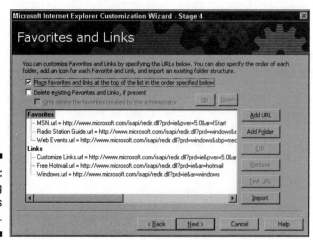

Figure 10-8:
Configuring
favorites
and links.

Don't overlook the opportunity that this screen provides for you to add value for your corporation. You can meet with representatives from several departments to determine the type of information that is beneficial to employees.

On the exam, you're likely to see a scenario question that describes a set of user requirements, including a need to retain existing favorites when the new browser is installed. You must be able to determine whether a series of defined actions satisfies the user requirements.

The Channels screen

You have the option to customize the channels that appear on user desktops. You can delete existing channels and turn on the Channel Bar by default. You can also import the channels that are configured in your own browser. Be prepared to specify channel configuration information.

Be sure to include the Offline Browsing Pack as a component in your Internet Explorer 5 package if you want users to be able to view channels. Why? Because if Internet Explorer 4 and the Active Desktop weren't installed before Internet Explorer 5, users can't use channels.

The Welcome Page screen

On the Welcome Page screen, you can choose one of three options:

- ✔ Display default Internet Explorer 5 Welcome page
- ✔ Do not display a Welcome page
- ✔ Use a custom Welcome page

The Welcome Page is the screen that you see when the browser is started for the first time. To use a custom welcome page, you must enter the URL of the page on this screen.

The User Agent String screen

Many Web developers use user agent strings to track site statistics, such as number of accesses, and type of browsers that are accessing their Web sites. The User Agent String screen in the Customization wizard lets you append information to the end of the user agent string.

You know that your Web site is being accessed by a computer with your custom browser package installed through the text that you added to the user agent string. Similarly, other companies see your custom text when your users access their sites.

For the exam, know that you can track site statistics (such as page hits) by using the User Agent String.

The Connection Settings screen

In the Connection Settings screen of the Customization wizard, you have the opportunity to import connection settings directly from your own system and include them in your customized browser package. You can modify your own connection settings from this screen by clicking the Modify Settings button.

On this screen, you can also choose to remove existing connection settings from user computers, or to not customize the connection settings at all.

Providing your user community with preconfigured connection settings has a direct impact on support costs by reducing the number of helpdesk calls and trouble tickets.

The Security screen

In the Security screen of the Customization wizard, you choose whether to customize certification authorities and Authenticode Security. Certification authorities and Authenticode Security help you to control the sites from which your user community can download content, such as programs and applets. A certificate (sometimes called a digital signature) provided by a certification authority provides information about where a program originated and whether the program is in its original form.

In the security screen are two panels:

✔ **Certification Authorities panel:** This panel contains a pair of radio buttons that allow you to choose whether to customize certification authorities for your users. You have the choice of not including certification authorities in the package or importing the certification authorities from the computer that you're using to create the package. Clicking the Modify Settings button starts the Certification Authorities Import wizard, in which you can make changes to the authorities that the wizard imports.

✔ **The Authenticode Security panel:** This panel contains a pair of radio buttons that enable you to choose whether to customize *Authenticode* security for your users. Authenticode allows you to specify certain software publishers and credentials agencies as *trusted,* which means that users aren't prompted before installing and using programs from these publishers. You can choose not to customize Authenticode security or to import the Authenticode security information from the computer that you're using to create the package. Click the Modify Settings button next to Authenticode security to display the Trusted Publishers and Issuers of Credentials list, where you can remove any publisher name that you don't want to be trusted on your users' computers.

The Security Settings screen

The last screen in Stage 4 is the Security Settings screen, which lets you import and modify security zone settings and content ratings settings. Security zones are areas that you define to which you can attach different levels of security. Content ratings allow you to filter Web sites based on rating information provided by the author of the site or, if sites are not rated, they may be blocked.

In the Security Setting screen are two panels:

✔ **The Security Zones panel:** This panel contains a pair of radio buttons that allow you to choose between the Internet Explorer 5 default Security Zones settings (by selecting the Do Not Customize Security Zones radio button) or to import the security zone information from the computer that you use to create the package. You can customize the security zone information by clicking the Modify Settings button in this panel.

✔ **The Content Ratings panel:** This panel contains a pair of radio buttons that allow you to choose between the default settings for content ratings (by selecting the Do Not Customize Content Ratings radio button) or to import the content rating information from the computer that you use to create the package. You can customize the content rating information by clicking the Modify Settings button in this panel.

Reviewing how to customize security zones and content ratings is time well spent. The exam has a variety of questions on both topics.

Stage 5: Configuring IE Components

Stage 5 deals with customizing the individual components that you include in your custom package. As usual, the options available for you to customize depend on whether you work as a corporate administrator, Internet content provider, or Internet service provider. The information in this section assumes the corporate administrator role.

The Programs screen

In the Programs screen, you choose whether or not to import the current default programs settings. These settings are the same ones that you see if you look at the Programs tab after choosing Internet Options from the Internet Explorer Tools menu. If you decide to import the Program settings, you can also modify them by clicking the Modify Settings button.

If you select the Import the Current Program Settings radio button, the wizard will attempt to use the settings on the computer that you're using to create the package for the following Internet services:

- ✔ HTML editor
- ✔ E-mail
- ✔ Newsgroups
- ✔ Internet call
- ✔ Calendar
- ✔ Contact list

The Outlook Express Accounts screen

In the Outlook Express Accounts screen, you can preset your users' mail and news settings. Think of the time this saves — you no longer go from desk to desk configuring Internet mail and news! Think of the reduction in helpdesk calls! In this screen, you can also lock down some settings so that users can't alter them. Figure 10-9 shows the Outlook Express Accounts screen.

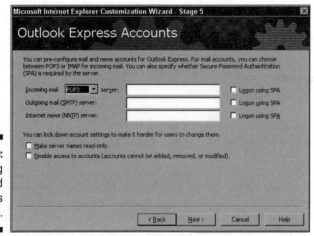

Figure 10-9:
Configuring
mail and
news
accounts.

If you don't elect to install or customize Outlook Express during Stage 1 of the Customization wizard, this setting screen doesn't appear in Stage 5.

The configurable options in the screen are the incoming mail server, outgoing mail server, and the news server. POP3 and IMAP are the two choices for incoming mail type. On all three of these options, you can specify whether or not to require secure password authentication by selecting the check box to the right of the option.

Near the bottom of the screen, you see the options to lock down settings by making the server entries read-only and by preventing modification of accounts.

The Outlook Express Custom Content screen

The Custom Content screen (see Figure 10-10) enables you to further customize Outlook Express by adding a custom InfoPane message and a welcome message for all new users.

Figure 10-10:
Customizing Outlook Express Content.

Microsoft Internet Explorer Customization Wizard - Stage 5

Outlook Express Custom Content

The InfoPane is a customizable pane that runs along the bottom of the Outlook Express window. You can customize this pane to display an HTML file. You can either point to an URL or a local file that will be included in your package.

- ○ URL:
- ⊙ Local file HTML path: _____ Browse
- Image path: _____ Browse

You can place a custom HTML welcome message in each user's inbox. If you use a custom message, you must supply the sender's name and address.

HTML path: _____ Browse
Sender: _____
Reply-to: _____

< Back   Next >   Cancel   Help

Customizing the InfoPane

The InfoPane is a small pane running along the bottom of the Outlook Express window. You add custom links, company information, help information, and other information to the pane by specifying either a local HTML file or a URL in the Outlook Express Custom Content screen.

If you add an HTML file, you copy the file from the original location and include it in the distribution package that you copy to all users. If you add a local HTML file, you can also add an image.

You can't add both a URL and an HTML file. Also, the InfoPane doesn't appear in the Outlook Express window if you don't choose either of the two options.

Creating a welcome message

You receive a welcome message when you initially set up your messaging client. You can configure a welcome message for Outlook Express in the bottom half of the Outlook Express Custom Content screen. After you identify an HTML file, a sender, and a reply-to address, the welcome message appears as the first message in each new user's Outlook Express mailbox.

The Outlook Express Custom Settings screen

In this screen (see Figure 10-11), you can make Outlook Express your default mail program and/or default newsreader. You can also subscribe to newsgroups that are distributed to all of your users.

The settings you customize here affect all users.

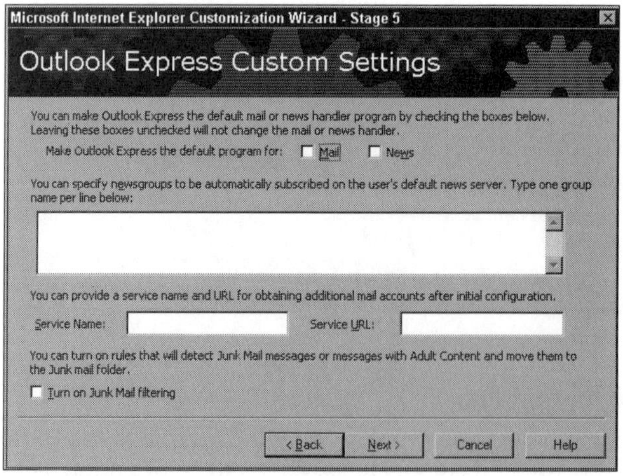

Figure 10-11: Customizing Outlook Express settings.

In the middle section of the screen you see blank text boxes for both Service Name and Service URL. These create an Outlook Express menu item that enables users to request an additional mail account.

The last entry in the screen is a Turn on Junk Mail Filtering check box. If you select this option, it turns on filtering rules to keep junk mail and mail containing adult content out of your Inbox by moving them to the Junk mail folder. This feature is hugely popular among Internet mail users! But be very cautious when attempting to filter junk mail for all users. Remember: One man's trash is another man's treasure!

The Outlook Express View Settings screen

This screen determines how Outlook Express appears on the user desktop. You decide how the Outlook Express interface appears to your users. Select the check box to include the element in the display; otherwise, it doesn't appear. Configurable elements are:

✔ Basic
   - Folder bar
   - Status bar
   - Outlook bar
   - Contacts
   - Folder list
   - Tip of the day

✔ Toolbar
   - Show toolbar
   - Show text on toolbar buttons

✔ Preview pane
   - Show preview pane below messages
   - Show preview pane beside messages
   - Show preview pane header

The Outlook Express Compose Settings screen

In the Outlook Express Compose Settings screen, you can configure a default signature message that appears in all mail messages, all news messages, or both.

You can also determine whether the default format for these messages is HTML or plain text. (The maximum size of the signature file is 1K. The default format for e-mail messages is HTML. The default format for news postings is plain text.)

Put some thought into these signature files, as they can serve a number of purposes. Some companies use signatures for marketing pitches and legal disclaimers. You have to determine if there's a good use for signature files within your organization.

The Address Book Directory Service screen

In the Address Book Directory Service screen, you can configure an LDAP (Lightweight Directory Access Protocol) server for all users. A directory service is like a searchable electronic phone book in which you look up users. For example, in NetMeeting you use an ILS server to locate and select users with whom to call or collaborate. Configuring a directory service on this screen provides your users with access to this directory service, enabling them to search for other users to whom they want to send e-mail messages.

The System Policies and Restrictions screen

The System Policies and Restrictions screen, as shown in Figure 10-12, looks similar to the IEAK Profile Manager screen. In the left pane, you select the component that you want to set policies and restrictions for. As you double-click components in the left pane, individual settings and restrictions appear in the right pane. You can import existing policy files (.adm files) from your own computer by clicking the Import button near the bottom left of the screen.

The policy and restriction settings you see in this screen are stored in administration files (.adm files) on your machine in the IEAK\policies folder. Administration files are default policy templates that the computer creates the first time that you run the IEAK Customization wizard or the IEAK Profile Manager.

After the IEAK Customization wizard finishes, the computer writes the settings to an .inf file and packages them with the .cab files for your custom built package. After users unpack them, the .inf files change the settings and restrictions on the users' workstations.

Table 10-1 shows each component and its associated .adm and .inf files. Know these for the exam.

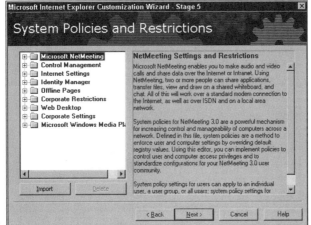

Figure 10-12:
Setting
policies and
restrictions.

**Table 10-1   .ADM Files, .INF Files, and Associated Policies
and Restrictions Components**

.ADM File	.INF File	Component
CONF.ADM	CONF.INF	NetMeeting
AXAA.ADM	AXAA.INF	Administrator approved controls
INETSET.ADM	INETSET.INF	Internet settings
OE.ADM	OE.INF	Identify manager
SUBS.ADM	SUBS.INF	Offline pages
INETRES.ADM	INETRES.INFL	Corporate restrictions
CHAT.ADM	CHAT.INF	Microsoft Chat
SP1SHELL.ADM	SP1SHELL.INF	Web Desktop
INETCORP.ADM	INETCORP.INF	Corporate
WMP.ADM	WMP.INF	Windows Media Player

Any settings or restrictions that you configure here affect all users and computers that receive your custom package. Plan carefully! Determine and configure a base build that is appropriate for the majority of your user community. After you build the initial browser package, you can use the IEAK Profile Manager to go back and set policies and restrictions for special groups of users.

Read the Customization wizard screens for each of the folders in the left pane. As you select different folders, notice that a definition screen appears in the right pane. This screen explains the settings, restrictions, and limitations configurable for the folder you select.

See Appendix C for a complete list of settings and restrictions.

Microsoft NetMeeting

Microsoft NetMeeting is a popular application that enables users to collaborate via the Internet (or intranet). Used correctly, NetMeeting is a valuable corporate tool that can help save on travel expenses.

But NetMeeting also places a heavy load on a network. Thus, corporate administrators need to pay careful attention and configure NetMeeting appropriately for their users and their network. Within the NetMeeting folder, you find configurable options for NetMeeting Settings and NetMeeting Protocols.

NetMeeting Settings, which are per-user settings, enable you to:

- Restrict the use of file transfer
- Restrict the use of application sharing
- Restrict the use of the options dialog
- Prevent the user from answering calls
- Prevent the user from using audio features
- Restrict the use of video
- Prevent the user from using directory services
- Set the default Directory Server
- Set Exchange Server Property for NetMeeting Address
- Preset User Information Category
- Set the NetMeeting home page
- Set limit for audio/video throughput

NetMeeting Protocol settings, which are per-machine settings, enable you to:

- Disable TCP/IP
- Disable null modem

The Wizard Complete screen

After you finish with Settings and Restrictions and click Next, you see a screen telling you that the IEAK Customization wizard is complete. Click Next to create your custom package.

To help you understand the entire process, I include a lab that takes you through the IEAK Customization wizard. For this exercise, assume the role of a corporate administrator. You are to create a custom package containing the Internet Explorer browser and NetMeeting. Make a hands-free install for this build so that the user can observe error and progress messages. I tell you which options to choose during each step of the lab.

Lab 10-1   Using the IEAK Customization wizard

1. **Start the IEAK Customization wizard.**

2. **Click Next in the Welcome screen and again in the Stage 1 Introductory screen.**

3. **For the Company Name, type** XYZ Corp. **Type the Customization Code that Microsoft gives you in the Customization Code text box. Click the Corporate Administrator button to choose the Corporate Administrator role and then click Next.**

4. **Select the Windows 9x/NT 4.0 platform and then click Next.**

5. **Type a destination folder for your custom package files. Click the Advanced Options button. Select the Enable Checking for Newest Versions Via AVS check box. Click OK and then click Next.**

   You experience a short wait while Language Selection choices compile.

6. **In the Language Selection screen, select English and then click Next.**

7. **In the Media Selection screen, select only CD-ROM and then click Next.**

8. **In the Feature Selection screen, select all features. Click Next to advance to Stage 2.**

9. **Read through the Stage 2 introductory screen and then click Next.**

10. **Choose a download site from the list (you may need to connect to the Internet at this point) and then click Next.**

11. **Review the information in the Automatic Version Synchronization screen. Update any files that are not current.**

    If you are downloading several files, you may have a long wait while the files download.

    After all files are synchronized, click Next.

12. **Click Next to advance past the Add Custom Components screen because you won't add custom components here.**

13. **After you read through the Stage 3 introductory information, click Next.**

14. **In the Title Bar text box, type** XYZ Corp. **Select the settings of your choice for the other fields and then click Next.**

15. **Deselect the Use Kiosk Mode Start Page check box and then click Next.**

16. In the Customize Setup screen, type any valid information in the blanks and then click Next.

17. In the Silent Install screen, select the Hands-free Install option and then click Next.

18. In the Installation Options screen, select the Typical option. Make sure to include NetMeeting in the Components to Install list and then click Next.

19. In the Component Download screen, use the default URL for the Windows Update. Select the Download Components from Microsoft After Install option. Click Next to advance to the next screen.

20. In the Installation Directory screen, deselect the Allow the User to Choose the Installation Directory check box. Click Install in the specified folder within the Program Files folder. Type Internet Explorer in the text box as the specified folder and then click Next.

21. In the Corporate Install Options screen, do not disable any of the options. Select the Internet Explorer is Set as the Default Browser check box and then click Next.

22. In the Advanced Installation Options screen, select the Select All check box and then click Next.

23. Click Next again to advance past the Connection Manager Customization screen.

24. Click No in the Windows Desktop Update screen. Click Next to advance to the next screen.

25. Do not enter any digital signature information. Click Next to advance to Stage 4.

26. After reading the Stage 4 introductory screen, click Next to advance.

27. Select the Customize Title Bars check box. In the Title Bar text box, type XYZ Corp. and then click Next.

28. In the Browser Toolbar Buttons screen, click Next.

29. Click Next in the Animated Logo screen.

30. Click Next in the Static Logo screen.

31. For the Home Page URL, enter the URL for your ISP or corporate home page. Leave the default settings in the other fields and then click Next.

32. Add or delete any Favorites and Links you desire and then click Next.

33. In the Channels screen, select the Delete Existing Channels check box and then click Next.

34. In the Welcome Page screen, click the Do Not Display a Welcome Page button and then click Next.

35. Type XYZ Corp. as the custom string and then click Next.

36. **Click the Import the Current Connection Settings button and select the check box labeled** Delete Existing Connection Settings, if Present. **Then click Next.**

37. **In the Security screen, click the Do Not Customize Option button for both choices and then click Next.**

38. **In the Security Settings screen, select the Import the Current Security Zones Settings check box and the Do Not Customize Content Ratings check box. Click Next.**

39. **Read through the Stage 5 introductory screen and then click Next.**

    This screen contains excellent descriptions on navigating the screen and on template files. Note: If you view any category of a restriction, the wizard copies all of the restriction values to your custom package.

40. **Import the current Program settings and then click Next.**

41. **In the Outlook Express Accounts screen, specify valid server names for the incoming and outgoing mail servers. Lock down both of the options at the bottom of this screen by selecting the check box next to each of the two options. Click Next to continue.**

42. **Click Next in the Outlook Express Custom Content screen.**

43. **In the Outlook Express Custom Settings screen, make Outlook Express the default for mail and news and then click Next.**

44. **Use the defaults in the Outlook Express View Settings screen and then click Next.**

45. **In the Outlook Express Compose Settings screen, select the Append a Signature to Each Message check box. Type** XYZ Corp. proprietary information **in the text field and then click Next.**

46. **Click Next in the Address Book Directory Service screen to skip customizing this screen.**

47. **In the System Policies and Restrictions screen, restrict the user from using FTP in NetMeeting by selecting the check boxes labeled** Prevent Users from Sending Files **and** Prevent Users from Receiving Files. **Also, select the check box labeled** Prevent Users from Configuring or Using Identities in the Identity Manager settings. **In the Offline Pages folder, disable adding and removing channels by selecting the check boxes next to these two options. Then click Next to continue.**

48. **Click Next to create the custom package.**

The IEAK Customization wizard is central to the exam. Be sure to create several packages so that you become familiar with the results of choosing different options. You should also install the packages you create so that you experience the custom setup process.

Prep Test

1 You can install Internet Explorer 5 custom packages on which of the following platforms? (Choose all that apply.)

A ❑ UNIX

B ❑ Windows 98

C ❑ Windows NT 3.51

D ❑ Windows NT 4.0

2 Joe is a corporate administrator preparing a custom Internet Explorer 5 package. Some of Joe's users speak Japanese; the rest speak English. Can Joe create one package that includes both languages?

A ○ Yes. Joe can select both languages in the Language Selection screen in Stage 1 of the Customization wizard.

B ○ No. Joe must run the Customization wizard once for each language that he must accommodate. Each version is a separate package.

C ○ Yes. Joe must run through Stage 1 of the Customization wizard twice, choosing a different language each time.

D ○ No. Joe can only create the package in English because he only has an English version of the IEAK.

3 Joe is building a new Internet Explorer package. He wants to make sure that only the latest versions of components are included. What should Joe enable in the Customization wizard to make sure he uses the most recent files?

A ○ Turn on the CMAK to be sure that only new files are used.

B ○ Turn on Completely Silent Install to make sure that users don't choose the wrong files.

C ○ Turn on AVS (Automatic Version Synchronization) to determine whether the newest files are being used.

D ○ Enable Compatibility Mode to assure that all files are compatible with previous versions.

4 As a corporate administrator, Sam has a user community with widely differing needs for Internet Explorer components. He wants to install only the components that each user needs. Can Sam create a single package that includes different installation options depending on the user's needs?

A ○ No. Sam must create a separate package for each user group.

B ○ Yes. Sam can identify ten different installation options and let users select the appropriate set of options for their needs.

C ○ Yes. Sam can specify up to ten different download sites so that users can select the package that they want to install.

D ○ No. Sam can specify only Minimal, Typical, or Full installation options.

5 (True/False). In a completely hands-free installation, users can still respond to error messages and progress indicators.

   A ○ True

   B ○ False

6 You plan to include a custom application in your custom browser package. What actions should you take while running the Customization wizard to assure that users are able to cleanly remove the custom application from their systems should the need arise?

   A ○ On the Add Custom Components screen of the Customization wizard, enter the name of an uninstall file in the Uninstall Key text box.

   B ○ Take no further action. Users are able to uninstall applications using the Uninstall feature in Control Panel.

   C ○ Take no further action. Users can simply delete the application files to completely remove the application from their system.

   D ○ On the Advanced Installation Options screen of the Customization wizard, select the Uninstall Application check box.

7 (True/False). Windows Desktop Update is not available in Internet Explorer 5.

   A ○ True

   B ○ False

8 (True/False). If you specify a Silent Install, the Customization wizard does not prompt you to fill in any further information.

   A ○ True

   B ○ False

Answers

1 *A, B, C, and D.* You can create Internet Explorer 5 packages for all of the platforms listed above. *Review "Stage 1: Gathering Information."*

2 *B.* Joe must run the Customization wizard twice to build packages in both languages. *Review "Stage 1: Gathering Information."*

3 *C.* AVS compares the downloaded files against the most recent files from the download site. If newer files are available, the administrator can choose to download them and include them in the package. *Review "Stage 1: Gathering Information" and "Stage 2: Specifying Setup Parameters."*

4 *B.* In the Installation Options screen in Stage 2, Sam can combine components into up to ten different installation options from which users can select. *See "Stage 2: Specifying Setup Parameters."*

5 *B.* In a hands-free installation, users see error messages and progress indicators but aren't able to interact at all in the installation process. *Review "Stage 2: Specifying Setup Parameters."*

6 *A.* The file that you name in the Uninstall Key text box should contain the appropriate uninstall subkey information to completely remove the components from the disk and from the system. *See "Stage 2: Specifying Setup Parameters."*

7 *B.* If you install Windows Desktop Update in Internet Explorer 4 and a user upgrades to Internet Explorer 5, the upgrade includes the Windows Desktop Update. If you install Internet Explorer 5 on the Windows 98 platform, you can also enable the Windows Desktop Update because it is included with Windows 98. *See "Stage 3: Customizing Setup."*

8 *B.* If you specify a Silent Install, the Customization wizard doesn't prompt users to supply information during the installation. The administrator uses the Customization wizard to specify all installation information. *Review "Stage 2: Specifying Setup Parameters."*

Chapter 11

Planning Browser Updates

· ·

Exam Objectives

▶ Choosing between automatic and manual configuration

▶ Selecting an automatic configuration method

▶ Using Profile Manager settings

· ·

*T*he Internet Explorer Administration Kit provides outstanding tools for customizing and managing Internet Explorer 5. With a little forethought and planning, you can deploy and manage a customized package that ideally suits your user community and saves your organization valuable time and money.

Before you build your custom browser package, you should plan how you intend to maintain the deployed browser. In this chapter, I help you determine whether you should use automatic configuration and which automatic configuration method is best for you.

Quick Assessment

Planning
Browser
Updates

1 _____ _____ _____ is a powerful IEAK feature that enables you to alter the configuration of deployed browsers from a central location.

2 Use an _____ _____ when you want to change only the proxy configurations of your users' browsers.

3 (True/False). A browser package can be configured to simultaneously use both an auto-proxy script and an auto-config URL.

Configuring
an Auto-
Proxy Script

4 An _____ _____ changes the browser's proxy settings without requiring that any other files be downloaded.

5 Although you can reconfigure deployed browsers for auto-proxy configuration, it's much more efficient to include the configuration in your customized browser package when you run the _____ _____ _____.

6 You use a _____ _____ to create an auto-proxy file.

7 Setting up an _____ _____ allows you much greater flexibility in changing your users' browsers than an auto-proxy file.

Configuring
Automatic
Browser
Updates by
Using the
Profile
Manager

Setting Up
an Auto-
Config URL

8 You enable automatic browser configuration from within the _____ _____.

9 You use the IEAK Profile Manager to update browser settings and create new _____ and _____ files.

Profile
Manager
Settings

10 When you open an _____ _____, Profile Manager reads the configuration and settings that the Customization wizard saved when you created the file using the wizard.

Answers

1   *Automatic browser configuration.* See "Automatic Browser Configuration versus Manual Updates."

2   *auto-proxy file.* See "Automatic Browser Configuration versus Manual Updates."

3   *True.* See "Automatic Browser Configuration versus Manual Updates."

4   *auto-proxy script.* See "Configuring an Auto-Proxy Script."

5   *IEAK Customization wizard.* See "Configuring an Auto-Proxy Script."

6   *text editor.* See "Configuring an Auto-Proxy Script."

7   *auto-config file.* See "Configuring Automatic Browser Updates by Using the Profile Manager."

8   *Customization wizard.* See "Setting up an auto-config URL."

9   *.ins and .cab.* See "Setting up an auto-config URL."

10   *.ins file or instruction file.* See "Profile manager settings."

Automatic Browser Configuration versus Manual Updates

As you plan your custom browser package, consider how you intend to manage updates to browsers after you deploy them to users. *Automatic browser configuration* is a powerful option that the Internet Explorer Administration Kit provides to allow you to alter any or all browser settings, system policies, and connections — including proxy settings — from a central location that houses a configuration file.

Automatic browser configuration saves countless hours and help desk tickets. With a bit of careful consideration, you can deploy a browser that's both full featured and easily managed from a central location.

Choosing automatic configuration makes sense in almost all cases. Why make configuration changes multiple times (as you would with manual configuration), when you can make them once and automatically distribute them to any number of other systems? As long as you have a central location to place the automatic configuration files, then automatic configuration is a good choice.

When would you choose *not* to use automatic browser configuration? If you have a small number of deployed browsers and all the computers are at a single location, you may opt for manual configuration. No matter how many deployed browsers you're supporting, however, you should consider configuring them via automatic browser configuration. Doing so ensures that you're always capable of distributing browser updates — whether any browser updates ever take place or not.

You must have a LAN server, intranet server, or Internet server to distribute configuration files in order to take advantage of automatic browser configuration.

You can configure automatic browser configuration in two ways, via an auto-proxy script or by using the automatic configuration URL. For the exam, know that you configure automatic browser configuration

- ✔ Using an auto-proxy file when you want to change only the proxy configurations of your users' browsers in the future.

- ✔ Using the IEAK Profile Manager when you want to change other browser settings instead of (or in addition to) proxy configurations.

You can also configure the browser to use both an auto-proxy file and an automatic configuration file. When only the proxy configuration changes, modify the auto-proxy script. Incorporate all other browser changes in the automatic configuration file.

Configuring an Auto-Proxy Script

If you only want to set up a file to update proxy settings on your users' browsers, then you should use an auto-proxy script. An auto-proxy script changes the browser's proxy settings without requiring any other files to be downloaded.

Follow the directions in Lab 11-1 to enable auto-proxy configuration:

Lab 11-1   Supporting Automatic Proxy Settings

1. **Using Microsoft Word or Notepad, type in a Jscript file that details the browser proxy configuration.**

   For example, the following text shows the JScript code necessary to configure my browser to use `proxy1.mrl.com`, port 80 as the proxy configuration.

   ```
   function FindProxyForURL(url, host) {
      if (isResolvable(host))
      return "DIRECT";
         else
            return "PROXY proxy1.mrl.com:80";
         }
   ```

2. **Save the file with the .js file extension (for example: proxy1.js).**

3. **Run the IEAK Customization wizard.**

   On the Automatic Configuration screen, select the Enable Automatic Configuration check box. In the Auto-proxy URL text box at the bottom of the screen, type a URL followed by the name of the auto-proxy file you saved in Step 2. Complete the Customization wizard and deploy the browser to a client computer.

4. **Copy the proxy.js file to the auto-proxy URL that you specified during the IEAK Customization wizard in Step 3.**

5. **On the client computer, restart the IE5 browser and check the proxy configuration to see that it matches the file you configured in Step 1.**

Planning for automatic configuration before creating a custom browser (rather than after its deployed) pays off in reduced administration. Although you can reconfigure deployed browsers for auto-proxy configuration, it's much easier to just include the configuration in your customized browser package when you run the IEAK Customization wizard, as shown in Figure 11-1.

You don't need any special utilities to create a Jscript auto-proxy file. Use any text editor to create the file and then save it with a .js, .jvs, or .pac file extension. (See Chapter 18 for more information about auto-proxy settings.)

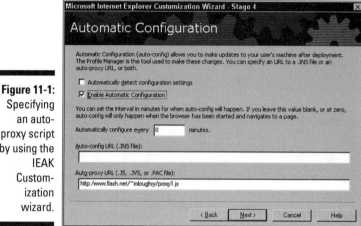

Figure 11-1:
Specifying
an auto-
proxy script
by using the
IEAK
Custom-
ization
wizard.

For the exam, you won't be asked questions about the JScript code. Instead, know the steps necessary to configure automatic proxy configuration.

Configuring Automatic Browser Updates by Using the Profile Manager

Setting up an auto-config file allows you much greater flexibility in changing your users' browsers than an auto-proxy file. As is the case with an auto-proxy file, you can update proxy settings via an auto-config file, but you can also accomplish much more. You can change any of the settings and parameters available in the IEAK Customization wizard from within the IEAK Profile Manager, including:

- ✔ Favorites and Links
- ✔ Connection settings
- ✔ Graphics and logos
- ✔ User agent strings
- ✔ Important URLs

Appendix C lists all the parameters that you can configure by using the Profile Manager. You should be familiar with these settings because many of the scenario questions ask whether particular steps involving particular changes made in the Profile Manager arrive at a desired outcome.

Setting up an auto-config URL

You enable automatic browser configuration from within the IEAK
Customization wizard, as shown in Figure 11-2. In the Automatic
Configuration screen, select the Enable Automatic Configuration check box
and then type a URL that points to the location where you intend to post configuration updates.

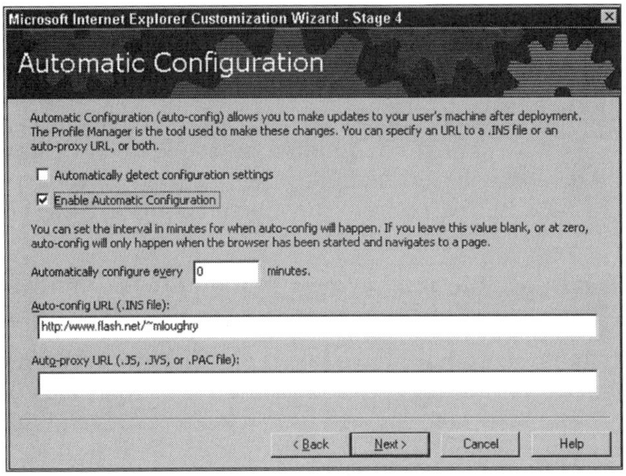

Figure 11-2:
Specifying
an auto-
matic
browser
configura-
tion URL
with the
Custom-
ization
wizard.

After you deploy your package, you can distribute changes to the custom
package by placing updated configuration files at your specified URL.
Whether or not you make changes to the configuration file later, you should
plan ahead and specify a location to store files when you run the
Customization wizard. Then you have the option to update browsers automatically, if you need to use it.

Lab 11-2 below shows you how to update the browser after it's deployed.

Lab 11-2   Updating a Deployed Browser

1. Use the IEAK Customization wizard to create a browser package.

On the Automatic Configuration screen, select the Enable Automatic
Configuration check box. In the Auto-config URL text box near the
bottom of the screen, type a URL. Leave the configuration interval set to
0 minutes. Complete the Customization wizard and deploy the browser
package to a client computer.

2. Start the IEAK Profile Manager and then choose File⇨Open to open the Install.ins file.

3. In the left pane of the Profile Manager, click the + sign next to `Wizard Settings` to expand the list of settings.

4. Under `Wizard Settings`, select Important URLs.

5. In the right pane of the Profile Manager, type `http://www.yahoo.com` in the Home Page URL text box.

6. In the left pane of the Profile Manager, under `Wizard Settings`, select Connection Settings.

7. In the right pane of the Profile Manager, select Import the Current Connection Settings.

8. From the Profile Manager menu bar, choose File⇨Save As. In the Save As dialog box, type a new name for the .ins file and type a URL for any .cab files that are created from the above changes. Click OK to save the files.

9. Copy the new .ins file and any new .cab files to the automatic configuration URL.

10. To verify that the updates have taken place, restart IE5 on the client computer that is running the deployed browser package. Check to see that the home page has changed to `www.yahoo.com` and that the connection settings from the build computer are incorporated into the browser.

You use the IEAK Profile Manager to update browser settings and create new .ins and .cab files.

Profile manager settings

You can update or add to the configuration of any browser settings, connection settings, system policies, or components of a customized browser package by using the Profile Manager. To start Profile Manager, choose Start⇨Programs⇨Microsoft IEAK⇨IEAK Profile Manager. When you open an .ins (instruction) file, Profile Manager reads the configuration and settings that the Customization wizard saved when you created the file by using the wizard. The parameters for each setting are displayed in the Profile Manager, where you can change them to reflect changes in your environment.

For example, look at the Profile Manager window, as shown in Figure 11-3. The Wizard Settings in the left pane reflect the settings that I set in the Customization wizard to create Figures 11-1 and 11-2. In the right pane of the Profile Manager are the parameters that I specified to configure automatic browser configuration.

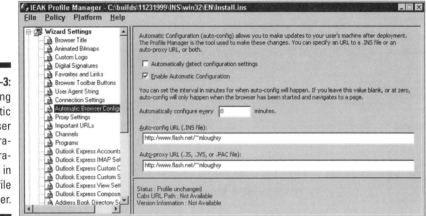

Figure 11-3: Viewing automatic browser configuration parameters in Profile Manager.

You can use the Profile Manager to create additional .ins files for multiple versions of the custom browser package, or you can use the Profile Manager to modify an already deployed browser package.

The IEAK Customization wizard creates a custom browser package. The IEAK Profile Manager *modifies* the browser package that you created with the Customization wizard.

To further illustrate this concept, read the following scenario:

You're the corporate administrator for ABC Affiliates. You use the IEAK Customization wizard to create a custom browser package. While using the wizard to create the package, you specify a custom title bar for the browser (see Figure 11-4).You deploy the custom browser to your company. Shortly after deployment, a larger firm purchases your company. The name of the company changes from ABC Affiliates to XYZ Affiliates. The new owner instructs you to change the title bar on all the deployed IE5 browsers to XYZ affiliates. Lab 11-3 takes you through the steps that you would need to follow if faced with this scenario.

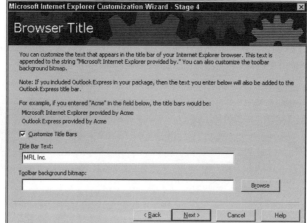

Figure 11-4:
Configuring
a cus-
tomized Title
Bar for the
IE5 browser.

Lab 11-3   Rolling Out a Change to the Title Bar via Automatic Configuration

1. **Using the IEAK Profile Manager, open the .ins file of a custom browser package.**

2. **In the left pane of Profile Manager, under** Wizard Settings, **click the Browser Title profile. You can see the setting that you originally configured in the Customization wizard in the right pane.**

3. **Highlight the setting in the right pane and type** XYZ Affiliates, **as shown in Figure 11-5.**

4. **Save the file (File⇨Save) as an .ins file and move it to the automatic browser configuration URL so that the deployed browsers can find the update.**

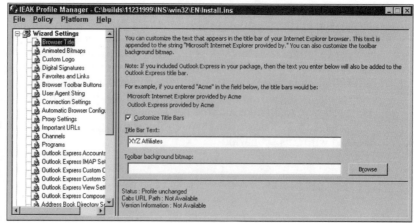

Figure 11-5:
Modifying
the Title Bar
with Profile
Manager.

Here's another scenario:

You're the system administrator for Cyber Cafe. At each of your store locations, you provide terminals that your customers use to browse the Internet while they enjoy their coffee and pastries. You spend a lot of time driving to each location and reinstating the original configuration settings of the IE5 browsers that you use on your terminals. You want to reduce these trips by preventing users from changing the browser configuration. In this scenario, you need to use the Profile Manager to modify the .ins file of your customized browser package: the steps are outlined in Lab 11-4.

Lab 11-4   Using the Profile Manager to Disable IE Configuration Changes

1. **Using the IEAK Profile Manager, open the .ins file of a custom browser package.**

2. **In the left pane of the Profile Manager, click the + sign beside Policies and Restrictions.**

3. **Click** `Corporate Restrictions` **and then** `Browser Menus`**. In the right pane, you select the check box labeled** `Disable Internet Options . . . menu option` **(see Figure 11-6).**

4. **Save the .ins file and move it to the URL for automatic browser configuration.**

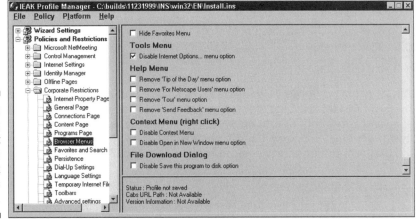

Figure 11-6:
Disabling
the Internet
Options
dialog box
on the Tools
menu.

On the exam, you see many scenarios like the examples above. You must be able to identify the tools and steps needed to make required changes.

Prep Test

1 Which of the following options can be configured by using the IEAK Profile Manager? (Choose all that apply.)

A ❑ Favorites and Links

B ❑ Connection settings

C ❑ Important URLs

D ❑ User agent strings

2 Which of the following steps are necessary to configure an auto-proxy URL? (Choose all that apply.)

A ❑ Using a text editor, create an auto-proxy script.

B ❑ Using the Customization wizard, enable automatic configuration.

C ❑ From the IE5 browser Tools menu, turn on Automatic Configuration.

D ❑ Copy the auto-proxy script file to the auto-proxy URL.

3 James is the corporate administrator at a large company. Using the IEAK, he creates and deploys a custom browser package that includes automatic configuration, enabling him to update the configuration of the deployed browsers. What file must James alter to update the deployed browsers?

A ◯ The IEAK Profile Manager

B ◯ The IEAK Customization wizard

C ◯ The .cab file

D ◯ The .ins file

4 James is the corporate administrator at a large company and is planning a custom browser package. James needs to create several versions of the package for the different operating system platforms used on the client computers throughout his company. Can James use the IEAK Profile Manager to change the platform option of the custom browser package?

A ◯ Yes

B ◯ No

5 James is the corporate administrator at a large company and is planning a custom browser package. James wants to include automatic configuration in the browser package, but is unsure how to configure the options. He knows that various browser settings may change in the future, but he is uncertain whether the proxy configuration will change. Which automatic configuration option(s) should James configure? (Choose all that apply.)

A ❏ James should configure the auto-proxy URL.

B ❏ James should configure the Jscript proxy URL.

C ❏ James should configure the auto-config URL.

D ❏ James should enable automatic configuration.

Answers

1 *A, B, C, and D.* Using the IEAK Profile Manager, you can configure or add any configuration or setting that is available in the Customization wizard. *See "Configuring Automatic Browser Updates by Using the Profile Manager."*

2 *A, B, and D.* To successfully configure an auto-proxy URL, you first enable automatic configuration in the Configuration wizard and specify an auto-proxy URL. Then create a script file and copy it to the auto-proxy URL. *Review "Configuring an Auto-Proxy Script."*

3 *D.* To update the browser configuration, James must modify the .ins file by using the IEAK Profile Manager. *See "Configuring Automatic Browser Updates by Using the Profile Manager."*

4 *A.* Using the IEAK Profile Manager, James can configure any of the options, features, or settings that are available in the Customization wizard. James can edit the .ins file of a browser package and specify a different platform. *See "Configuring Automatic Browser Updates by Using the Profile Manager."*

5 *A, C, and D.* Before James can specify either URL, he must enable automatic configuration. The auto-config URL holds the automatic browser configuration files used to update the browser's settings. The auto-proxy URL holds the auto-proxy script. James should configure both because he knows that the browser settings may change and is uncertain whether the proxy settings may change. He can configure the auto-proxy URL whether the proxy settings change or not. *See "Configuring Automatic Browser Updates by Using the Profile Manager."*

Chapter 12

Configuring with CMAK

. . . .

Exam Objectives

▶ Understanding the role of the CMAK

▶ Building service profiles

▶ Using the CMAK wizard

▶ Developing CMAK strategies for PPTP, Dial-Up Networking, and user security

. . . .

*T*he Connection Manager Administration Kit, or CMAK, is a component of the Internet Explorer Administration Kit (IEAK). (You should get extra credit on the exam for remembering all these acronyms!) The CMAK, like the IEAK, is a wizard. The CMAK enables you to centrally manage the connection settings on all your client computers from a single location.

Using the CMAK, corporate administrators and ISPs can preconfigure connections for their users and then distribute them to the client computers. Just like the IEAK, the CMAK is a great support tool that can save you both money and time by easing the administrative workload.

In this chapter, I introduce you to the CMAK wizard. I also discuss strategies for using the CMAK with different types of connections.

Quick Assessment

IP Config-
uration Tools

1 Like the Internet Explorer Administration Kit, the Connection Manager Administration Kit (CMAK) is a _____.

2 Using the CMAK, you can preconfigure _____ before the IE5 browser is deployed.

3 One advantage of the CMAK is the ability to create and manage a _____ _____ of contact information for your organization.

4 Each time that you run the CMAK wizard, you create a _____ _____.

5 When creating a custom IE5 browser package, you can access the CMAK while using the _____ _____ _____.

6 A VPN emulates a _____ _____ _____.

7 VPN stands for _____ _____ _____.

8 Microsoft VPN support uses _____ to create a secure connection across the Internet.

9 In addition to running TCP/IP and PPTP, the client computer must run the same _____ _____ as the destination network.

10 When accessing a network by using dial-up VPN, the client computer connects to a _____ _____ attached to the private network.

Answers

1   *wizard.* See "Configuring with CMAK."

2   *connections.* See "Advantages."

3   *phone book.* See "Advantages."

4   *service profile.* See "Using the CMAK Wizard."

5   *IEAK Customization wizard.* See "Preparing to Use the CMAK."

6   *secure private network.* See "Configuring VPN Support."

7   *virtual private network.* See "Configuring VPN Support."

8   *PPTP (or point-to-point tunneling protocol).* See "Configuring VPN Support."

9   *network protocol.* See "Configuring VPN Support."

10   *VPN server.* See "Configuring VPN Support."

CMAK Overview

The Connection Manager Administration Kit helps administrators create, customize, and distribute Microsoft Connection Manager dialers and phonebooks to their users. Connection Manager is similar to Windows Dial-Up Networking but contains more features, such as allowing both remote and local connections, enabling VPN connections, and providing the ability to specify automatic connect actions that run before or after the user connects.

Although the exam covers the CMAK, it assumes that you're familiar with Connection Manager 1.2.

Purpose

The concept behind the CMAK is the same as the IEAK. Just as you use the IEAK to configure and deploy a custom browser package, you use the CMAK to configure and deploy customized Connection Manager dialer settings.

Using the CMAK, you can customize the appearance and function of Connection Manager. Customization features include:

- Graphics
- Icons
- Logos
- Help files
- Support files
- Phone books

Advantages

If you've ever supported RAS, Dial-Up Networking, or VPN connections, the advantages of using the CMAK are clear. System administrators and ISPs spend a great deal (lots and lots!) of time troubleshooting connections for their users. Using the CMAK, you can preconfigure these connection settings before they're deployed. And, by using the IEAK, you can lock down the settings that you configure in the CMAK so that users can't alter them. You save the initial visit to the computer to configure the connection and subsequent visits to fix connections that are "broken."

Another advantage of the CMAK is the ability to create and manage a phone book of contact information for your organization. This provides a great service to your users, and support is minimal because you manage the phone book entries from a central location. With the CMAK, your whole organization can do things faster and better!

Using the CMAK Wizard

Each time that you run the CMAK wizard, you create a service profile that consists of options that you select while running the wizard. Each service profile contains the installation instructions and necessary files for a user to connect to your service.

The CMAK wizard creates a self-extracting executable file and four additional files that contain the settings you select during the wizard. For example, if you run the CMAK wizard and create a service profile called Profile1, the wizard creates the following files:

- ✔ Profile1.exe
- ✔ Profile1.cms
- ✔ Profile1.cmp
- ✔ Profile1.inf
- ✔ Profile1.sed

To create additional service profiles, run the wizard again and create a new profile or edit an existing profile. If you edit an existing service profile, be sure to save it with a new name to avoid overwriting the existing service profile.

Preparing to use the CMAK

You can launch the CMAK independently from the IEAK, or you can run it as part of the Customization wizard. The Customization wizard gives you the option of importing the connection settings from the build computer or running the CMAK to create the connection settings. Make sure to plan ahead before creating your connection settings. Microsoft recommends the following phases when using the CMAK:

- ✔ **Phase 1 — Planning:** During the planning phase, identify the elements that you want to customize. A planning worksheet is included in the online documentation that comes with the CMAK. I advise you to use the planning worksheet before you run the CMAK wizard.

✓ **Phase 2 — Creating custom elements:** If you plan to include custom elements in your package, such as bitmaps, logo, support messages, or a phone book, prepare them before you begin running the wizard so that they can be included in the package.

✓ **Phase 3 — Running the CMAK wizard:** Use the wizard to create a service profile that enables connection to your network.

✓ **Phase 4 — Preparing deliverables:** You can deliver the Connection Manager and service profile as a separate package or include them with a custom browser package created by using the IEAK. File preparations depend on the distribution method. If you're just distributing the service profile, distribution options are CD and download only.

✓ **Phase 5 — Testing the package:** Test the custom package extensively before attempting to distribute it to your users.

✓ **Phase 6 — Ongoing support:** After you deploy the Connection Manager and service profile, you manage and maintain the files as the environment changes.

Running the wizard

For the test, you want to practice running the CMAK wizard several times, varying the options you choose and noting the results. Lab 12-1 presents a set of options to get you started. Be prepared (come test day) to be able to identify whether a particular set of steps fulfills a particular scenario objective.

Lab 12-1   Using the CMAK

1. **Start the Connection Manager Administration Kit by choosing Start⇨Programs⇨Connection Manager Administration Kit.**

2. **Click Next to move from the Welcome screen to the Service Profile Source screen.**

3. **On the Service Profile Source screen, select a radio button to specify whether you're creating a new service profile or modifying an existing profile. Click Next to advance to the Service and File Names screen.**

4. **On the Service and File Names screen, you must type the name for the service profile and a filename for all the resulting files. Type** Profile1 **in both text boxes.**

   (The service profile name can be up to 40 characters long, and the filename up to eight characters long.)

   Click Next to advance to the Merged Service Profiles screen.

5. **If you're merging an existing service profile into the profile that you're currently creating, enter the name(s) of those profiles on the**

Merged Service Profiles screen. Because you haven't run the wizard before and have no existing profiles, click Next to advance to the next wizard screen.

6. The Support Information screen (see Figure 12-1) enables you to add a 50-character line of support information to the Connection Manager logon screen. Type the following in the Support Information text box: Call 1-800-*xxx-xxxx* for customer service. **Click Next to advance to the Realm Name screen of the wizard.**

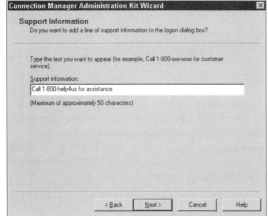

Figure 12-1: Adding support information.

7. On the Realm Name screen, select the Add a Realm Name option to specify a realm name (which provides additional network authentication information) and then select either the Prefix or Suffix option. Then type the prefix or suffix into the Realm Name box, such as the suffix @mrl.com (see Figure 12-2). Be sure to include separator characters, such as @ or /, in the Realm Name text box. Realm-name prefixes and suffixes work as follows:

   • **Prefix:** The prefix is normally used to add a company name as a prefix to the user-name. For example, typing **Northwest/** as the prefix to a username results in `Northwest/username`. The user isn't required to type the prefix prior to the username each time they use the service profile.

   • **Suffix:** Adding the *@company.com* suffix to the end of a username is the most common suffix. When a user employs such a service profile, the profile automatically appends the domain name to the end of his username. This adds the full domain name or security authentication information without the user needing to type it.

   Click Next to advance to the next wizard screen.

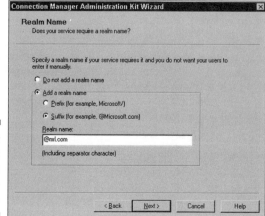

Figure 12-2:
Including a
realm name
in the ser-
vice profile.

8. **On the Dial-Up Networking Entries screen, you have an opportunity to create Dial-Up Networking entries for your users. The entries that you add here (see Figure 12-3) must match specific entries in your phone book. You can also specify DNS, WINS, and Dial-Up Networking scripts as you add each entry. Leave this screen blank, and click Next to advance to the VPN Support screen.**

Figure 12-3:
Adding
Dial-Up
Networking
entries.

9. **On the VPN Support screen (see Figure 12-4), specify whether you want to establish a VPN connection over the Internet. You establish a VPN connection by selecting the This Service Profile check box. Doing**

so brings up the VPN Connection screen shown in Figure 12-5. Check out the section titled "Supporting VPN with the CMAK," later in this chapter, for more information on configuring VPN.

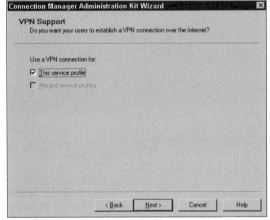

Figure 12-4:
Enabling
VPN support
for the ser-
vice profile.

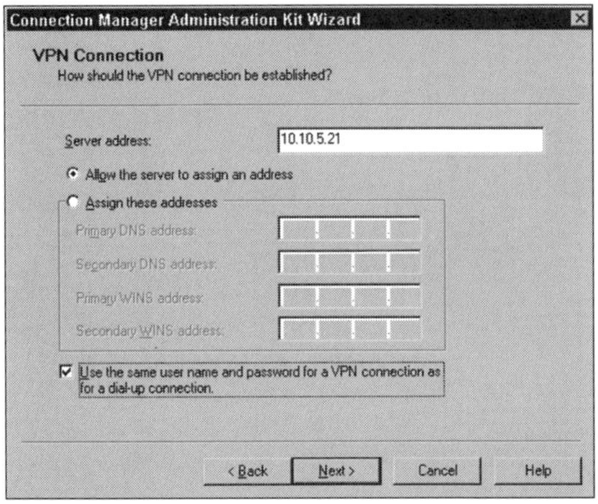

Figure 12-5:
Entering
configura-
tion
information
for the VPN
connection.

10. **If you don't specify VPN support, you see the Connect Actions screen, as shown in Figure 12-6. (Otherwise, you'd see the VPN Connection screen next. You only see the VPN Connection screen if you specify VPN support.) For each connect action that you select on this screen, you will see an additional screen where you specify which programs you want to run before or after the connect action that you checked.**

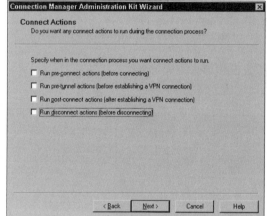

Figure 12-6:
Choosing
connect
actions for
the service
profile.

11. **After you specify connect actions, use the Auto-Applications screen (see Figure 12-7) to enter any programs that you want to run while the user is connected with this service profile.**

Figure 12-7:
Including
auto-
applications
in the
service
profile.

12. **On the next two screens, you specify which bitmaps you want to appear on the logon dialog box and on the phone book dialog box. These screens are self-explanatory — you either use the default bitmaps or enter a path and filename for a custom bitmap of your choosing. Click Next to advance to the next wizard screen.**

13. **On the Phone Book screen (Figure 12-8), you can include a custom phone book in the service profile. A custom phone book is handy if your users need to choose from a variety of access numbers.**

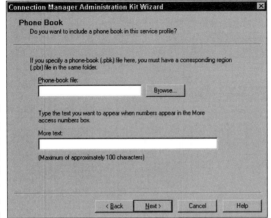

Figure 12-8:
Including a
custom
phone book
in the ser-
vice profile.

14. **The next two screens are icon screens. The first screen enables you to select the icon that will represent Connection Manager. The second lets you select an icon that allows users to access the Connection Manager status area.**

15. **The Help File screen (see Figure 12-9) appears. You can choose the default Connection Manager Help file, or you can specify a custom help file that you create for your users. Click Next to move to the next wizard screen.**

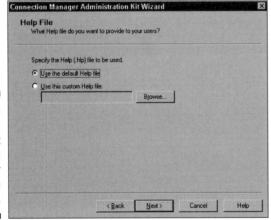

Figure 12-9:
Choosing
the default
or a custom
Help file for
the service
profile.

16. **On the Connection Manager Software screen (see Figure 12-10), select the Include the Connection Manager 1.2 Software check box to include the Connection Manager 1.2 software with the service profile. Click Next to continue.**

If Connection Manager is already installed on your client computers, you don't need to include Connection Manager 1.2 software. Otherwise, you need to include the software with the service profile for users to connect to your service.

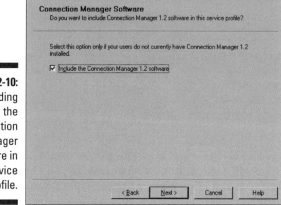

Figure 12-10: Including the Connection Manager software in the service profile.

17. **The License Agreement screen appears. Indicate whether or not you want each user to accept a license agreement before they can use the service profile. If you want users to accept a license agreement before installing the service profile, enter the filename of the License agreement in the text box. Leave the box blank and click Next to continue.**

You can use any text-editing software to create your own license agreement. If you include a license agreement, users must accept it in order to install the service profile. If they do not accept the agreement, the installation stops.

18. **The Additional Files screen appears. This screen gives you the opportunity to include any files or programs that you didn't specify earlier in the wizard. If any other programs are required for use of your service, enter the programs on this screen. Click Next to continue.**

Clicking the Add button opens a browse window where you can select the files or programs that you want to include in the service profile.

19. **Finally! The Ready to Build Service Profile screen appears, which means that you've completed the wizard. Click Next to build the service profile and watch the makecab application create the .cab files for your service profile.**

Remember that the wizard builds five files that are named according to the service profile name. The default location for the built files is

```
C:\Program Files\CMAK\Profiles\<ProfileName>
```

I created a service profile named Profile1. After the wizard completed, I was able to view the files at C:\Program Files\Cmak\Profiles\Profile1. As you see in Figure 12-11, the wizard built five files.

Figure 12-11:
Viewing the installation files for the service profile Profile1.

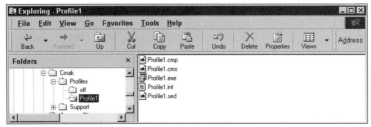

CMAK Strategies

As you can see from the preceding section, you can't run the CMAK wizard without doing quite a bit of advance planning. As a corporate administrator or ISP, your role is to

- ✔ Determine what types of connections are required.
- ✔ Determine how many service profiles are needed.
- ✔ Create or prepare custom elements for the service profile.
- ✔ Determine how to distribute the service profile.
- ✔ Determine how to maintain the service profile.

If you're distributing service profiles outside of an IEAK custom package, your distribution options are limited to CD and download. If you include the service profiles within an IEAK custom package, you can use any of the IEAK distribution methods: CD, download, or floppy disk.

Be certain that you plan for all the service profiles that you must create. Different profiles may require different preparation. For example, before you can enable VPN support for a service profile, you must configure a VPN server. Similarly, if you plan to include Dial-Up Networking connections, you must create the appropriate phone book entries.

On the exam, expect to see scenario questions that describe a particular environment and a required result. Be prepared to identify the correct steps and components to achieve the required result.

Supporting VPN with the CMAK

A virtual private network (or VPN) emulates a secure point-to-point private link between two computers. A VPN connection enables a remote user to securely access a private network by creating a virtual link across the Internet. For example, a user in Atlanta dials a local ISP and forms a virtual connection to his corporate network in Los Angeles instead of dialing a long-distance number and connecting to a modem on the Los Angeles network. Rather than paying long-distance rates and supporting an ever-growing number of modems, the company deploys a VPN server accessible via the Internet.

Virtual private networking is very cost-effective for your company, and less work for you! Instead of maintaining all those modems, you maintain a single VPN server. And with the help of the Connection Manager Administration Kit, you can effortlessly configure and deploy VPN connections to all your users. You use the CMAK to configure and distribute VPN connections just as you do regular dial-up connections. All the wizard screens and steps are the same, until you reach the VPN Support screen, where you add the particulars for your VPN server.

Using the CMAK to configure PPTP

With use of the Internet growing by leaps and bounds, you may need to configure VPN support for a service profile. Before you run the wizard and enable VPN support (refer to Figure 12-4), you should create your phone book entries and set up a VPN server.

Microsoft VPN support uses PPTP (Point-to-Point Tunneling Protocol) to create a secure connection across the Internet from your dial-in location to a VPN server. Usually, users access the Internet through an ISP, tunnel across the Internet to a corporate VPN server, and connect to the private corporate network.

Note that in addition to running TCP/IP and PPTP, the client computer must run the same network protocol as the destination network. For example, if you're using a dial-up VPN connection to access a NetWare network, your client computer must support TCP/IP, PPTP, and IPX/SPX.

For the exam, you must know how to configure a VPN service profile.

Refer to Step 9 of Lab 12-1 to see how to enable VPN support for a service profile. As you use the wizard to create the service profile, select the This Service Profile check box on the VPN Support screen. Click Next to advance to the VPN Connection screen.

In the Server Address text box on the VPN Connection screen, type the IP address or fully qualified domain name of the VPN server that connects to the private network. Specify that you want the VPN server to provide DNS and WINS server addresses automatically by selecting the Allow the Server to Assign an Address option. If you select the Assign these Addresses option, you can enter the IP addresses of a primary and a secondary DNS server and a primary and a secondary WINS server.

Using the CMAK to validate user security

At the bottom of the VPN Connection screen, check the box labeled `Use the same user name and password for a VPN connection as for a dial-up connection` to indicate that users can use a single ID and password to access both the VPN connection and the dial-up connection.

If you don't select this option, then users must enter an additional ID and password to be authenticated by the VPN server. (If security is a primary concern, a separate logon at the VPN server isn't a bad idea.)

Planning to support Dial-Up Networking

Planning is crucial to configuring a Dial-Up Networking (DUN) connection. Before you can configure Dial-Up Networking in a service profile, you must create phone book entries for the dial-up connections. If you plan to include WINS, DNS, and dial-up script support, you must have this information in advance as well. Refer back to Figure 12-3, which shows the Dial-Up Networking Entries screen. The entries that you add on this screen *must* match the entries in the phone book.

Prep Test

1 John is a corporate administrator preparing a customized IE5 browser package. Which IEAK component can he use to customize both the IE5 browser and connections?

A ○ Connection Manager 1.2

B ○ The IEAK Toolkit

C ○ The IEAK Customization wizard

D ○ The IEAK Profile Manager

2 Which of the following items cannot be customized by using the CMAK?

A ○ Graphics

B ○ User agent strings

C ○ Help files

D ○ Icons

3 John is using the CMAK to create a new service profile that includes Dial-Up Networking connections. What must John create prior to creating the Dial-Up Networking connections?

A ○ A custom IE5 browser

B ○ A VPN connection

C ○ A VPN server

D ○ Phone book entries

4 Which IEAK component do you use to create and distribute a VPN connection to your users?

A ○ IEAK Profile Manager

B ○ IEAK Connection Manager Administration Kit

C ○ IEAK VPN Toolkit

D ○ CMAK VPN Connector

5 John is the system administrator for an ISP. He's using the CMAK to create dial-up connections for the ISP's customers. John wants his connections to be user friendly. He doesn't want users to be required to type the domain name behind their user name when they enter their logon ID. Can John configure the dial-up connections to automatically include the domain name?

A ○ No, John cannot configure the connections to automatically include the domain name.

B ○ Yes, John can configure the connections to automatically include the domain name.

6 John is a corporate administrator supporting 10 Windows 95 clients, 50 Windows 98 clients, and 6 Windows NT clients on a Windows NT 4.0 network. The network is connected to the Internet, but protected by a corporate firewall. John is creating a custom IE5 browser to distribute to all clients. Many employees using the custom browser travel frequently, and John must configure a secure means of remote access for these employees. How can John best provide secure remote access for the employees who travel?

A ○ John should purchase several modems so that users can dial long distance to access the modems and log into the corporate network. He should also configure dial-up connections to distribute with the custom IE5 browser.

B ○ John should remove the firewall so users can access the corporate network from the Internet.

C ○ John should configure a VPN server that securely connects the corporate network to the Internet. He should also configure VPN connections to distribute with the custom IE5 browser.

D ○ John can do nothing to provide secure access for the employees who travel.

7 What information is contained in a service profile?

A ○ All the instructions and files necessary to establish a connection to your service.

B ○ The .ins and .cab files required to install an IE5 package.

C ○ The setup files for IE5.

D ○ A phone book entry.

Answers

1 *C.* The Customization wizard includes the CMAK, which is used to customize connections. Answer A is incorrect because Connection Manager 1.2 doesn't enable you to customize the browser. Answers B and D are incorrect because they don't enable you to customize connections. *Review "Preparing to use the CMAK."*

2 *B.* A user agent string can only be customized by using the IEAK. Graphics, logos, help files, support files, icons, and phone books can all be customized with the CMAK. *See "Purpose."*

3 *D.* Before you can configure Dial-Up Networking in a service profile, you must create phone book entries for the dial-up connections. The entries that you add on the CMAK Dial-Up Networking Entries screen *must* match the phone book entries. Answer A isn't correct because you aren't required to create a custom browser in order to create dial-up connections. Answers B and C aren't required for dial-up connections. *Review "Planning to support Dial-Up Networking."*

4 *B.* The CMAK is a component of the IEAK and is used to create dial-up and VPN connections. Answer B is incorrect because the Profile Manager is used to edit profiles for custom browser packages. Answers C and D aren't legitimate components of the IEAK. *See "Configuring with CMAK."*

5 *B.* On the Realm Name screen of the CMAK, John can select the Add a Realm Name option, and then type the domain name in the suffix text box. This automatically appends the domain name to the end of the user name when the customer logs on using this connection. *Review "Running the Wizard."*

6 *C.* Although answer A is technically feasible, it's not the best solution because it requires long-distance access. VPN connections provide secure access without incurring long-distance charges. Answer B isn't a secure solution. Answer D is incorrect. *Review "Supporting VPN with the CMAK."*

7 *A.* Answers B and C are incorrect because service profiles don't install IE5. Answer D is incorrect because a service profile contains much more than phone book entries. *Review "Using the CMAK Wizard."*

Part III
Installing and Configuring

The 5th Wave   By Rich Tennant

" Get ready, Mona—here come the test results."

In this part . . .

Part III includes further information on installing and configuring Internet Explorer 5. Options for customizing and installing IE5 using the Internet Explorer Administration Kit vary according to administrative role. This part includes a chapter on the differences between administrative roles and how those differences affect the installation and configuration of IE5. I've also included a chapter on creating and maintaining an IE5 installation site that supports multiple platforms and multiple languages.

Chapter 13

Assuming an Identity!

* *

Exam Objectives

▶ Selecting the appropriate role

▶ Identifying the key features of the three roles

* *

*I*n this chapter, I discuss selecting the proper role so that you can license and use the correct version of the Internet Explorer Administration Kit (IEAK).

When you use the IEAK, you must select one of three roles:

✔ Corporate Administrator

✔ Internet Service Provider (ISP)

✔ Internet Content Provider (ICP) or developer

Depending on which role you select, you'll see differing versions of the IEAK. Each version of the IEAK offers somewhat different customization options. In this chapter, I explain the purpose of each version and the differences in the available options.

The exam includes many scenario questions that describe an organization's requirements for a customized Internet Explorer 5 browser. You must be able to recognize the options for each role so that you can choose the correct answer.

Quick Assessment

Replacing
Netscape
Navigator

1   Before you can run the IEAK Customization wizard, you must register with Microsoft and obtain a _____ _____.

2   The _____ role provides Internet service to customers and is available for 32-bit and 16-bit versions of Internet Explorer 5.

3   The _____ role provides custom content and functionality to users and is available for 32-bit and 16-bit versions of Internet Explorer 5.

4   The Corporate Administrator role manages software and applications for a company or organization and is available for 32-bit, 16-bit, and _____ versions of Internet Explorer 5.

5   _____ often use single-disk branding to customize their users' IE5 browsers.

6   As an ISP, you have additional customization options that enable users to _____ _____ for your Internet services.

7   ISPs can provide a _____ sign-up package, a _____ sign-up package, or choose not to include a sign-up feature in the package at all.

8   Server-based sign-up by using the _____ _____ _____ is the sign-up method that Microsoft recommends.

9   When using the _____ sign-up method, you enter all the connection variables (password, gateway, and dialing information) into the IEAK Customization wizard.

10   Only a _____ _____ can distribute a customized IE5 browser to UNIX clients.

Answers

1 *customization code.* See "Identifying Your Role."

2 *ISP.* See "Identifying Your Role."

3 *ICP.* See "Identifying Your Role."

4 *UNIX.* See "Identifying Your Role."

5 *ICPs.* See "Content Provider/Developer Features."

6 *sign up.* See "Internet Service Provider (ISP) Features."

7 *server-based, serverless.* See "Internet Service Provider (ISP) Features."

8 *Internet Connection wizard.* See "Internet Service Provider (ISP) Features."

9 *serverless.* See "Internet Service Provider (ISP) Features."

10 *corporate administrator.* See "Internet Service Provider (ISP) Features."

Identifying Your Role

The Internet Explorer Administration Kit is available in three different versions. You select a version depending on the role that you play for your organization. Before you can run the IEAK Customization wizard, you must register with Microsoft and obtain a customization code. (See Chapter 2 for directions on registering and obtaining a code.) Then when you run the Customization wizard, you select the same role that you indicated when you applied for your license agreement.

The role you choose in the Customization wizard must match the license agreement. The customization code, which is tied to the role, determines which IEAK options you can access.

IEAK has three licensing options, as shown in Figure 13-1:

- ✓ **Content Provider/Developer:** Provides custom content and functionality to users. Available for 32-bit and 16-bit versions of Internet Explorer 5.

- ✓ **Internet Service Provider (ISP):** Provides Internet service to customers. Available for 32-bit and 16-bit versions of Internet Explorer 5.

- ✓ **Corporate Administrator:** Manages software and applications for a company or organization. Available for 32-bit, 16-bit, and UNIX versions of Internet Explorer 5.

Microsoft Internet Explorer Customization Wizard - Stage 1 ☒

Company Name and Customization Code

Please identify yourself with your company name and respective customization code. You cannot continue without entering a valid customization code.

You should have received your personal 10-digit customization code via mail or email. This is your own personal code. Keep this code secure and do not distribute it.

Company name: MRL

Customization code: ********   Get Customization Code

The title that best fits your role is:
- ○ Content Provider/Developer
- ○ Service Provider
- ⦿ Corporate Administrator

< Back   Next >   Cancel   Help

Figure 13-1:
Selecting
a role.

Choose the licensing option that most closely matches the role of your organization. Not all roles provide the same configuration options, so choose carefully. The Corporate Administrator role provides the most choices, although it may not include all the options that you require.

Corporate Administrator Features

The Corporate Administrator role offers the most features of the three options. This role is intended for use by system administrators who work for a single organization and plan to distribute IE5 only within their organization.

Corporate administrators can distribute IE5 packages through a variety of installation methods:

- ✔ CD-ROM
- ✔ Download
- ✔ Multiple floppy disks
- ✔ Single floppy disk
- ✔ Single-disk branding

If you choose to use single-disk branding, remember that it only customizes the browser. It does not distribute any application code.

In addition, a browser package can be deployed across the following platforms:

- ✔ 16-bit Windows
- ✔ 32-bit Windows
- ✔ UNIX

The other roles, ICP and ISP, don't allow for deployment on UNIX platforms.

Content Provider/Developer Features

Internet Content Providers/Developers (ICPs) provide customized browsers to users who already have Internet accounts. Alternately, an ICP can deploy a custom browser that includes a link to the Microsoft referral server, which provides contact information about Internet Service Providers.

ICPs use the IEAK to customize setup, customize the browser and channels, and deploy their custom packages. ICPs can select the single-disk branding method to customize a browser. Single-disk branding enables the ICP to customize the browser without reinstalling Internet Explorer 5. But with single-disk branding, custom components cannot be included in the package. Single-disk branding setup files can be distributed on any media.

ICPs use the following distribution methods to deploy their custom browser:

- ✔ Multiple floppy disks
- ✔ CD
- ✔ Download

For the exam, know which media options are available for an ICP to deploy a customized browser.

Internet Service Provider (ISP) Features

Internet Service Providers (ISPs) provide Internet access services to their customers. An ISP uses the IEAK to customize IE5 and distribute it to its customers. These customers aren't within any particular organization and can be geographically dispersed in a variety of locations. Customers dial the ISP to connect to the Internet.

As an ISP, you have additional customization options that allow users to sign up for your Internet services. ISPs can provide a server-based sign-up package, a serverless sign-up package, or choose not to include a sign-up feature in the package at all. To create a server-based sign-up, you enter connection information via the IEAK, as shown in Figure 13-2. This info is then stored on your sign-up server in an .INS file.

- ✔ **Server-based sign-up using the Internet Connection wizard:** This is the sign-up method that Microsoft recommends. This sign-up method creates server solutions that interact with Internet Connection wizard screens.

- ✔ **Server-based sign-up using full-screen kiosk mode:** By using this sign-up method, you create server solutions that interact with the browser in kiosk mode.

- ✔ **Serverless sign-up:** This method requires no sign-up server. Instead, you enter all the connection variables (password, gateway, and dialing information) into the IEAK Customization wizard. You can't use this method to customize the Internet Connection wizard.

- ✔ **No sign-up:** Use this method if you don't require users to go through a sign-up process when they install the browser. (You cannot use this method if you specify the single floppy disk distribution method.)

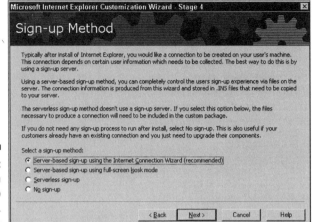

Figure 13-2:
Selecting an
ISP sign-up
method.

Like ICPs, ISPs can distribute 32-bit and 16-bit versions of Internet Explorer 5. However, distribution to UNIX clients is not available.

The recommended installation methods for the ISP role are:

- ✔ CD-ROM
- ✔ Web download
- ✔ Single-disk branding

The other customization options — customizing logos, title bars, and other browser features — remain the same as those available in the corporate administrator role.

Prep Test

1 Mary is the system administrator at an ISP, and she is preparing a customized IE5 package to distribute to customers. Mary wants customers to use the Internet Connection wizard to sign up for her ISP's service. Aside from creating the custom browser, what else must Mary do to enable this sign-up feature?

A ○ Mary need do nothing else.

B ○ Mary must distribute the media on a single floppy disk.

C ○ Mary must install a sign-up server.

D ○ Mary must install an ILS server.

2 Mary is a corporate administrator for a global firm with over 10,000 employees. She plans to distribute a customized IE5 browser package to Windows 98, Windows NT 4.0, and UNIX computers throughout the organization. While running the IEAK Customization wizard, Mary is unable to configure a sign-up method. What could be causing the problem?

A ○ The sign-up feature is not available on UNIX computers.

B ○ The sign-up feature is not available in the Corporate Administrator role.

C ○ Mary must select Sign-up Settings on the Feature Selection screen of the Customization wizard.

D ○ Mary had not deployed a sign-up server.

3 As a corporate administrator using the IEAK, Mary can distribute a custom IE5 package to which platforms? (Choose all that apply.)

A ❑ 16-bit Windows

B ❑ 32-bit Windows

C ❑ UNIX

D ❑ NetWare

4 Toni is a system administrator for an ICP. Toni must create a custom version of IE5 to distribute to the company's customers. Toni plans to use the single-disk branding method for packaging and distributing IE5. What features will Toni be able to include in the package? (Choose all that apply.)

A ❑ Outlook Express 5

B ❑ Custom graphics and logos

C ❑ Custom title bars

D ❑ NetMeeting

5 Toni is a system administrator for an ICP. Toni must create a custom version of IE5 to distribute to the company's customers. Toni plans to use the single-disk branding method for packaging and distributing IE5. What media can Toni use to distribute the package? (Choose all that apply.)

A ❑ Download

B ❑ CD-ROM

C ❑ Multiple floppy disks

6 Which of the following are sign-up methods available to an ISP? (Choose all that apply.)

A ❑ Server-based sign-up using the Internet Connection wizard

B ❑ Server-based sign-up using full-screen kiosk mode

C ❑ Server-based sign-up using single-task mode

D ❑ Serverless sign-up

Answers

1 C. Server-based sign-up using the Internet Connection wizard is the sign-up method that Microsoft recommends. This sign-up method creates server solutions that interact with Internet Connection wizard screens. *See "Internet Service Provider (ISP) Features."*

2 B. Only the ISP role includes the sign-up feature. This feature is used for ISP customers to sign-up for Internet services. *See "Internet Service Provider (ISP) Features."*

3 A, B, and C. A corporate administrator using the IEAK can distribute to UNIX computers as well as Windows computers. The ICP and ISP roles, however, cannot distribute to UNIX computers. *See "Corporate Administrator Features."*

4 B and C. As an ICP, Toni can only customize currently installed IE5 browsers. Single-disk branding allows an ICP to customize the browser without reinstalling Internet Explorer 5. But with single-disk branding, custom components cannot be included in the package. *See "Content Provider/Developer Features."*

5 A, B, and C. Single-disk branding setup files can be distributed on any media. *See "Content Provider/Developer Features."*

6 A, B, and D. ISPs can also use the No Sign-up method if they don't require users to go through a sign-up process when they install the browser. Answer C is not a legitimate sign-up method — I made it up to throw you off! *See "Internet Service Provider (ISP) Features."*

Chapter 14

Deploying IE5 Using the IEAK

• •

Exam Objectives

▶ Distribution media for Internet Explorer 5

▶ Using the IEAK to deploy Internet Explorer 5

• •

*A*fter you plan and customize an IE5 browser package, you have a custom build that you can distribute to your users. Now all you have to do is figure out how to get it to them!

Fortunately, in this chapter I go over the steps required in order to distribute IE5 via:

✔ Download

✔ CD-ROM

✔ Multiple floppy disks

✔ Single floppy disk

✔ Flat

✔ Single-disk branding

Quick Assessment

Deploying IE5

1 Depending on the distribution methods that you specify in Stage 1 of the Customization wizard, your destination directory has one or more corresponding _____.

2 Every destination folder, no matter what the distribution media, contains _____ _____ _____.

3 You can't select _____ as the distribution media unless you also select _____ download.

4 Destination directories, language selection, and media selection all take place while using the _____ _____ _____.

Network Download

5 The _____ file contains a list of all the download sites that you enter into the Customization wizard.

6 _____ media distribution works much the same as the download distribution.

7 With the _____ distribution method, all the files are placed into the destination directory in a flat-file structure with no subfolders.

CD-ROM

8 The _____ file contains the CD autorun information.

Floppy Disk

9 When using the _____ _____ distribution method, you install the entire package from floppy disk.

10 The single floppy distribution method places all the setup files into a subfolder called _____.

Answers

1 *subdirectories.* See "Deploying IE5."

2 *an INS directory.* See "Deploying IE5."

3 *single, floppy.* Review "Deploying IE5."

4 *IEAK Customization wizard.* See "Deploying IE5."

5 *IE5SITES.DAT.* See "Network Download."

6 *Flat-file.* Review "Network Download."

7 *flat-file.* See "Network Download."

8 *AUTORUN.INF.* See "CD-ROM."

9 *multiple floppy.* Review "Floppy Disk."

10 *Disk1.* See "Floppy Disk."

Distribution Media

Stage 1 of the Customization wizard presents features that work together to determine which distribution media are available for distributing an IE5 package. In combination, the IEAK role and the platform selected determine the distribution media.

The platforms available in the corporate administrator role are:

- ✔ Windows 9x/NT 4.0 (32-bit browsers)
- ✔ Windows 3.1/WFW/NT 3.51 (16-bit browsers)
- ✔ UNIX

Platforms available in the ISP and ICP roles are:

- ✔ Windows 9x/NT 4.0 (32-bit browsers)
- ✔ Windows 3.1/WFW/NT 3.51 (16-bit browsers)

For example, a corporate administrator creating a package for 16-bit platforms (Windows 3.1/WFW/NT 3.51) can choose either download, CD-ROM, or flat as the distribution options. Similarly, an ISP administrator creating a package for 16-bit platforms can select download, CD-ROM, flat, or multiple floppy disks as the distribution media.

Table 14-1 shows the distribution options available according to role and platform selections. Notice that the table does not list distribution media options for the UNIX platform in the corporate administrator role. This is because the UNIX files are packaged into a single folder and are distributed across the network from one computer to another.

Table 14-1	Distribution Media Options					
Role/Platform	*Download*	*CD*	*Flat*	*Multiple Floppy*	*Single Floppy*	*Single-Disk Branding*
Corp. Admin/32-bit	X	X	X			X
Corp. Admin/16-bit	X	X	X			
ISP/32-bit	X	X	X	X	X	X
ISP/16-bit	X	X	X	X		
ICP/32-bit	X	X	X	X		X
ICP/16-bit	X	X	X	X		

Deploying IE5

When you run the IEAK Customization wizard, you specify a destination directory in which to place the files of your custom build after you complete the package. Depending on distribution methods that you specify in Stage 1 of the Customization wizard, your destination directory has one or more corresponding subdirectories.

As an example, look at the subdirectories shown in Figure 14-1. The first subdirectories are the result of my running the Customization wizard and specifying D:\builds\02091999 as the destination directory. For my distribution media, I chose download and CD.

Figure 14-1:
Viewing the destination directory and subdirectories.

As you can see, the destination directory contains several subdirectories:

- ✔ Download
- ✔ CD
- ✔ INS

The download directory contains all the .CAB files that I need to download my custom package via the Internet or intranet. The CD directory contains all the .CAB files that I need to distribute my package via CD-ROM.

Every destination folder, no matter what the distribution media, contains an INS directory. This directory contains — can you guess? — the .INS file that contains the customization info for your package.

Look at Figure 14-1 again. The second time that I ran the Customization wizard, I specified my destination directory as D:\builds\04201999. I chose single-disk branding and flat-file as the distribution media. As you see in Figure 14-1, the directories on my hard drive are

- ✔ BrndOnly
- ✔ Flat
- ✔ INS

The third time that I ran the Customization wizard, I specified D:\builds\ 04211999 for a destination directory and multiple floppy and single floppy as the distribution media. As shown in Figure 14-1, the resulting directories are

- ✔ Download
- ✔ INS
- ✔ Mfloppy
- ✔ Sfloppy

Network Download

If you intend for users to download your package for installation, you need to specify one or more download sites when you run the Customization wizard. To make the files in the Download folder available for installation, move the files to the URL that you specify as a download site and make sure that the users have access to the location.

Look at the directory structure under the Download folder in Figure 14-2. First, you see a folder labeled Win32. This folder corresponds to my platform selection — Win9x/NT 4.0 — while running the Customization wizard. Within the Win32 folder is the En folder (because English was the language I chose for the package) and the IE5SITES.DAT file.

The En folder contains the .CAB files that the computer requires for installing my package by download. You can place the setup file from the En folder on a Web site for download or you can copy it to a floppy disk for distribution. After the user executes the setup file, the installation from the download site commences.

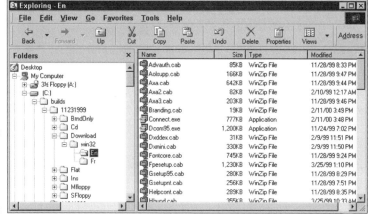

Figure 14-2:
Viewing the
.CAB file
location.

The IE5SITES.DAT file contains a list of all the download sites that you enter into the Customization wizard.

Flat-file media distribution works much the same as download distribution. But in this case, the wizard places all the files into the destination directory in a flat-file structure — there are no subfolders. You commonly use this distribution method when installing from a network server. The setup file resides in the destination directory with all other package files.

CD-ROM

Distribution via CD-ROM is similar to the download option. The CD folder contains the required files to install the package from CD-ROM:

- ✔ Win32 folder — (once again I selected the Win9x/NT 4.0 platform) contains the files for the custom package

- ✔ AUTORUN.INF — contains the CD autorun information

- ✔ CDSETUP.EXE — the setup file to begin the CD installation of the custom package

Copy the files in the CD folder to CD-ROM and distribute throughout your organization.

Floppy Disk

Single floppy distribution is also similar to distribution via download. The En folder contains all the files that you need for the setup floppy in a subfolder with the label Disk1. Copy the files to a floppy disk, and then distribute the disk to users. Users start package installation from the floppy disk, which contains connection information to the package files on a server.

Multiple floppy installations work similarly. Within the En folder is a series of subfolders with the labels Disk1, Disk2, and so on. Copy these files to disks and distribute them to the users. In this case though, users install the entire package from the floppy disks.

Single-disk branding is another distribution option. With single-disk branding, the wizard places a single setup file in the En subfolder. This file contains features that customize setup for the service provider.

Prep Test

1 Which of the following are valid distribution media in the IEAK? (Choose all that apply.)

A ❑ CD-ROM

B ❑ Multi-disk branding

C ❑ Download

D ❑ Multiple floppy

2 You want to distribute your custom package via single floppy distribution media. Which other distribution option must you select in order to use the single floppy media?

A ○ CD-ROM

B ○ Flat

C ○ Download

D ○ Single-disk branding

3 (True/False). If you want to distribute your custom package via download or via CD-ROM, you must run the Customization wizard once for each distribution method.

A ○ True

B ○ False

4 While running the Customization wizard, John specifies the destination folder as C:\builds\IE5. He enters `http://www.install1.com/ie5` as the download site. After completing the Customization wizard, what else does John need to do so that users can download his custom package? (Choose all that apply.)

A ❑ John must modify the IE5SITES.DAT file to include the destination directory.

B ❑ John must copy or move the files from the destination directory to the download site.

C ❑ John must place a setup file on a Web page or on a disk so that users can initiate the setup.

D ❑ John must make the download directory accessible to all users.

5 You are a system administrator for a service provider who wants to distribute a custom version of Internet Explorer 5 to your users via single floppy disk media. Which role should you select when you run the Customization wizard?

A ○ Corporate Administrator

B ○ Service Provider

C ○ Content Developer

D ○ Web Master

6 Sharon is an administrator at an ICP. She is creating a custom IE5 package for customers using Windows 3.1 and NT 3.51. Which distribution methods can Sharon select? (Choose all that apply.)

A ❑ Download

B ❑ CD-ROM

C ❑ Flat

D ❑ Multiple floppy disks

E ❑ Single floppy disk

F ❑ Single-disk branding

7 Jane is an administrator at an ISP. She is creating a custom IE5 package for customers using Windows 98 and NT 4.0. Which distribution methods can Jane select? (Choose all that apply.)

A ❑ Download

B ❑ CD-ROM

C ❑ Flat

D ❑ Multiple floppy disks

E ❑ Single floppy disk

F ❑ Single-disk branding

8 Clay is a corporate administrator. He is creating a custom IE5 package for customers using Windows 98 and NT 4.0. Which distribution methods can Clay select? (Choose all that apply.)

A ❑ Download

B ❑ CD-ROM

C ❑ Flat

D ❑ Multiple floppy disks

E ❑ Single floppy disk

F ❑ Single-disk branding

Answers

1 *A, C, and D.* Answer B is not correct because only single-disk branding is a distribution option, not multi-disk branding. Single floppy and flat are also valid distribution methods. *Review "Deploying IE5," "Network Download," "Floppy Disk,"* and *"CD-ROM."*

2 *C.* To use the single floppy distribution media, you must also select download. You copy only the setup files to floppy disk. The user has to download the rest of the files from a server. *Review "Floppy Disk."*

3 *B.* You can specify both download and CD-ROM distribution media within the same custom package. You can even send the files to the same destination directory. (You can't, however, select more than one platform or language. You have to run the Customization wizard once for each language and platform choice.) *See "Deploying IE5."*

4 *B, C, and D.* Answer A is not a correct answer because the Customization wizard automatically creates the IE5SITES.DAT file. The IE5SITES.DAT file contains the list of download sites that you enter when using the Customization wizard. *See "Network Download."*

5 *B.* The Service Provider role is the best choice if you plan to distribute a custom browser package by using single floppy distribution. *See "Floppy Disk."*

6 *A, B, C, and D.* Download, CD-ROM, flat, and multiple floppy disks are all viable distribution methods for Sharon's custom package. *Review "Distribution Methods."*

7 *A, B, C, D, E, and F.* All of the above are available selections for distributing Jane's IE5 package. *Review "Distribution Media."*

8 *A, B, C, and F.* Download, CD-ROM, flat, and single-disk branding are all available distribution methods. Review *"Distribution Methods."*

Chapter 15

Configuring an Installation Site

● ●

Exam Objectives

▶ Configuring an installation site for multiple languages
▶ Configuring an installation site for multiple platforms
▶ Updating and managing an installation site

● ●

*I*n this chapter, I tell you how to create an installation site for your customized Internet Explorer 5 browser package. I discuss how to prepare an
installation site that supports installations on multiple platforms, such as
Windows 98 or Windows 3.1. I also cover how to prepare a site that can
install the package in multiple languages. Finally, I tell you how to maintain
the site as you introduce updated versions of the browser package.

Quick Assessment

1   From the information that you supply, the _____ _____ _____ creates the appropriate installation files for the custom package.

2   After you create the installation files for a custom package, you _____ the files to the installation site specified during the Customization wizard.

3   When users install your package, they initiate the installation by running the _____ file.

4   The setup file begins placing temporary files on the PC and reads the _____ file to locate the download sites from which the installation files can be loaded.

5   The setup program downloads and extracts _____ files to complete the installation.

6   You must run the _____ _____ once for each platform or language created.

7   When you run the Customization wizard and specify multiple distribution methods, all the resulting files go to the same _____ _____.

8   If you plan to have users install the IE5 package from a LAN server, you must specify the _____ distribution method when you run the Customization wizard.

9   _____ _____ doesn't install a new version of IE5, but merely customizes an already existing version.

10   The _____ _____ distribution method places only the setup and sign-up information on the disk.

Answers

1   *IEAK Customization Wizard.* See "Creating an Installation Site."

2   *copy.* See "Creating an Installation Site."

3   *ie5setup.exe.* See "Understanding setup."

4   *ie5sites.dat.* See "Understanding setup."

5   *.cab (or cabinet).* See "Understanding setup."

6   *Customization Wizard.* See "Supporting Multiple Platforms."

7   *destination directory.* See "Other Distribution Methods."

8   *flat.* See "Other Distribution Methods."

9   *Single-disk branding.* See "Other Distribution Methods."

10   *single disk.* See "Other Distribution Methods."

Creating an Installation Site

After you create a custom IE5 (Internet Explorer 5) browser package, the next step is to place the package in a location that users can access for installation. Sometimes the location is a CD or floppy disk; other times it's a server or a Web site. This chapter covers an Internet or intranet installation site. (Chapter 2 introduces and explains the purpose of the IEAK Customization wizard. The Customization wizard is used to create and customize an IE5 browser package. I take you through the Customization wizard in Chapter 10.)

Remember that while running the IEAK Customization wizard, you provide information, such as:

- ✔ The destination folder for completed IE packages
- ✔ The URL or address of a download server (if using download distribution method)
- ✔ Which platform the package is to support
- ✔ Which languages the package is to support

From the information that you supply, the IEAK Customization wizard creates the appropriate installation files for the custom package. Now you must move those files from your hard drive or network drive to an intranet or Internet server.

Take a moment to look at the files that the Customization wizard places in the destination folder. First, you see subdirectories for each distribution method that you selected while running the wizard. (See my example in Figure 15-1.) If you specified distribution by download, you see a Download directory. Within the Download directory are subdirectories for each platform that your package supports. Within each platform directory is a subdirectory for every language that the platform supports. Figure 15-1 shows a win32 platform directory and En (English language) subdirectory. The En folder contains the installation files for your custom package.

Figure 15-1:
Examining
the files
in the
destination
folder.

Understanding setup

When users install your package, they initiate the installation by running the ie5setup.exe file. The Customization wizard creates this setup file for your package and places it in the language folder of the destination folder.

Using the example shown in Figure 15-1, the path for the setup file is:

```
C:\builds\11231999\Download\Win32\En
```

The setup file begins placing temporary files on the PC and reads the ie5sites.dat file to locate the download sites from which the installation files can be loaded. Looking at Figure 15-1 again, you find the ie5sites.dat file in the following path:

```
C:\builds\11231999\Download\Win32
```

Setup presents these download sites for the user to select from and then downloads and extracts the cabinet files (also called .cab files) to complete the installation.

For the exam, know the contents of the ie5sites.dat file. You must also be familiar with the process for creating an installation site because you're likely to see at least one question on this topic on the exam.

Location, location, location!

To develop an installation site, you must copy all files created by the IEAK Customization wizard to a Web site that users can access to install the browser package. When you run the IEAK Customization wizard to create the browser package, you specify the download site for the installation files (see Figure 15-2). Therefore, you must copy the installation files to the location specified as the download site. The easiest way to do this is to copy the entire download directory to the download site.

In the example in Figure 15-2, the destination site is a Microsoft Internet Information Server at www.na.com. During the Customization wizard, I specified the download URL as http://www.na.com/ie5. I copy the download directory from the destination directory on my hard drive to the ie5 directory on the Web server. The actual path on my Web server is:

```
C:\InetPub\wwwroot\ie5
```

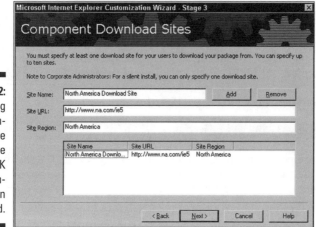

Figure 15-2:
Specifying
the down-
load site
during the
IEAK
Custom-
ization
wizard.

Of course, depending on the type of Web server that you use and the directory structure on your server, your path may be different.

When you copy installation files to a Web server for Internet or intranet download, you don't need to copy the files for alternate distribution methods. You need only copy the files from the download folder.

Supporting Multiple Platforms

If you need to create a custom browser package for more than one operating system, run the IEAK Customization wizard once for each version that you need to create. For example, if you need to customize IE5 for both Windows 98 and Windows 3.1 systems, you run the Customization wizard once to build the Windows 98 version, then again to build the Windows 3.1 version. Specify the same destination folder for both versions.

You might be thinking that you can use the IEAK Profile Manager to create a second package for another platform. This is true, but for the exam they want you to know that you have to run the Customization wizard once for each version that you need to create.

After you create both packages, the directory structure of the destination folder resembles the example in Figure 15-3. In my destination folder named 11231999, I created a Windows 98 version (in the win32 directory) and a Windows 3.1 version (in the win16 directory). The win32 directory contains the cabinet and setup files for the Windows 98 platform, while the win16 directory contains the cabinet and setup files for the Windows 3.1 platform.

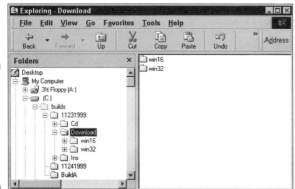

Figure 15-3:
Creating a
download
site
supporting
multiple
platforms.

After you create all the versions that you require, copy the download directory to the destination site that you specified in the Customization wizard.
Again, by using the example in Figure 15-2, the destination site is a Microsoft
Internet Information Server at `www.na.com`. During the Customization wizard,
I specified the download URL as `http://www.na.com/ie5`. I copy the download directory from the destination directory on my hard drive to the ie5
directory on the Web server at:

```
C:\InetPub\wwwroot\ie5
```

What if you don't create all your custom packages at the same time? Suppose
you already deployed a Windows 98 package within your organization and
then discover that you need to create and deploy a Windows 3.1 version. You
can create the second package by running the IEAK Customization wizard
and specifying the same destination folder as the initial package. Then simply
move the new win16 subdirectory from the download directory on your hard
drive to the download directory on the Web site.

If you see a question on the exam that presents a scenario describing a need
for a custom browser package for multiple platforms, realize that they want
to know if you understand that you need a separate package for each platform version. Read the question carefully. In all probability, the correct
answer for this scenario is to run the Customization wizard once for each
platform version required or to create a separate custom package for each
platform version required.

Supporting Multiple Languages

Supporting multiple language versions of an IE5 package is similar to supporting multiple platform versions. You must run the Customization wizard
once for each language supported by IE5. Specify the target language for the

IE5 browser during the Customization wizard, as shown in Figure 15-4. Specify the same destination folder that you used for the English language version (or whichever version you ran first) of the package.

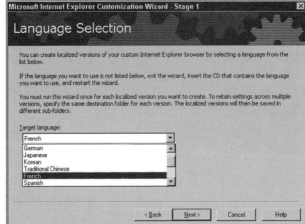

Figure 15-4: Specifying the target language for an IE5 browser package.

The Customization wizard places the files for the second version in the same download directory as the English version. In the example shown in Figure 15-5, I created a second Windows 98 version of my browser package in French. The download directory now contains a win16 and a win32 directory. The win32 directory contains both an English (En) directory and a French (Fr) directory. Each contains installation and setup files for its target language.

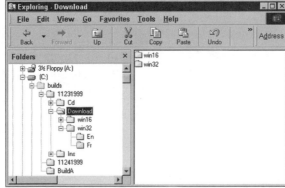

Figure 15-5: Installation files for different languages are stored in separate folders.

To create an installation site, copy all the files created by the Customization wizard to the Web site that you specified as the download site (refer to Figure 15-2). During the Customization wizard, I specified the download URL as `www.na.com/ie5`. I copy the download directory from the destination directory on my hard drive to the ie5 directory on the Web server. The actual path on my Web server is:

```
C:\InetPub\wwwroot\ie5
```

To add a French language browser package to an existing Web installation site, I simply copy the Fr directory from my hard drive to the correct location on the Web server. The path on my hard drive is:

```
C:\builds\11231999\Download\Win32\Fr
```

And the new location on the Web server is:

```
C:\InetPub\wwwroot\ie5\Download\Win32\Fr
```

Maintaining an Installation Site

Maintaining the installation site for your IE5 package isn't difficult. Each time that you create a new version of the IE5 package, you need to copy the new files to the Web server. If you add new versions to support different languages or platforms, create the files and place them on the installation site, as I explain in the preceding sections. If you create a new version to replace a previously deployed package, replace the files on the installation site with the new files created by the Customization wizard.

Other Distribution Methods

When you run the Customization wizard and specify multiple distribution methods, all the resulting files go to the same destination directory. If you name the destination folder `11231999`, for example, then that directory contains subdirectories for CD, download, multiple floppy, and flat distribution methods, in addition to the Ins folder, which contains the instruction file (.ins file).

CD

To prepare for a CD-ROM distribution, copy the contents of the `C:\builds\<build number>\CD` directory to the root of the CD. The contents of the CD should look like Figure 15-6, which contains a win32 installation directory, an autorun.inf file, and a cdsetup.exe file.

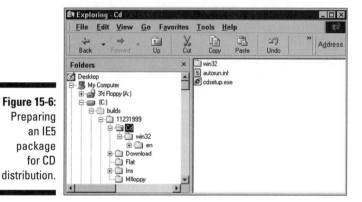

Figure 15-6:
Preparing
an IE5
package
for CD
distribution.

Multiple floppy

You seldom see IE5 distributed on multiple floppy disks, but it can be done! If some of your systems don't have CD-ROM drives or network connectivity, create multiple (maybe I should say a multitude!) floppy disks and copy the installation files to the disks. The IEAK Customization wizard places these installation files in the following path:

```
C:\builds\<build number>\Mfloppy
```

The Customization wizard arranges the files created for an English language version of IE5 running on the Windows 95 platform by disk within the \win32\En subdirectory. To create the installation disks, copy the contents of each folder to the root directory of a diskette. You need a large number of disks for this distribution method.

Flat (or LAN) distribution

If you plan to have users install the IE5 package from a LAN server, you must specify the flat file distribution method when you run the Customization wizard. All the files are placed into a single subdirectory:

```
C:\builds\<build number\Flat\win32\En
```

To prepare for installation from a LAN server, copy all the files from this folder into a target directory on the LAN server.

Single floppy

If you select the single floppy distribution method, the Customization wizard places files in the following path:

```
C:\builds\<build number\Sfloppy
```

Obviously, you can't fit all the IE5 installation files on a single disk. The single disk distribution method places only the setup and sign-up information on the disk. To create the distribution disk, copy the contents of the \Disk1 subdirectory to a floppy disk.

Single-disk branding

Single-disk branding doesn't install a new version of IE5, but merely customizes an already existing version. The Customization wizard places the branding files in the following directory path:

```
C:\builds\<build number>\BrndOnly
```

The BrndOnly folder contains a single setup file, which you copy to a floppy disk for distribution.

Prep Test

1 Greg is an ISP administrator preparing a custom package for distribution to the ISP's customers. Greg plans to use the single-disk branding distribution method so that he is only customizing existing versions of IE5. What should Greg do to distribute the package on a disk after he creates it using the Customization wizard?

A ○ Copy the .ins and .cab files from the distribution folder to the floppy.

B ○ Copy the single setup file from the `BrndOnly` folder to the floppy.

C ○ Use the IEAK Profile Manager to create a setup file and copy it to the floppy.

D ○ Move the setup file from the `BrndOnly` folder to the auto-config URL.

2 As system administrator at an ISP, John is creating a custom IE5 browser package. He wants to distribute the package via CD-ROM. John copies the destination folder created by the Customization Wizard to the CD-ROM, but is unable to install the package from the CD. What did John do wrong?

A ○ John cannot create a CD-ROM for installation because he is using the ISP role.

B ○ John must run the IEAK Profile Manager to create the correct setup files.

C ○ John should have copied only the contents of the CD folder in his destination directory to the root of the CD-ROM.

D ○ John should have run the Customization wizard in the corporate administrator role.

3 While running the Customization wizard, you can specify up to ten download sites from which users can install a custom browser package. When the wizard is complete, which file contains the download sites information?

A ○ .cab files

B ○ .inf file

C ○ .ins file

D ○ ie5sites.dat file

4 Joan is a corporate administrator for an international firm. Joan is planning a custom browser package, which must be available in three languages. How does Joan create a browser package for three different languages?

A ○ Joan just selects the target languages in the Customization wizard. Users will then select the target language during setup.

B ○ Joan must run the Customization wizard once for each language, creating three separate browser packages.

C ○ Joan must run the Customization wizard once, and then use the IEAK Profile Manager to edit the .ins file to create new packages.

D ○ Joan must run the Customization wizard in each of the target languages and create a custom browser package in each language.

5 Sam is a corporate administrator planning a custom IE5 browser package. Client computers in Sam's corporation run Windows 98, Windows NT 4.0 and UNIX. Can Sam create one browser package that will install IE5 on all of these platforms?

A ○ Yes.

B ○ No.

Answers

1 *B.* Copy the single setup file from the BrndOnly folder to the floppy. When you choose Single-Disk Branding, the Customization Wizard creates a single setup file in the BrndOnly folder. You must copy the setup file to the floppy. *Review "Single-disk branding."*

2 *C.* John should have copied only the contents of the CD folder in his destination directory to the root of the CD-ROM. The Customization Wizard creates a CD folder in the destination directory. The CD directory contains a win32 installation directory, an autorun.inf file, and a cdsetup.exe file that must be copied to the root of the CD-ROM. *See "CD."*

3 *D.* ie5sites.dat file. When users install your package, they initiate the installation by running the ie5setup.exe file. The setup file then begins placing temporary files on the PC and reads the ie5sites.dat file to locate the download sites from which the installation files can be loaded. *Review "Understanding setup."*

4 *B.* Joan must run the Customization Wizard once for each language, creating three separate browser packages. She doesn't need to run the IEAK Customization Wizard in the target language, but rather select the target language while running the wizard. She cannot use the IEAK Profile Manager to edit the language option for the browser package. *Review "Supporting Multiple Languages."*

5 *B. No.* Sam must run the Customization Wizard once for each platform that he must support. He will require two packages, one for the 32-bit operating systems and one for UNIX. *Review "Supporting Multiple Platforms."*

Configuring an Installation Site

Part IV
Configuring and Managing Resource Access

The 5th Wave   By Rich Tennant

Tarzan - Lord of the Web

©RICHTENNANT

"... and then one day it hit Tarzan, Lord of Jungle - where future in that?"

In this part . . .

Part IV explains how to use the Internet Explorer Administration Kit tools to manage IE5 once the browser is deployed and in use. In Chapter 16, you learn about policies, profiles, and logon scripts — the tools that help you centrally administer IE5 after deployment. Chapter 17 explains the intricacies of configuring security zones that protect resources while maximizing Web features. Chapter 18 tells you how to manage automated connection settings using scripts, profiles, and policies.

Chapter 16

Managing Configuration Updates

· ·

Exam Objectives

▶ Enabling automatic configuration

▶ Creating profiles

▶ Configuring logon scripts

▶ Changing system policies

· ·

*I*n this chapter, I tell you how to use profiles, system policies, and logon scripts to maintain your deployed IE5 browsers. Microsoft provides several methods for managing Internet Explorer 5 after it's deployed in your organization. Rather than visit each workstation to change configurations or install an updated browser, automatic configuration options enable system administrators to make changes quickly and economically. As always, advance planning helps you properly configure the browser for best results.

Quick Assessment

Automatic
Configur-
ation
Concepts

1 _____ _____ is the process of updating the settings of the Internet Explorer 5 browser from a centrally located source file.

2 You can change settings on all your deployed IE5 browsers by altering the _____ file and having the browsers read the new configuration from this altered file.

Enabling
Automatic
Configuration

3 Enabling automatic configuration in the IEAK Customization Wizard causes the deployed IE5 browsers to periodically check a specified _____ to look for an updated .ins file.

4 _____ uses a centrally located JScript file to alter the proxy settings of the browser.

Editing .ins
Files

5 Some changes to the .ins file require that the IEAK create new _____ files.

6 Administrators must place .ins and .cab files at the _____ _____ _____ so that the deployed browsers can access the files.

Creating
Profiles and
Policies

7 The first time that you run the IEAK Customization Wizard or the Profile Manager, the system creates administration file templates (_____ files) that contain the Internet Explorer 5 settings and restrictions.

8 _____ _____ specify environment settings on a per-user basis.

9 Registry settings that control what settings the users can and cannot alter are called _____ _____.

10 You use the _____ _____ _____ to manage IE5 profiles and policies of previously configured custom browser packages.

Answers

1 *Automatic configuration.* See "Automatic Configuration Concepts."

2 *.ins.* See "Automatic Configuration Concepts."

3 *URL.* See "Enabling Automatic Configuration."

4 *Auto-proxy.* See "Enabling Automatic Configuration."

5 *.cab.* See "Editing .ins Files."

6 *automatic configuration URL.* See "Editing .ins Files."

7 *.adm.* See "Creating Profiles and Policies."

8 *User profiles.* See "Creating Profiles and Policies."

9 *system policies.* See "Creating Profiles and Policies."

10 *IEAK Profile Manager.* See "Creating Profiles and Policies."

Automatic Configuration Concepts

Automatic configuration is the process of updating the settings of the Internet Explorer 5 browser from a centrally located source file. When you run the IEAK Customization Wizard, it creates an instruction file (.ins file) that specifies the browser configuration settings that you select during the wizard. You can later change settings on all your deployed IE5 browsers by altering this .ins file and having the browser read the new configuration from this altered file. Or, you can create different .ins files for groups of users requiring specific configuration changes.

Enabling automatic configuration involves several steps:

- ✔ When initially creating the custom IE5 package with the IEAK Customization Wizard, check the box marked Enable automatic configuration on the Automatic Configuration screen.

- ✔ Use the IEAK Profile Manager to edit or create an .ins file with the updated configuration settings.

- ✔ Place the new .ins file in a network accessible location.

- ✔ At a specified interval, or when IE5 starts, the browser checks for a new configuration file and changes the browser settings according to the information in the file.

Enabling automatic configuration

Enabling automatic configuration in the IEAK Customization Wizard causes the deployed IE5 browsers to periodically check a specified URL to look for an updated .ins file. By including automatic configuration in the original IE5 browser package, you create automatic centralized management of all the deployed IE5 browsers.

Obviously, automatic configuration requires some advance planning. You must determine whether to use automatic configuration files before you create the custom package. And when you run the Customization Wizard, you need to know the URL for the location of the automatic configuration files. Figure 16-1 shows the Automatic Configuration screen of the Customization Wizard.

Don't confuse the auto-proxy configuration and the automatic browser configuration — they're two distinct settings. Auto-proxy uses a centrally located JScript file to alter only the proxy settings of the browser. The automatic configuration file, however, includes all possible settings for customizing the IE5 browser.

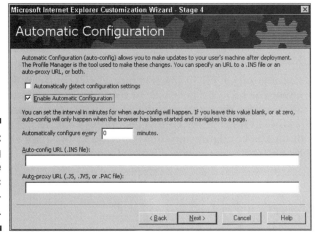

Figure 16-1:
Specifying
the
automatic
configura-
tion URL.

Use an auto-proxy script if you need to change only a proxy setting. Use an automatic configuration file when you change other settings in your custom browser.

The automatic configuration file can contain proxy settings as well as browser configuration settings. But the auto-proxy file contains only proxy setting information.

To enable automatic configuration, select the Enable Automatic Configuration check box, as shown in Figure 16-1. This provides access to the other settings on the screen, which remain grayed out unless you enable automatic configuration.

If your browser package changes often, configure the browser to check the auto configuration URL for an updated file at a specified time interval. In most cases, configuration changes are infrequent and you can leave the interval blank, or set it to zero. A blank or zero setting causes the system to check for a new auto configuration file each time that IE5 starts.

Examples of the type of events that may result in browser package configuration changes are:

✔ New mail servers or NetMeeting servers

✔ New URLs for download sites, search pages, or support pages

✔ Changes to security zones or security levels

✔ Adding components to a browser package

✔ Changes to graphics and logos

✔ Changing connection settings

✔ Adding/deleting favorites and links

I find it hard to believe that anyone would need to check for an updated configuration file every few minutes. But if that is the case, the IEAK enables you to configure the browser to do so.

At the bottom of the Automatic Configuration screen, you type the URL for the automatic configuration file in the text box labeled Auto-config URL. This is the location that the browser accesses to read new configuration settings from an .ins file. You also have the option to type a URL for an auto-proxy file in the text box labeled Auto-proxy URL. Again, don't confuse the auto-proxy file with the automatic configuration (.ins) file. You can specify either URL, you can specify both URLs, or you can leave them blank.

.ins Files: Powerful Magic!

Each time that you build a customized IE5 package by using the IEAK Customization wizard, the wizard generates a file called Install.ins. This .ins file contains all the configuration settings that you specified by using the wizard. After the .ins file is created, you can edit the file to change those configuration settings. Or, you can save an edited version of the file under a new name — thereby creating a different version of the customized browser.

Each .ins file creates an IEAK profile, also called a profile. An environment with multiple IE5 configurations has multiple .ins files, thus multiple profiles.

Locating Install.ins

The Install.ins file is located in the destination folder that you specified during the Information Gathering stage of the Customization wizard. I use the default settings when saving my customized packages, so my Install.ins file is located here:

```
C:\Builds\11231999\Ins\Win32\En
```

In the example above, 11231999 reflects the date that I built the package, Win32 shows that I distributed a 32-bit browser, and En demonstrates that I used an English language browser. Change the name of the destination folder to place the Install.ins file in a different path. For example, if IE5Ver1 is the destination folder, the path looks like this:

```
C:\IE5Ver1\11231999\Ins\Win32\En
```

Opening an .ins file

When you're ready to edit your original Install.ins file, start the IEAK Profile Manager and open the .ins file (see Figure 16-2). Until the file is open, all of the policies, restrictions and settings are grayed out in the Profile Manager window. Once the .ins file is open, you can select any of the settings, policies, or restrictions and view the settings you originally configured for your customized browser package.

You cannot run the IEAK Customization Wizard and the IEAK Profile Manager on your computer at the same time. You must close the Customization Wizard before you can start the Profile Manager.

Figure 16-2:
Loading the
Install.ins
file into the
Profile
Manager.

Editing .ins files

After you open the .ins file in the Profile Manager, you can alter any of the settings that are included in the customized browser package. For example, say that you created a customized IE5 browser package for the Windows 95 computers in your organization. But new computers shipped to you are preinstalled with Windows 2000, so now you want to create an IE5 browser package for the Windows 2000 platform.

Lab 16-1   Configuring an IE5 Browser Package for Windows 2000

1. **Start the IEAK Profile Manager and then choose File⇨Open to open the Install.ins file.**

2. **Once the .ins file is open, select the Profile Manager Platform menu. The drop-down menu lists the following platform options (as shown in Figure 16-3):**

    Windows 95/NT 4.0

    Windows 3.1/WFW/NT 3.51

    UNIX

    Windows 2000

Notice in Figure 16-3 that there is a check mark next to the Windows 95/NT 4.0 option. This indicates that this .ins file was created for the Windows 95/NT 4.0 platform.

3. Choose Windows 2000.

4. Save the .ins file with a new name.

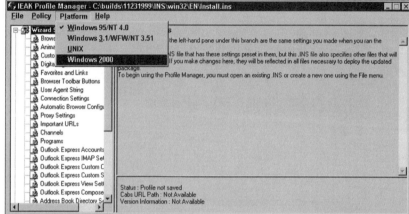

Figure 16-3:
Creating an .ins file for another platform.

Other changes to the .ins file are just as simple as Lab 16-1. You can modify any of the policies, restrictions, and settings of the .ins file by selecting a setting in the left pane of the Profile Manager window. The configurable options for the setting then display in the right pane of the window (see Figure 16-4). Configure the settings as needed; then save the .ins file with a new name.

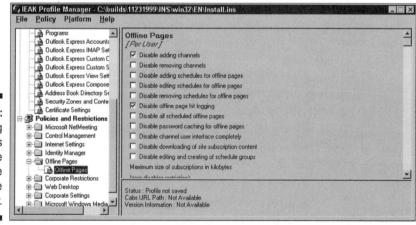

Figure 16-4:
Changing the settings in an .ins file by using the Profile Manager.

If you configured automatic configuration by using the IEAK Customization Wizard (see the preceding section), you can use the IEAK Profile Manager to create a new .ins file with browser configuration changes. If, for example, you need to change the names of the mail servers, you can use the Profile Manager to edit the .ins file to reflect the new names, as shown in Figure 16-5.

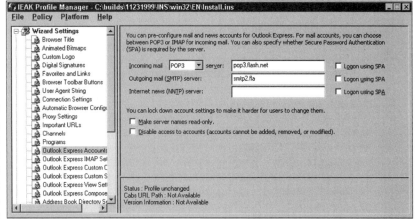

Figure 16-5:
Using
Profile
Manager to
edit the
.ins file.

After you edit the .ins file, save it with a new filename. Some changes to the .ins file require that new .cab files be created. The IEAK Profile Manager recognizes these situations and creates the files when you save the new .ins file. (If the changes to the .ins file don't require new .cab files, none are created.) Specify the location for the new .cab files, as shown in Figure 16-6. You must specify the location from which the .cab files are to be installed because the .cab file location is contained in the .ins file.

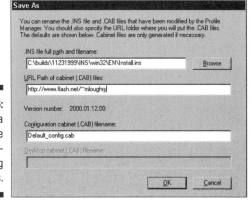

Figure 16-6:
Creating a
new .ins file
and corre-
sponding
.cab files.

Once the .ins file and .cab files are in place at the automatic configuration URL, browsers automatically access these files and are reconfigured according to the new .ins file settings.

Creating Profiles and Policies

Perhaps you're familiar with system policies and user profiles as they're used in Windows NT domains. System administrators use these files to manage user configurations and restrictions throughout a domain. By controlling user settings and restrictions with profiles and policies, you greatly limit the number of support calls to your help desk. You can also use profiles and policies to manage your deployed Internet Explorer 5 browser package.

Below is a brief review of profiles, policies, and logon scripts:

- **User profiles:** Specify environment settings on a per-user basis. These settings are made up of desktop and environment settings that the user has configured and the system policies that determine which settings are available to users.

- **System policies:** Registry settings that control what settings the users can and cannot access.

- **Logon scripts:** A series of commands that execute at logon and further define the user environment. For example, a logon script can start an application at logon.

The first time that you run the IEAK Customization Wizard or the Profile Manager, the system creates administration file templates (.adm files) that contain the Internet Explorer 5 settings and restrictions. (Figure 16-7 shows the .adm files created when I initially ran the Customization Wizard.) When you create a new IE5 package, the information from these .adm template files is read into the Customization Wizard, where you select parameters for the settings.

Figure 16-7:
Exploring the .adm files in the Internet Explorer Administration Kit.

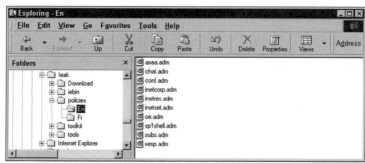

The Customization Wizard saves these settings and restrictions in .inf files that correspond to each of the .adm files, then packages the .inf files into .cab files. The deployed IE5 browsers download the .cab files along with the .ins file to reconfigure the browser. Figure 16-8 illustrates the use of .adm files to create policy and .cab files.

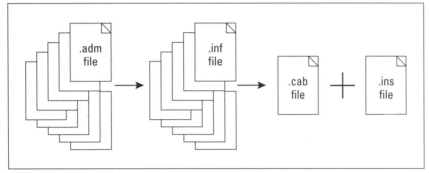

Figure 16-8:
The Custom-
ization
Wizard
creates .ins
and .cab
files from
.adm files.

You use the IEAK Profile Manager to manage IE5 profiles and policies. Profile Manager enables you to edit all previously configured settings, including system policies and restrictions. You do this by editing an .ins file, or by importing policy (.adm) files into Profile Manager and creating new .ins files from them.

You can create multiple profiles for different users in your organization by editing .ins files with Profile Manager. Begin by creating a custom package with the Customization Wizard. Then use Profile Manager to create additional profiles by modifying the .ins file of the original package — saving the .ins file with a new name each time. You can then distribute multiple versions of an IE5 package to different users and groups by assigning these new profiles to individual users and groups.

Prep Test

1 What type of browser package configuration changes would indicate creating a new automatic configuration file?

A ❑ The proxy server's name has changed.

B ❑ The port number for the FTP protocol has changed on the company proxy server.

C ❑ There are new URLs for download sites, search pages, or support pages.

D ❑ The connection settings have changed.

2 What type of browser package configuration changes would indicate creating a new auto-proxy script file?

A ❑ The proxy server's name has changed.

B ❑ The port number for the FTP protocol has changed on the company proxy server.

C ❑ There are new URLs for download sites, search pages, or support pages.

D ❑ The connection settings have changed.

3 May is a corporate administrator at a large firm. She created a custom browser package using the IEAK. The package included an automatic configuration URL. Now May has made changes to the browser package. What file(s) does May need to place at the automatic configuration URL to enable automatic configuration to work?

A ❑ .adm files

B ❑ .inf files

C ❑ .cab files

D ❑ .ins file

4 Bob is a corporate administrator and has created a custom browser package that is deployed to his user community. When he created the custom browser, he included both auto-proxy and automatic configuration URLs. Bob is preparing to install a new proxy server for the company. He knows that he must create a new auto-proxy file. What else does Bob need to do to make the proxy configuration change?

A ○ Copy the new auto-proxy file to the auto-config URL.

B ○ Copy the new auto-proxy file to the auto-proxy URL.

C ○ Copy the new .ins file to the auto-proxy URL.

D ○ Copy the new .ins file to the auto-config URL.

5 Which of the following steps are required to enable automatic browser configuration of a custom IE5 package?

A ❑ Copy .ins file to the automatic configuration URL.

B ❑ During the IEAK Customization Wizard, enable automatic configuration.

C ❑ Enter an automatic configuration URL while running the Customization Wizard.

D ❑ Copy the .cab files to the automatic configuration URL.

Answers

1 *A, B, C, and D.* All the changes listed would create the need for a new automatic configuration file. The files placed at the auto-config URL are the .ins and .cab files created by running the IEAK. Since all of the settings listed above are included in the .ins and .cab files, all or any of them would indicate the need for a changed browser configuration. *Review "Enabling Automatic Configuration."*

2 *A and B.* Only the proxy configuration settings are included in an auto-proxy script. Although the automatic configuration files can include changes to proxy settings, the auto-proxy script file contains only proxy related information. *Review "Enabling Automatic Configuration."*

3 *C and D. .cab files and .ins file.* The Customization Wizard saves settings and restrictions in .inf files that correspond to each of the .adm file templates, then packages the .inf files into .cab files. The deployed IE5 browsers download the .cab files along with the .ins file to reconfigure the browser. Answers A and B are incorrect because only the .cab and .ins files need be placed at the automatic configuration URL. *See "Editing .ins Files."*

4 *B.* Copy the new auto-proxy file to the auto-proxy URL. To change proxy settings using an auto-proxy file, the file must be copied to the auto-proxy URL. In contrast, .ins and .cab files are copied to the auto-config URL. *See "Enabling Automatic Configuration."*

5 *A, B, C, and D.* All of the answers listed are steps in the process of enabling automatic configuration for a custom browser. *Review "Enabling Automatic Configuration."*

Chapter 17

Zoning Out! (Configuring Security Zones)

Exam Objectives

▶ Reviewing standard security zones
▶ Creating new security zones
▶ Assigning security levels

*W*ould any discussion of an Internet technology be complete without discussing security? I think not!

Nefarious minds (I've always wanted to use that word!) are creating applets, scripts, and viruses whose sole purpose is to wreak havoc on your computer. At the very least, they give you a major headache. At their worst, they destroy data.

The truth about Internet security is this: If you proceed with caution, you can safely enjoy many of the conveniences that the Internet has to offer. Fortunately, Internet Explorer 5 has many security features to help you safeguard your users and still let them access the Net. In this chapter, I help you understand and configure appropriate security strategies.

Quick Assessment

Under-
standing
Security
Zones

1 The four default security zones of Internet Explorer 5 are: _____ zone, _____ zone, _____ zone, and _____ zone.

2 Each zone has a different level of security, with the _____ zone having the most stringent settings, and the _____ zone having the least restrictive settings.

3 The four security levels associated with all security zones are: _____, _____, _____, and _____.

4 To enable users to access full browser features while maintaining some degree of safety, select the _____ security level.

Internet
Zone

5 The default security level for the Internet zone is _____.

Local
Intranet
Zone

6 The default security level for the Local Intranet zone is _____.

7 Sites on your corporate intranet should be added to the _____ zone.

Restricted
Sites Zone

8 When using the _____ level security setting, the ActiveX, Java, and scripting features on Web sites are disabled and do not work correctly.

Adding Web
Sites to a
Zone

9 If a Web site contains content that you don't trust, add it to the _____ zone.

10 When you're accessing a site, the _____ _____ _____ is displayed in the bottom-right corner of the browser window.

Answers

1 *Internet, Local Intranet, Restricted Sites, Trusted Sites.* See "Understanding Security Zones."

2 *Restricted Sites, Trusted Sites.* See "Understanding Security Zones."

3 *High, Medium, Medium-Low, Low.* See "Understanding Security Zones."

4 *Medium.* See "Understanding Security Zones."

5 *Medium.* See "Internet zone."

6 *Medium-Low.* See "Local Intranet zone."

7 *Local Intranet.* See "Local Intranet zone."

8 *High.* See "Restricted Sites zone."

9 *Restricted Sites.* See "Adding Web Sites to a Zone."

10 *security zone status.* See "Adding Web Sites to a Zone."

Understanding Security Zones

As a system administrator, you're required to appropriately configure security levels and security zones for custom IE5 packages. (This is true for the test and in the field!) Using the IEAK, you create a custom package with the security configuration that meets the requirements of your organization. After you configure the security levels and zones, you can use the IEAK policies and restrictions (in the Customization wizard or the Profile Manager) to lock down the security configuration so that users can't alter it. The information in this section will help you to determine the appropriate security zones and levels for a custom package.

Internet Explorer 5 is preconfigured with four default security zones, as shown in Figure 17-1:

- ✔ Internet zone
- ✔ Local Intranet zone
- ✔ Trusted Sites zone
- ✔ Restricted Sites zone

Each zone has a different level of security, with the Restricted Sites zone having the most stringent settings, and the Trusted Sites zone having the least restrictive settings.

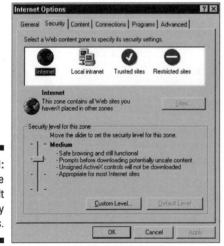

Figure 17-1:
Viewing the
default
security
zones.

You can modify the security setting of a zone by moving a slide bar up (higher security) and down (lower security). The four security levels associated with the slide bar are:

✔ High

✔ Medium

✔ Medium-Low

✔ Low

You can also click the Custom Level button near the bottom of the screen. This takes you to the Security Settings window (see Figure 17-2), where you can enable and disable features to customize security settings so that they're appropriate for your users. Through the Default Level button, you can reset the security settings to the default configuration if you have altered them.

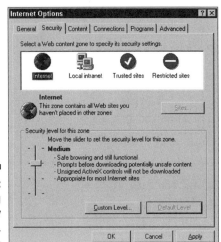

Figure 17-2:
Customizing
security
settings.

For the exam, know the default settings for each of the four security zones. You need to examine all the options for each of the security settings so that you can identify the correct settings when they're described in a scenario question on the exam.

Internet zone

The Internet zone includes all the sites on the Internet, excluding those that you've placed into one of the other zones. The default security level for the Internet zone is Medium security, and is set as follows:

- ✔ Download signed ActiveX controls: Prompt
- ✔ Download unsigned ActiveX controls: Disable
- ✔ Initialize and script ActiveX controls not marked as safe: Disable
- ✔ Run ActiveX controls and plug-ins: Enable
- ✔ Script ActiveX controls marked safe for scripting: Enable
- ✔ Allow cookies that are stored on your computer: Enable
- ✔ Allow per-session cookies (not stored): Enable
- ✔ File download: Enable
- ✔ Font download: Enable
- ✔ Java permissions: High safety
- ✔ Access data sources across domains: Disable
- ✔ Drag-and-drop or copy and paste files: Enable
- ✔ Installation of desktop items: Prompt
- ✔ Launching programs and files in an IFRAME: Prompt
- ✔ Navigate sub-frames across different domains: Enable
- ✔ Software channel permissions: Medium safety
- ✔ Submit nonencrypted form data: Prompt
- ✔ Userdata persistence: Enable
- ✔ Active scripting: Enable
- ✔ Allow paste operations via script: Enable
- ✔ Scripting of Java applets: Enable
- ✔ Logon: Automatic logon only in Intranet zone

You can customize the Internet zone security settings to make them lower or higher. I recommend that you not change them at all, unless you increase the security level. Weakening the security on the Internet zone can enable users to inadvertently download and run malicious content.

Local Intranet zone

The Local Intranet zone includes sites on your local area network. You can usually feel comfortable that sites on your private network are safe. For this reason, the security level is set to Medium-Low (see Figure 17-3). This is similar to the Medium level, but runs most content without prompts.

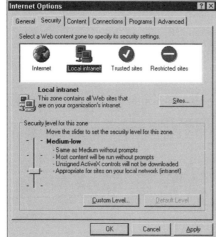

Figure 17-3:
Viewing
Local
Intranet
security
levels.

Medium-Low level security is configured as follows:

- Download signed ActiveX controls: Prompt
- Download unsigned ActiveX controls: Disable
- Initialize and script ActiveX controls not marked as safe: Disable
- Run ActiveX controls and plug-ins: Enable
- Script ActiveX controls marked safe for scripting: Enable
- Allow cookies that are stored on your computer: Enable
- Allow per-session cookies (not stored): Enable
- File download: Enable
- Font download: Enable
- Java permissions: Medium safety
- Access data sources across domains: Prompt

✔ Drag-and-drop or copy and paste files: Enable

✔ Installation of desktop items: Prompt

✔ Launching programs and files in an IFRAME: Prompt

✔ Navigate sub-frames across different domains: Enable

✔ Software channel permissions: Medium safety

✔ Submit nonencrypted form data: Enable

✔ Userdata persistence: Enable

✔ Active scripting: Enable

✔ Allow paste operations via script: Enable

✔ Scripting of Java applets: Enable

✔ Logon: Automatic logon only in Intranet zone

I never recommend weakening these security levels. But if your private network is protected by a firewall and you're totally comfortable that all the content on your sites is safe, you can weaken the security settings if you choose.

Trusted Sites zone

The Trusted Sites zone consists of Web sites that you add to a list of sites that you feel confident can be trusted. Only sites that you're absolutely certain that you can trust should go into this zone! The default security level is Low (see Figure 17-4), allowing you to freely run ActiveX content and download files. The configuration settings for the Trusted Sites zone are:

✔ Download signed ActiveX controls: Enable

✔ Download unsigned ActiveX controls: Prompt

✔ Initialize and script ActiveX controls not marked as safe: Prompt

✔ Run ActiveX controls and plug-ins: Enable

✔ Script ActiveX controls marked safe for scripting: Enable

✔ Allow cookies that are stored on your computer: Enable

✔ Allow per-session cookies (not stored): Enable

✔ File download: Enable

✔ Font download: Enable

✔ Java permissions: Low safety

✔ Access data sources across domains: Enable

✔ Drag-and-drop or copy and paste files: Enable

✔ Installation of desktop items: Enable

✔ Launching programs and files in an IFRAME: Enable

✔ Navigate sub-frames across different domains: Enable

✔ Software channel permissions: Low safety

✔ Submit nonencrypted form data: Enable

✔ Userdata persistence: Enable

✔ Active scripting: Enable

✔ Allow paste operations via script: Enable

✔ Scripting of Java applets: Enable

✔ Logon: Automatic logon with current username and password

Be certain that you're familiar with configuration options for User Authentication, Java permissions, and ActiveX controls and plug-ins. These differ from the typical Disable/Enable/Prompt choices and may appear on your exam.

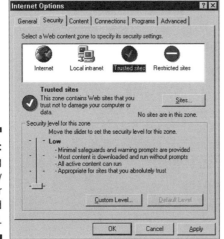

Figure 17-4:
Viewing security settings for the Trusted Sites zone.

Restricted Sites Zone

Restricted sites (see Figure 17-5) are those that you don't want to trust. For some reason, you feel reluctant to allow users to download information or run scripts from these locations. These sites justify the High security level, which is configured as follows:

- Download signed ActiveX controls: Disable
- Download unsigned ActiveX controls: Disable
- Initialize and script ActiveX controls not marked as safe: Disable
- Run ActiveX controls and plug-ins: Disable
- Script ActiveX controls marked safe for scripting: Enable
- Allow cookies that are stored on your computer: Disable
- Allow per-session cookies (not stored): Disable
- File download: Disable
- Font download: Prompt
- Java permissions: High safety
- Access data sources across domains: Disable
- Drag-and-drop or copy and paste files: Prompt
- Installation of desktop items: Disable
- Launching programs and files in an IFRAME: Disable
- Navigate sub-frames across different domains: Enable
- Software channel permissions: High safety
- Submit nonencrypted form data: Prompt
- Userdata persistence: Disable
- Active scripting: Enable
- Allow paste operations via script: Disable
- Scripting of Java applets: Disable
- Logon: Prompt for username and password

Anytime you're uncertain about a site's content, add it to the Restricted Sites zone. This still allows users access to the site, but prevents them from unintentionally accessing malicious content.

When using the High level security setting, the ActiveX, Java, and scripting features on Web sites are disabled and do not work correctly.

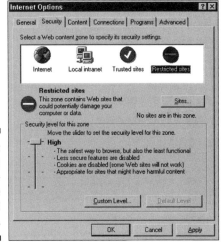

Figure 17-5:
Viewing
security set-
tings for the
Restricted
Sites zone.

Adding Web Sites to a Zone

In the "Internet zone" section earlier in this chapter, I told you that the
Internet zone consists of all the sites on the Internet, excluding those that
you've placed into one of the other zones. Although you can't add Web sites
to the Internet zone, you *can* add sites to each of the other three zones.

For example, if you know of a site that is absolutely trustworthy and you
don't want users to be prompted while accessing content on that site, you
can add it to the Trusted Sites zone. Similarly, if a Web site contains content
that you don't trust, add it to the Restricted Sites zone. You can also add sites
to the Local Intranet zone, but you cannot add sites to the Internet zone.

Internet Explorer 5 autodetects Internet and intranet Web sites. Pages in the
Trusted Sites and Restricted Sites zones are identified according to the sites
you add to their lists. When you're accessing a site, the security zone status
is displayed in the bottom-right corner of the browser window.

Lab 17-1 takes you through the steps of adding a site to a security zone. In
this exercise, you are to add two Web sites — www.idgbooks.com and
www.dummies.com — to your Trusted Sites zone.

Lab 17-1   Adding Web Sites to a Security Zone

1. **After opening the IE5 browser, choose Tools⇨Internet Options. Click
   the Security tab.**

2. **Click the Trusted Sites icon, and then click the Sites button. This
   brings up the Trusted sites window.**

3. **In Add this Web Site to the Zone text box, type** www.dummies.com.

4. **Click the Add button.**

   This adds www.dummies.com to the text box labeled Web sites.

5. **Now type** www.idgbooks.com **in the Add this Web Site to the Zone text box. (Your configuration looks like Figure 17-6.)**

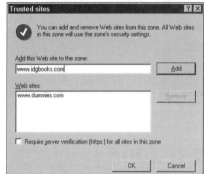

Figure 17-6: Adding Web sites to a security zone.

6. **Click the Add button.**

   Both Web sites are now included in the Trusted Sites zone, and can be accessed using Low level security.

7. **Click OK to close the Trusted Sites window.**

8. **Click OK to close the Internet Options window.**

Altering Security Levels

Sometimes the default security levels aren't exactly right for your user community. In these situations, you can adjust the individual security settings for a zone to more closely match your needs.

You can weaken the security settings for the Internet and Restricted Sites zones, but I strongly discourage you from doing so! Always put safety of data and corporate resources ahead of convenience while accessing the Internet.

Suppose you want to alter the security configuration for your Local Intranet zone. You can simply move the slide bar on the Local Intranet options screen (see Figure 17-3) to the Low security level. Or, you could use the Custom Level button to access the individual settings for the zone.

Altering the individual settings gives you flexibility in selecting the right security measures for your organization. For example, perhaps you want to permit users to download unsigned ActiveX controls on your intranet sites. Changing the security level to Low weakens security too much, because it changes more than just the ActiveX controls settings. Instead, you configure a Custom Level by simply changing the Download Unsigned ActiveX Controls setting to Enable. Lab 17-2 below shows you how to make this configuration change.

Lab 17-2   Customizing Security Levels

1. **Choose Tools⇨Internet Options.**

2. **Click the Security tab, and then select the Local intranet icon.**

3. **Click the Custom Level button to access the Security Settings window.**

4. **Under Download Unsigned ActiveX Controls, click the Enable radio button.**

5. **Click OK to close the Security Settings window.**

6. **Click OK to close the Internet Options window.**

Prep Test

1 Ann is a corporate administrator preparing a custom IE5 browser package. She wants to make certain that users can take advantage of IE5 active content features on Web sites that are safe. What steps should she take to configure security for this purpose? (Choose all that apply.)

A ❑ Configure the browser to prompt before running active content on Internet sites.

B ❑ Add the known safe sites to the Trusted Sites zone.

C ❑ Add the safe sites to the Local Intranet zone.

D ❑ Change the security level on the Internet zone to Low.

2 Ann is a corporate administrator and is preparing a custom IE5 package for users at her company. Security is a primary consideration at the company, and she wants to take no chances on users being affected by malicious content. Ann wants to prevent users from downloading and running ActiveX content from Internet sites. Which security level should she select for the Internet zone?

A ○ Low

B ○ Medium-Low

C ○ Medium

D ○ High

3 Ann has created a custom IE5 package for her corporation. Before she deploys the package, she wants to make certain that users will not be able to change the security levels she has configured for the IE5 browser. What tool should Ann use to prevent users from altering the browser's security configuration?

A ○ IEAK Security Configurator

B ○ IEAK Customization wizard

C ○ IEAK Profile Manager

D ○ IEAK Toolkit

4 Ann created a custom IE5 package with the High security level for Internet sites. Users are complaining that they can't take advantage of site cookies to customize the content that they access at various Internet sites. How can Ann let users download cookies without further weakening the security level?

- A ○ Ann cannot make this change without changing to another security level for the Internet zone.
- B ○ Ann can customize the security level to enable downloading and storing cookies without altering other security policies or other zones.
- C ○ Ann must change from the High to the Medium security level in the Internet zone.
- D ○ Ann must add the sites with cookies to the Trusted Sites zone.

5 Paul is the system administrator at a large corporation. Some of the users at Paul's company routinely access a business partner's Web site throughout the day. The users complain about being prompted before every action they take on the partner's Web site. What security zone should Paul place the business partner's Web site into?

- A ○ Restricted Sites zone
- B ○ Internet zone
- C ○ Local Intranet zone
- D ○ Trusted Sites zone

6 Paul is a corporate administrator at a large corporation. He knows that some users have complained of receiving malicious content from a Web site that they accessed. What actions should Paul take to prevent users from accessing damaging content from this site? (Choose all that apply.)

- A ❑ Add the site to the Restricted Sites zone.
- B ❑ Change the Internet zone security level to High.
- C ❑ Use the IEAK Profile Manager to restrict users from adding or deleting sites from a security zone.
- D ❑ Use the IEAK Profile Manager to restrict users from altering the security policies of security zones.

Answers

1 *A and B.* Answer C is incorrect because the only sites appropriate for the Local Intranet zone are those within Ann's own organization. Answer D is incorrect because a Low security level on the Internet zone will permit unrestricted access to potentially harmful content. *Review "Adding Web Sites to a Zone" and "Altering Security Levels."*

2 *D.* The High security level disables downloading and running ActiveX content. The default setting for the Internet zone is Medium, which enables users to run some ActiveX content after being prompted. Answers A, B, and C are all incorrect because the ActiveX settings are too permissive. *Review "Internet zone."*

3 *C.* Because Ann has already created the custom browser package, she should use the IEAK Profile Manager to edit the package .ins file. Answer B is not correct because the Customization wizard is used to create a package, and Ann has already created her package. Answer A is not a legitimate tool. Answer D is incorrect because the IEAK Toolkit doesn't enable you to make changes to a custom package. *Review "Understanding Security Zones."*

4 *B.* By clicking the Custom Level button on the Internet Options Security tab, Ann can enable cookies without affecting any of the other policies for this zone, or the policies of any other zone. Changing the security level or adding the sites to the Trusted Sites zone would excessively weaken the browser security. Therefore, answers A, C, and D are incorrect answers. *Review "Understanding Security Zones."*

5 *D.* Because the users access the content on this page frequently and it is required for their work, Paul should place the site in the Trusted Sites zone. *Review "Understanding Security Zones."*

6 *A, C, and D.* If Paul only adds the site to the Restricted Sites zone, users can still access content at this site by removing the site from the zone on their browser. If he doesn't want users to be able to alter his configuration, Paul must also select actions C and D. Changing the Internet zone's security level to High (answer B) also restricts access to content at all other Internet sites. Answer B, therefore, isn't an appropriate action. *Review "Adding Web Sites to a Zone."*

Chapter 18

Automating Connection Settings

• •

Exam Objectives

▶ Using Jscript configuration files

▶ Configuring connection settings with .ins files

▶ Using policy templates (.adm files) to configure connection settings

• •

1 don't believe that any task is more commonly repeated by system admin- istrators than troubleshooting connection settings. Users are continually altering their dial-up or Internet connection settings, only to be unable to remember the original configuration. Then too, organizations frequently change their access methods, creating the need to reconfigure connection settings on a multitude of workstations.

Fortunately, the Internet Explorer Administration Kit includes several tools that you can use to automatically configure (or reconfigure) the connection settings for a deployed browser. In this chapter, I tell you how to use auto- matic configuration files to manage connection settings.

Quick Assessment

Reviewing Automatic Configuration Methods

1 _____ _____ enables you to make changes to a custom browser after it's been deployed.

2 If your proxy configuration changes frequently, a _____ file may be the most efficient method of managing connection settings. For more static environments, editing the _____ file is probably the best choice.

Using .adm Templates

3 _____ files are templates that contain system policy settings.

4 The IEAK _____ wizard uses .adm template files to create the .ins and .cab files required for a custom browser installation.

5 The customized parameters selected during the Customization wizard are saved as _____ files, which are then compacted into _____ files for easy download.

Creating .ins Files

6 The easiest way to include the various connection settings that your organization requires is to create them on your build computer and then _____ them into the package during the Customization wizard.

7 Leaving the update interval blank or set to zero causes the system to check for a new configuration file _____.

8 You can edit the _____ file of the custom package to alter the connection settings after the package is created and deployed.

Using Jscript Auto-proxy Files

9 The file extension of an auto-proxy file can be _____, _____, or _____.

10 Both Jscript and auto-proxy URLs are entered on the _____ _____ screen of the Customization wizard.

Answers

1   *Automatic configuration.* See "Reviewing Automatic Configuration Methods."

2   *Jscript, .ins.* See "Reviewing Automatic Configuration Methods."

3   *.adm.* See "Using .adm templates."

4   *Customization.* See "Using .adm templates."

5   *.inf, .cab.* See "Using .adm templates."

6   *import.* See "Creating .ins files."

7   *each time IE5 is started.* See "Creating .ins files."

8   *.ins.* See "Creating .ins files."

9   *.js, .jvs, or .pac.* See "Using Jscript auto-proxy files."

10 *Automatic Configuration.* See "Using Jscript auto-proxy files."

Reviewing Automatic Configuration Methods

Automatic configuration enables you to make changes to a custom browser after it's been deployed. You can set up automatic configuration of connections in a couple of ways:

- ✔ **You can use a Jscript file to specify a proxy configuration.** By placing the script file in a network accessible location, browsers can access the script file and obtain up-to-date proxy settings.

- ✔ **You can use the .ins file created with the IEAK to automatically change the proxy configurations in your organization.** If your proxy configuration changes frequently, a Jscript may be the most efficient method of managing connection settings. For more static environments, editing the .ins file is probably the best choice.

Regardless of the method you use, automatic configuration of connection settings is a huge advantage for the user community. By including preconfigured connections, the user is saved the task of struggling with these configurations. And the system administrator is saved dozens of potential help desk calls.

Using .adm templates

In Chapter 16, I explain how the Customization wizard uses .adm template files to create the .ins and .cab files required for a custom browser installation. To briefly review, .adm files are templates that contain system policy settings. The Customization wizard reads the settings contained in the .adm files and presents them to the system administrator to choose configuration parameters. The customized parameters selected during the wizard are saved as .inf files, which are then compacted into .cab files for easy download.

Some of the system policies and restrictions contained in the .adm files deal with connection settings and proxy settings. System administrators can lock down the connection settings so that users cannot alter them, as shown in Figure 18-1.

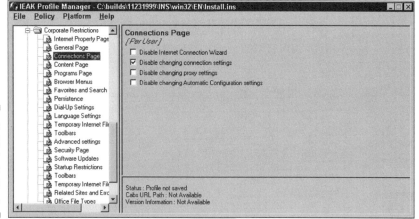

Figure 18-1:
Locking
down set-
tings with
system
policies.

Creating .ins files

When you run the Customization wizard, you're presented with options for configuring connection settings in your custom package. The easiest way to include the various connection settings that your organization requires is to create them on your build computer and then import them into the package during the Customization wizard. You can also edit the .ins file of the custom package to alter the connection settings after the package is created and deployed (see Figure 18-2).

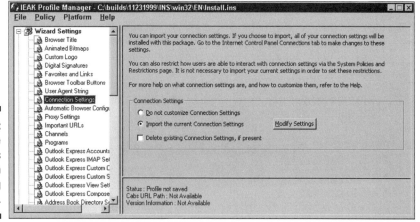

Figure 18-2:
Editing the
.ins file's
connection
setting
parameters.

After the .ins file contains the desired connection settings, place the .ins file at the URL you specified when you configured automatic configuration. In Chapter 16, I provide specific instructions on setting up automatic configuration. As a refresher, look at Figure 18-3.

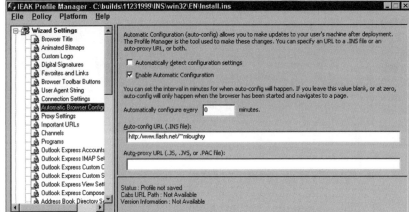

Figure 18-3:
Configuring
automatic
browser
configura-
tion.

As you see in the figure, first you select the Enable Automatic Configuration check box. Then you specify an update interval (leaving the interval blank or set to zero causes the system to check for a new configuration file each time IE5 is started) and a URL for the configuration file. Finally, the last text box on the screen enables you to enter the location for an auto-proxy script, which lets you automatically change proxy settings from one central location.

For the exam, know what steps are required to enable automatic browser configuration. You're likely to see a scenario question that asks you to indicate all the steps necessary to enable automatic configuration of connection settings.

Lab 18-1 below is an example of configuring automatic browser configuration for connection settings. Please follow along and complete the lab.

Lab 18-1   Automating Connection Settings

You're the system administrator for a large corporation and have deployed a custom version of IE5. You want to update the deployed browsers to include the settings for a dial-up connection. When users dial in, they don't use a proxy server to access the Internet. When users access the Internet from the LAN, however, they must use a proxy configuration.

1. Using the IEAK Profile Manager, open the .ins file of your custom browser package.

2. Under the wizard Settings, select Connection Settings in the left pane of the Profile Manager.

3. In the right pane, select Import the current Connection Settings.

4. Click the Modify Settings button.

5. In the Internet Properties Screen, click the Add button next to Dial-up Settings.

6. On the Make New Connection screen, enter Office in the text box for the connection name. Select your modem from the drop-down list under Select a device. Click Next.

7. Enter the area code, telephone number, and country code in the appropriate text boxes on the Telephone Number screen. Click Next.

8. On the Internet Properties screen, select the Office Dial-Up Setting that you just created. Then click the Settings button.

9. On the Office Settings screen (shown in Figure 18-4), select the Use Automatic Configuration Script check box. Enter the URL for your automatic configuration file in the Address text box. Make sure that the Use a Proxy Server check box is deselected. Click OK to return to the Internet Properties screen.

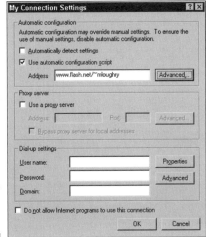

Figure 18-4:
Configuring
the auto-
matic con-
figuration
files for
a dial-up
connection.

10. Near the bottom of the Internet Properties screen, click the LAN Settings button.

11. On the LAN Settings screen, configure automatic browser configuration just as you did in Step 10. Select the Use a Proxy Server check box and enter the address and port number of your proxy server. Click OK to return to the Internet Properties screen.

12. On the Internet Properties screen, click OK to return to the Profile Manager.

13. In the Profile Manager, choose File⇨Save As. On the Save As screen, enter a new name for the altered .ins file. Enter the URL for the .cab files. Click OK to save the file.

14. Copy the new .ins file to the automatic configuration URL that you specified for the package.

Using Jscript auto-proxy files

Configuring an auto-proxy file is similar to configuring an automatic configuration file. In fact, both files are specified on the same screen of the Customization wizard (shown in Figure 18-5). Enter the path to the auto-proxy file in the Auto-proxy URL box at the bottom of the screen.

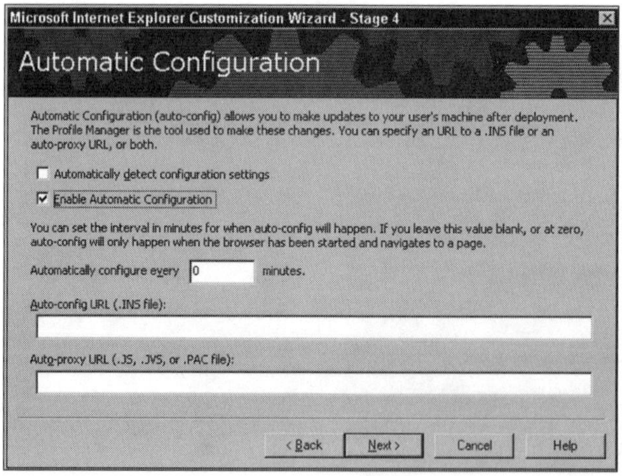

Figure 18-5: Configuring an auto-proxy URL.

After you configure the browser to use an auto-proxy file, the next step is to create the file! The auto-proxy file is a text file containing Jscript code that specifies how the browser accesses the Internet. The file extension can be .js, .jvs, or .pac (.pac files are recognized by Netscape browsers).

For the exam, you won't be asked questions about the Jscript code. Instead, know the steps necessary to configure automatic proxy configuration.

The example below shows the Jscript code necessary to configure my browser to use `proxy1.mrl.com`, port 80 as the proxy setting.

```
function FindProxyForURL(url, host) {
    if (isResolvable(host))
    return "DIRECT";
        else
            return "PROXY proxy1.mrl.com:80";
        }
```

Save the above code as a file with the .js, .jvs, or .pac file extension and place the file at the URL indicated on the automatic browser configuration screen.

Prep Test

1 Pam is the system administrator for a large corporation and is preparing a custom version of IE5. After creating the custom package, she finds that there is an additional connection that she should also deploy to the users. Which IEAK tool should Pam use to include the additional connection?

A ○ Connection Manager Administration Kit

B ○ IEAK Profile Manager

C ○ IEAK Customization wizard

D ○ IEAK Toolkit

2 Pam is the system administrator for a large corporation and has deployed a custom version of IE5 that included an auto-proxy script. Now Pam must change the proxy configuration for all the deployed browsers. How can Pam best make this change on all the deployed browsers?

A ○ Use the IEAK to modify the proxy configuration and redistribute the browser to all users.

B ○ Use the IEAK to modify the auto-proxy script and redistribute the browser to all users.

C ○ Use a text editor to modify the auto-proxy script and place the new script at the auto-proxy URL.

D ○ Use a text editor to modify the auto-proxy script and place the new script at the automatic configuration URL.

3 Pam wants to include an auto-proxy script in her custom IE5 package. What steps must she take to configure the auto-proxy script while running the Customization wizard? (Choose all that apply.)

A ❑ On the Automatic Configuration screen, check the Enable Automatic Configuration check box.

B ❑ On the Automatic Configuration screen, check the Enable Auto-Proxy check box.

C ❑ Enter a URL in the Auto-Proxy URL text box of the Automatic Configuration screen.

D ❑ Enter a URL in the Automatic Configuration URL text box of the Automatic Configuration screen.

4 Pam is configuring a custom browser package to include automatic configuration. She sets the auto-config interval to 0 minutes. How often will the browser check for a new auto-config file?

A ○ Never.

B ○ At the default interval of 10 minutes.

C ○ The browser will continually check for a new auto-config file.

D ○ Each time the browser is started and navigates to a page.

5 Pam is creating a custom IE5 package by using the IEAK Customization wizard. She plans to include two connections that are already configured on her build machine. What is the easiest way to include these connections in the custom IE5 package that she distributes to her users?

A ○ She can import the connections on the build machine into the package by using the Customization wizard.

B ○ She cannot include connections in a custom IE5 package.

C ○ She can import the connections by using the Connection Manager Administration Kit.

D ○ Pam must recreate the connections on each workstation.

6 Pam has configured a custom IE5 package to include an auto-proxy script. Now the corporate proxy configuration has changed, and Pam must change the script file. What file extensions are valid for the new file Pam places at the auto-proxy URL? (Choose all that apply.)

A ❑ .txt

B ❑ .js

C ❑ .jvs

D ❑ .pac

7 Jenni is a corporate administrator for a corporation that has grown to over 500 users. Much of her day is spent troubleshooting connection settings on users' IE5 browsers. Jenni wants to create a custom IE5 package that will prevent users from altering their connection settings. Which is the best option for achieving Jenni's goal?

A ○ Disable Internet Connection wizard.

B ○ Disable changing connection settings.

C ○ Disable changing proxy settings.

D ○ Disable changing Automatic Configuration settings.

8 Jenni is a corporate administrator creating a custom IE5 package. What steps must Jenni take to include automatic browser configuration in the IE5 package? (Choose all that apply.)

A ❑ Enable Automatic Configuration.

B ❑ Create a JScript auto-proxy file.

C ❑ Specify an auto-config URL.

D ❑ Place modified .ins and .cab files at the auto-config URL.

Answers

1 *B.* After a custom package is created, you use the IEAK Profile Manager to modify the package. Answer C is incorrect because the IEAK Customization wizard creates the custom browser package. Answers A and D are incorrect because the Connection Manager Administration Kit and the IEAK Toolkit are not used to modify a custom browser package. *Review "Creating .ins files."*

2 *C.* Answer A works, but it is not the best way to make this change because the auto-proxy script is already configured. Answer B is incorrect because the IEAK doesn't modify auto-proxy scripts. Answer D is incorrect because the auto-proxy script must be placed at the auto-proxy URL. *See "Using Jscript auto-proxy files."*

3 *A and C.* Answer B is not a legitimate option on the Automatic Configurations screen. Answer D is not correct because the auto-proxy script must be entered in the Auto-Proxy URL text box, not the Automatic Configuration URL text box. *Review "Using Jscript auto-proxy files."*

4 *D.* By default, setting the auto-config interval to 0 minutes causes the browser to check for a new auto-config file at startup. Therefore, A, B, and C are incorrect answers. *See "Creating .ins files."*

5 *A.* Answers B and D are incorrect because Pam can import the settings from the build machine into her custom package while running the IEAK Customization wizard. Answer C is incorrect because the Connection Manager Administration Kit is not the correct tool for importing connections into a custom package. *See "Creating .ins files."*

6 *B, C, and D.* Although you can edit a script file by using any text editor, .txt is not a valid auto-proxy file extension. *Review "Using Jscript auto-proxy files."*

7 *B.* Answers A, C, and D are incorrect because they don't prevent the users from changing their connection settings. *See "Using .adm templates."*

8 *A, C, and D.* Answer B is not a correct answer because a Jscript auto-proxy file is not required for automatic configuration. The auto-proxy file is used only to change proxy settings — not to change the browser configuration. *See "Creating .ins files."*

Part V
Integration and Interoperability

The 5th Wave   By Rich Tennant

"Before the Internet, we were only bustin' chops locally. But now, with our Web site, we're bustin' chops all over the world."

In This Part...

Controlling access to the Internet and to private networks is part of the job of a system admininstrator — an important part of the job! Whether using IE5 to connect through a proxy server, a dial-up solution, or through VPN, you must know the appropriate strategies for controlling access. In Part V, I tell you how to use the Internet Explorer Administration Kit to create secure access to the Internet and to intranets.

Chapter 19

Controlling Access!

· ·

Exam Objectives

▶ Controlling access to an intranet by using Dial-Up Networking and PPTP

▶ Controlling access to the Internet with Dial-Up Networking, PPTP, and proxy server

· ·

System administrators are painfully aware of the need to configure secure access to the Internet and to their private intranets. Pick up the newspaper any day — or better yet, read the news online — and you see story after story about security holes and hackers. In addition, the profusion of malicious content on the Web makes the system administrator's job quite a bit tougher.

In this chapter, I discuss controlling access to intranets and to the Internet over various connection methods. Whether users access a network through Dial-Up Networking, VPN, or a through a proxy server, you have to configure the appropriate security controls for them.

Quick Assessment

Dial-Up Networking

1 The _____ enables administrators to customize graphics, icons, support files, and phone books.

2 In most cases, an ISP administrator configures _____ connections for users to access their services.

3 While running the _____ _____, you can import the connection settings from the build computer.

4 When using the Customization wizard to create and distribute the connections, the connection settings are incorporated into the _____ file created by the wizard.

5 When using the CMAK to create and distribute the connections, the connections settings are incorporated into the _____ _____ created by the wizard.

PPTP

6 _____ connections use PPTP to create a secure, private connection across the Internet.

7 To use PPTP, users dial a service provider and then connect across the Internet via a secure, private connection (or tunnel) to a _____ _____ attached to a private network.

8 Administrators use the _____ to create VPN connections for distribution with custom IE5 browser packages.

Proxy Server

9 The role of the proxy server is to _____ the addresses of the client computers on the private network by substituting its own IP address in place of the client computer's address.

10 On a network that uses a _____ _____, client computers cannot access the Internet unless they are correctly configured to do so via the proxy server.

Answers

1   *CMAK.* See "Dial-Up Networking."

2   *dial-up.* See "Dial-Up Networking."

3   *Customization wizard.* See "Dial-Up Networking."

4   *.ins.* See "Dial-Up Networking."

5   *service profile.* See "Dial-Up Networking."

6   *VPN.* See "PPTP."

7   *VPN server.* See "PPTP."

8   *CMAK or Connection Manager Administration Kit.* See "PPTP."

9   *mask or hide.* See "Proxy Server."

10   *proxy server.* See "Proxy Server."

Dial-Up Networking

Most people became familiar with Microsoft Dial-Up Networking as long ago as Windows 95. Dial-Up Networking is one of the most common means of accessing the Internet, and it's the means that most users are familiar with. A system administrator distributing IE5, whether to corporate users or to ISP customers, must be able to appropriately configure Dial-Up Networking. System administrators use several tools to create, distribute, and manage Dial-Up Networking connections to the Internet:

  ✓ Dial-Up Networking

  ✓ Internet Explorer Administration Kit

  ✓ Connection Manager Administration Kit

Use of the Connection Manager Administration Kit (or CMAK) isn't necessary to distribute connections to users. Administrators can simply create the desired connections and then import them into a custom IE5 package by using the IEAK. But the CMAK allows further customization features by enabling administrators to customize graphics, icons, support files, and phone books.

Lab 19-1 takes you through the steps of building a connection with secure access and integrating it into a custom browser package by using the IEAK.

Lab 19-1   Creating a Dial-Up Connection

1. **On your build computer, click My Computer; then click Dial-Up Networking to open the folder.**

2. **Double-click the Make New Connection icon to start the Connection wizard.**

3. **In the Type a Name for the Computer You Are Dialing text box, type** Connect2. **In the Select a Device text box, select your modem from the drop-down list of devices. (See Figure 19-1.) Click Next.**

Figure 19-1: Configuring the new connection name and device.

4. **Enter the area code, telephone number, and country code in the labeled text boxes. Click Next.**

5. **The last screen of the wizard shows the name of the new connection (Connect2) and instructs you to click the Finish button to save the connection to the Dial-Up Networking folder. Click Finish.**

6. **Using Explorer, access the Dial-Up Networking folder on the build computer once again. In the Dial-Up Networking folder, right-click the Connect2 connection; then select Properties from the pop-up menu.**

7. **On the Server Types tab of the Connect2 Properties dialog box, as shown in Figure 19-2, select the Log on to Network check box and the Require Encrypted Password check box. At the bottom of the dialog box, in the Allowed Network Protocols section, make certain that only the TCP/IP check box is selected. Click OK to close the Connect2 Properties dialog box.**

Figure 19-2:
Configuring
secure
access
through
Dial-Up
Networking.

In Lab 19-1, you create a dial-up connection setting that can be imported into the IEAK Customization wizard. While running the Customization wizard, you can import these connection settings from the build computer (see Figure 19-3). The connection settings are incorporated into the .ins file created by the wizard. When users install the custom package, they also receive the configured connections. Note that these connections are preconfigured for the user, but not customized with special graphics and icons.

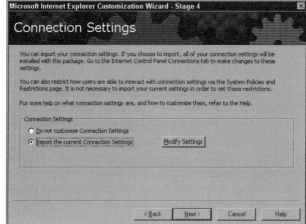

While the IEAK enables you to customize Internet Explorer 5, the CMAK
enables you to customize and configure the Connection Manager dialer for
the end user. You can create and independently distribute service profiles by
using the CMAK, but including the service profiles in an IE5 custom package
by using the IEAK is more common. You can do this by launching the CMAK
from the IEAK Customization wizard, as shown in Figure 19-4.

ISP administrators typically configure Internet access through a dial-up connection. The administrators set up and distribute connections through which their
customers access their services. Corporate administrators follow essentially
the same process as ISP administrators to create Dial-Up Networking connections. Corporate administrators, however, create dial-up connections through
which their users access the corporate intranet when away from the office.

PPTP

System administrators also use the IEAK and the CMAK to create and distribute VPN (Virtual Private Network) connections. VPN connections use PPTP (Point-to-Point Tunneling Protocol) to create a secure, private connection across the Internet. To use PPTP, users dial a service provider, and then connect across the Internet via a secure, private connection (or tunnel) to a VPN server attached to a private network. All data passing through the tunnel is encrypted. VPN is considered an extremely safe means of using public networks to transfer secure data.

VPN users usually go through two authentication steps: first, when they call the service provider and log in; second, when they connect to the VPN server. Administrators use the Connection Manager Administration Kit (CMAK) to create VPN connections for distribution with custom IE5 browser packages.

You encounter several VPN questions on the exam. Know the steps required to enable VPN connections and to recognize when a VPN connection meets the specified requirements.

Lab 19-2 takes you through the steps of configuring a VPN connection. In Step 7, you're instructed not to select the check box labeled Enable users to use the same ID and password for their dial-up connection as for their VPN connection. Having a second ID and password at the VPN server increases security. Anyone attempting to access a private network through the VPN connection configured in this lab is required to have an ID and password to authenticate at dial-up, and a second ID and password to authenticate at the VPN server.

Lab 19-2   Creating a Secure VPN Connection

1. **Start the Connection Manager Administration Kit by choosing Start⇨Programs⇨Connection Manager Administration Kit.**

2. **On the Welcome screen, click Next.**

3. **On the Service Profile Source screen, select the Create a New Service Profile check box. Click Next.**

4. **On the Service and File Names screen, type VPN1 in the Service Name text box. Type VPN1 in the File Name text box. Click Next three times.**

5. **On the Realm Name screen, select the Do Not Add a Realm Name check box. Click Next twice.**

6. **On the VPN Support screen, select the This Service Profile check box. Click Next.**

7. **On the VPN Connection screen (see Figure 19-5), type a server name or address in the Server Address text box. Do not select the option at the bottom of the screen that enables users to use the same ID and password for VPN authentication as they do for dial-up authentication. Make sure the check box is blank. Click Next.**

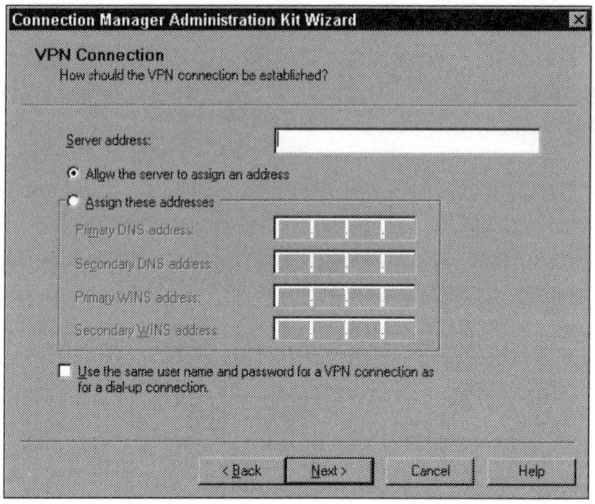

Figure 19-5:
Configuring
VPN
authentica-
tion.

8. **On the Connect Actions screen, clear all the check boxes. You don't need to run any connection actions in this lab. Click Next twice.**

9. **On the Logon Bitmap screen, select the default bitmap. Click Next.**

10. **On the Phone Book Bitmap screen, select the default bitmap. Click Next twice.**

11. **On the Icons screen, select the Use the Default Icons for All Icons check box. Click Next twice.**

12. **On the Help File screen, select the Use the Default Help File check box. Click Next.**

13. **On the Connection Manager Software screen, make sure that the Include the Connection Manager 1.2 Software check box is not selected. Click Next three times.**

14. **On the Ready to Build Service Profile screen, click Next and wait while the CMAK builds the service profile.**

15. **The final screen of the wizard shows the path and file name of the new service profile. Click Finish to close the wizard.**

Completing the CMAK wizard successfully creates a VPN service profile. After the service profile is distributed via the IEAK, users simply click the connection's icon to establish a VPN connection to their intranet. VPN connectivity is becoming increasingly popular because of its security benefits and ease of use, so administrators are configuring these connections quite often.

Remember that one of the components necessary to create a successful VPN connection is a VPN server situated between the Internet and the private network.

Proxy Server

A proxy server is a security device that sits between a private network and the Internet. The role of the proxy server is to mask the addresses of the client computers on the private network by substituting its own IP address in place of the client computer's address. Proxy servers can also be used to filter access to and from specific IP addresses and Web sites.

On networks that utilize a proxy server, when a client computer sends a request for a Web page, the request first passes through the proxy server. The proxy server inserts its own IP address in place of the client computer's IP address before forwarding the request to the Internet. Web site responses are returned to the proxy server, which then forwards the responses onto the client computer. This provides a high degree of security because Internet sites never receive client IP addresses from the private network. The only address that the public sees is the proxy server address.

Client computers cannot access the Internet on networks that use a proxy server unless they are correctly configured to do so via the proxy server. Figure 19-6 shows the IE5 proxy server settings for a LAN connection.

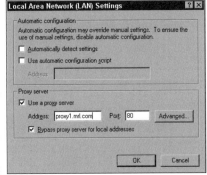

Figure 19-6: Configuring proxy server settings.

A corporate administrator configures a custom IE5 browser package with the correct proxy settings before deploying the browser to a user community. This assures that each browser is using secure access to the Internet. To make sure that the configuration isn't changed and that the proxy server isn't bypassed, corporate administrators often choose to lock down the proxy settings by using policies and restrictions.

Policies and restrictions are implemented by using either the IEAK Customization wizard or the IEAK Profile Manager. To lock down the proxy configuration for a browser, consider the following policies and restrictions:

- **Corporate Restrictions⇨Connections Page: Disable changing proxy settings.** Use this restriction to disable the users' ability to alter the proxy settings of the IE5 browser. Users can still view the Internet Options Connections page and view the proxy settings, but they cannot change the proxy settings.

- **Corporate Restrictions⇨Connections Page: Disable changing connection settings.** This restriction enables users to view the connection settings, but they are unable to alter any of the connection settings. Note that this affects more than just the proxy settings for the connection. This option may be too restrictive in an environment where users are allowed to configure their own connections.

- **Corporate Restrictions⇨Internet Property Pages: Disable viewing the Connections Page.** Use this restriction to prevent users from accessing or seeing any of the connection settings. This may be too restrictive in environments where users are allowed to configure connections.

- **Corporate Restrictions⇨Browser Menus: Disable Internet Options menu option.** Disabling Internet Options on the IE5 Tools menu is a very restrictive setting. This prevents the user from accessing the Connections page, but also prevents accessing Home Page, Temporary Internet Files, and History settings as well as many other features. This is a very restrictive setting and may prove too restrictive in some environments — but it certainly prevents users from altering their browser configuration!

Lab 19-3 guides you through configuring proxy settings for the IE5 browser.

Lab 19-3   Configuring Secure Proxy Server Access

1. **In IE5, choose Tools⇨Internet Options. Click the Connections tab.**

2. **Click the LAN Settings button.**

3. **In the LAN Settings dialog box, select the Use a Proxy Server check box.**

4. **In the Address text box, type proxy1.test.com. (Note that you can also type the IP address of the proxy server in the Address text box.) In the Port text box, type 80. (The default port number for IP is port 80.)**

5. **Click OK to close the LAN Settings dialog box.**

6. **Click OK to close the Internet Options dialog box.**

After you configure the proxy settings in the IE5 browser on a build computer, you can create a custom IE5 package with these proxy settings, restricting access to the settings as needed.

Prep Test

1 What components are needed to create and distribute a customized, precon-figured dial-up connection with a custom IE5 package? (Choose all that apply.)

A ❏ Internet Connection Manager Toolkit

B ❏ Dial-Up Networking

C ❏ Internet Explorer Administration Kit

D ❏ Connection Manager Administration Kit

2 Connie is a corporate administrator creating a custom IE5 browser package. Several of Connie's corporate users travel with their Windows 98 laptops. These users need secure access to the company's private network while traveling. What type of connection should Connie provide for these users?

A ○ VPN

B ○ PPTP

C ○ Dial-Up Networking

D ○ RAS

3 Mary is a corporate employee using a custom IE5 browser on her Windows 98 computer. Mary is trying to access a series of Internet sites while logged on to the corporate LAN, but she is unable to connect to any of them. She is, however, able to connect to intranet sites. What is causing this problem?

A ○ Her VPN connection is not secure.

B ○ Mary must use Dial-Up Networking to connect to Internet sites.

C ○ The proxy server configuration of Mary's IE5 browser is wrong.

D ○ Mary doesn't have an IP address configured on her computer.

4 Ted is a corporate administrator creating a custom IE5 package. Ted must include connections in the package so that users who travel can remotely access the corporate network. Ted has determined that a VPN connection is most appropriate. What components must Ted prepare so that the VPN connection will work? (Choose all that apply.)

A ❏ A connection within the browser

B ❏ A phone book

C ❏ A VPN server

D ❏ A RAS server

5 Terri is creating a custom IE5 browser package for corporate users. She must include several Dial-Up Networking connections in the package so that users can dial in to her private network. What is the most efficient way for Terri to include the connections in her custom browser package?

A ○ Terri should create and distribute the connections by using the CMAK.

B ○ Terri should create the connections by using the CMAK and distribute them from an auto-config URL.

C ○ Terri should create the connections on her build computer, import them into the package during the Customization wizard, and distribute them as part of the custom package.

D ○ Terri should first create the custom package and then include the connections by using the IEAK Profile Manager.

6 Terri is a corporate administrator creating a custom browser package. Terri has configured proxy access to the Internet for the browser package and does not want users to alter the proxy settings. Which method of restricting access to proxy settings should Terri use?

A ○ Corporate Restrictions⇨Connections Page: Disable changing proxy settings.

B ○ Corporate Restrictions⇨Connections Page: Disable changing connection settings.

C ○ Corporate Restrictions⇨Internet Property Pages: Disable viewing the Connections Page.

D ○ Corporate Restrictions⇨Browser Menus: Disable Internet Options menu option.

Answers

1   *B, C, and D.* Using Dial-Up Networking, the Internet Explorer Administration Kit, and the Connection Manager Administration Kit, administrators can create and customize preconfigured connections for distribution with an IE5 browser package.

2   *A.* Connie should provide a VPN connection for her traveling users. Dial-Up Networking and RAS aren't as secure as VPN.

3   *C.* Because Mary is able to connect to intranet sites, the problem involves the configuration for accessing sites outside the corporate network. The fact that she is a corporate employee usually indicates a proxy server or firewall, which indicates checking the proxy configuration. Answers A and B are not correct because they don't make sense in this question. Answer D is incorrect because she is able to access other sites on the network. *Review "Proxy Server."*

4   *A, B, and C.* Because Ted decides to use a VPN solution, a RAS server is unnecessary. Users dial in to a service provider by using the connection Ted creates. The phone book he creates provides access numbers for various parts of the United States. Ted must also consider a VPN server so that users can access his private network. *Review "PPTP."*

5   *C.* Although answer A is a valid way to distribute connections, it does not include them in the custom browser package. Answer B is incorrect because files created by using the IEAK (not the CMAK) are distributed from the auto-config URL. Answer D is also incorrect because the more efficient method is to include the connections during the IEAK Customization wizard. *Review "Dial-Up Networking."*

6   *A.* Answer A enables Terri to accomplish her objective without restricting any other settings. The other three answers restrict some settings, but the requirements of the question only mention limiting access to the proxy settings. *Review "Proxy Server."*

Part VI
Monitoring and Optimization

The 5th Wave   By Rich Tennant

OK, one of you will stay in the field, but the other one will handle clients over the Internet.

But which one?! Brad or Igor?! Brad or Igor?!

In This Part...

Optimizing the user experience is one of the best parts of customizing IE5! Here in Part VI, you learn tricks and tweaks to enhance the performance of IE5 for different types of users. IE5 performance requirements vary between ISP end-users, general business users, and single-task business users. Here you learn to optimize cache settings and tune system performance to suit a variety of user requirements.

Chapter 20

Optimizing Caching and Performance

Exam Objective

▶ Optimize IE5 cache settings

▶ Optimize IE5 performance settings

. . . .

Definition: *Cache* (verb) — to hide. *Cache* (noun) — a hidden reserve.

Four words with a lot of impact: optimize caching and performance. Most end users measure their satisfaction (or displeasure!) with a network by the performance of the computer on their desktop. Many factors affect network and system performance, and some of those factors are outside a system administrator's control. End users, however, care chiefly about how swiftly and reliably their desktop applications respond.

Because Internet Explorer 5 is one of the most widely deployed applications worldwide, understanding how to optimize its performance is a good idea (not to mention the matter of the IEAK5 exam you plan to pass!). This chapter covers the tools and methods for optimizing the performance of Internet Explorer 5 on the desktop.

Quick Assessment

Optimize Cache

1 You can increase the speed in which a user accesses a frequently used Web page by altering the _____ configuration.

Locate the Cache

2 The cache on a Windows 95 or Windows 98 computer is located in a folder called _____ _____ _____.

3 Choose the _____ menu to access Internet options and cache settings.

Configure the Cache

4 The default size of the cache is _____ percent of total disk space.

5 Increasing the cache _____ is one way to optimize browser performance without negatively affecting network bandwidth.

6 To completely prevent caching, set the cache _____ to _____.

7 To view the objects in the cache, click the _____ _____ button.

8 (True/False). Increasing the amount of disk space used for caching increases demand on network bandwidth.

9 (True/False). You cannot rename or relocate the cache.

Optimize Caching and Performance

10 Efficient caching is a balance between _____ _____ _____ and _____ _____ _____ _____.

Answers

1 *cache.* See "Optimize Caching."

2 *Temporary Internet Files.* See "Where is the cache?"

3 *Tools.* See "Where is the cache?"

4 *2.* See "How do I configure the cache?"

5 *size.* Review "How do I configure the cache?"

6 *size, zero.* See "How do I configure the cache?"

7 *View Objects.* See "How do I configure the cache?"

8 *False.* See "How do I configure the cache?"

9 *False.* Review "How do I configure the cache?"

10 *page access time, network bandwidth demand.* See "Caching and Performance."

Optimize Caching

The route to optimized caching varies from one user to another. For a help desk administrator needing quick access to a Web page of static information, infrequent updates to cached pages are acceptable. But for the financial analyst needing up-to-the-minute quotes, an optimized cache means continual cache updates — or even no caching at all. Obviously, you need to define optimized caching differently for these two users. Knowing the requirements of your user community allows you to determine the proper cache settings.

On the IEAK5 exam, know the methods for increasing performance by adjusting cache settings. Read questions carefully to determine whether you are optimizing network performance or the speed of Web page access.

What is the cache?

The cache is a folder on the hard disk that stores previously viewed Web pages for faster access on subsequent viewings. When you initially view a Web page, the content is downloaded to your computer and is stored in the cache. Each time you access a cached page, the browser checks the Web site for updated content. If the content is the same, the cached page loads from your disk. Internet Explorer 5 caches only one page for each Web page that you visit. After the cache fills, the newer pages replace the oldest cached pages. (A first in, first out rotation.)

Where is the cache?

Internet Explorer caches (or hides) previously viewed Web pages in the Temporary Internet Files folder. You can locate the cache by choosing Tools⇨Internet Options. Locate the Temporary Internet Files section of the dialog box and click the Settings button. Near the middle of the Settings dialog box is the Temporary Internet Files folder information. IE5 displays the current location of the cache in the Current location field.

Expect to see a test question that asks you to identify the location of the Internet Explorer cache. The default location for Windows 95/98 computers is:

```
c:\windows\Temporary Internet Files
```

The default location for a Windows NT computer is:

```
c:\WINNT\Profiles\userID\Temporary Internet Files
```

How do I configure the cache?

You control a number of options that relate to the status of the cache. Both the size and location of the cache can be adjusted by choosing Tools⇨Internet Options and clicking the Settings button on the General tab.

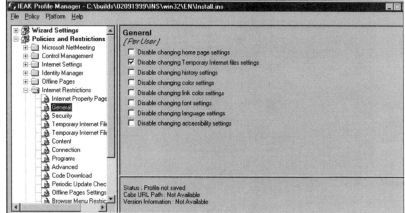

Figure 20-1:
Controlling
the cache
size and
location.

In the Settings dialog box, click the Move Folder button to move the cache to a different location on the hard drive (see Figure 20-1). Change the maximum size of the cache by moving the slide bar in the center of the dialog box to the left or the right. Moving the slidebar to the left makes the maximum cache size smaller. Moving it to the right increases the maximum cache size. You can view the files in the cache by clicking the View Files button. Similarly, you can click the View Objects button to see objects that are cached.

The default cache size for Internet Explorer is two percent of total disk capacity. If disk space is in short supply, decrease the maximum amount of disk space allocated for cached files. You can even set the cache size to zero, which completely prevents caching. Again, you should know the needs of the individual users to determine which requirement has priority.

One method to increase perceived Web page access time and simultaneously reduce network bandwidth demand is to increase the size of the cache. Cached pages load faster and don't access the Web to retrieve content.

Another option is to delete files from the cache. To quickly delete all the files from the cache, click the Delete Files button on the General tab of the Internet Options dialog box. (See Figure 20-2.)

Remember to weigh the benefits of increased disk space versus downloading all those Web pages again!

Figure 20-2:
Deleting
files from
the cache.

Lab 20-1 gives you an opportunity to become familiar with the various cache settings. Practice moving the cache location, changing the cache size, and viewing the cached files.

Lab 20-1   Viewing and Moving the Internet Explorer Cache

1. **In Internet Explorer, choose Tools⇨Internet Options to display the Internet Options dialog box.**

2. **Click the General tab (if it isn't already visible).**

3. **In the Temporary Internet Files panel, click the Settings button to display the Settings dialog box.**

   In the Temporary Internet Files Folder panel, you can see the current location of the cache, which, by default, is c:\windows\Temporary Internet Files.

4. **Click the View Files button to view the contents of the cache folder.**

5. **Click the Close button to return to the Settings dialog box.**

6. **In the Settings dialog box, click the Move Folder button to display the Browse for Folder dialog box.**

7. **Select the C:\My Documents folder and then click OK to return to the Settings dialog box, which reflects the new location of the cache folder.**

8. Click OK in the Settings dialog box to return to the Internet Options dialog box.

9. In the Temporary Internet File Folder panel, click the Delete Files button.

10. Click the Settings button and then click the View Files button to view the contents of the cache folder.

The Temporary Internet Files folder is empty except for "cookie" files, which Microsoft prefers that you not delete.

Caching and Performance

While Internet Explorer introduces many features that increase productivity, those same features introduce new strains on network bandwidth and desktop performance. Memory, disks, and processors are relatively inexpensive and effective desktop computer upgrades. But upgrading a network is time-consuming, expensive, and often impossible. With proper planning and configuration, Internet Explorer caching allows you to manage desktop performance and network bandwidth demands.

On the IEAK5 exam, one or more questions are on the speed of page load versus the demand for network bandwidth. Know that more caching usually equals less demand for bandwidth. Conversely, less caching (more frequent access of online Web sites) equals more demand for bandwidth.

After you determine the level of caching that is most beneficial for your users, you can further control caching through the following options on the Settings screen. Use these definitions to help you determine the appropriate caching level:

 ✔ **Every visit to the page:** Each time a user accesses the page, it checks for updated content on the Web site.

 ✔ **Every time you start Internet Explorer:** Each time a user starts Internet Explorer, the browser checks the cached Web pages for updated content.

 ✔ **Automatically:** Updates the Web page according to a schedule that the content provider determines.

 ✔ **Never:** Updates don't occur for cached pages.

Managing Caching and Performance with IEAK

After you determine the appropriate cache configuration for your users, you can use IEAK to prevent users from changing those settings. Figure 20-3 shows the location of the settings on the IEAK Profile Manager screen.

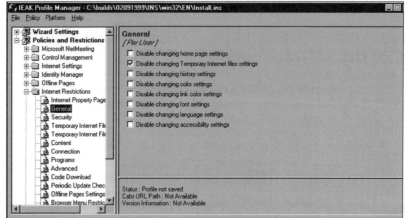

Figure 20-3:
Restricting changes to the cache settings with IEAK.

You can also use the IEAK Profile Manager to make changes to the size of the cache and the frequency of Web page updates. In Lab 20-2, I walk you through the steps of modifying an .INS file to change cache settings. Let's go!

In Lab 20-2, you use the IEAK Profile Manager to optimize the cache settings in an .INS file and then configure the profile so that the user can't change those settings. Before you begin this lab, you need to run the IEAK Customization wizard to create an IE5 package. You need the .INS file from the package to complete this lab.

**Lab 20-2   Optimizing the Cache Settings in an .INS File
by Using IEAK Profile Manager**

1. **Start the IEAK Profile Manager by choosing
   Start➪Programs➪Microsoft IEAK➪IEAK Profile Manager.**

2. **Within IEAK Profile Manager, choose File➪Open. Select an .INS file
   that you created earlier with the IEAK Configuration wizard.**

3. Locate the Policies and Restrictions settings in the left pane of the IEAK Profile Manager. Click the plus sign to expand the list of settings.

4. Locate Corporate Settings in the left pane and click the plus sign to view the list of configurable settings.

5. Choose Temporary Internet Files (User) in the left pane. In the right pane, change the amount of disk space to be used to 10,240 kilobytes by typing 10240 in the Set Amount of Disk Space to Use (in Kilobytes) text box.

6. In the left pane, select Temporary Internet Files (User). From the Check for Newer Versions of Stored Pages drop-down list box, select Every Time You Start Internet Explorer.

7. In the left pane, under Corporate Restrictions, locate and select General Page. Select the Disable Changing Temporary Internet Files Settings check box to prevent users from changing the Temporary Internet Files settings.

8. Save the changes by choosing File⇨Save.

Prep Test

1 John is planning an Internet Explorer 5 deployment for 50 Windows 98 users in the Sales Department. He is concerned about the effect of the users' Internet browsing on network bandwidth. What method should he use to minimize the effect of Web browsing on network bandwidth?

A ○ Increase the size of the Temporary Internet Files folder.

B ○ Increase the size of the Cache folder.

C ○ Select the Never option in the Check for Newer Versions of Stored Pages panel of the Internet Options dialog box.

D ○ Select the Automatically option in the Check for Newer Versions of Stored Pages panel of the Internet Options dialog box.

2 Cathy works in the Shipping Department and uses Internet Explorer 5 to access Zip code information on the Web. She complains that access to this information is too slow. After checking her machine, you find that the Temporary Internet Files folder is empty. What is the best way to speed her access to the zip code Web page?

A ○ Relocate the cache to a different partition.

B ○ Increase the size of the cache.

C ○ Select the Every Time You Start Internet Explorer option in the Check for Newer Versions of Stored Pages panel of the Internet Options dialog box.

D ○ Set the cache size to zero.

3 Your company has grown rapidly and is taxing the capacity of its network. You plan to use the Internet Explorer Administration Kit to optimize caching, and you want to avoid increased demand on network bandwidth. Which cache settings create an increased demand on network bandwidth? (Select all that apply.)

A ❏ Setting the cache size to zero.

B ❏ Increasing the size of the cache from two percent to five percent.

C ❏ Deleting all the files in the Temporary Internet Files folder.

D ❏ Selecting Never under the Check for Newer Versions of Stored Pages option.

4 Fred is unable to download a large document to his hard drive because the disk is full. He asks your assistance in determining which files he can remove. What is the quickest way to remove cached files and objects from Fred's computer?

A ○ Use Explorer to access the Temporary Internet Files folder and then delete all the files.

B ○ Increase the size of the cache from two percent to five percent.

C ○ Set the cache size to zero.

D ○ Click the Delete Files button in the Internet Options dialog box.

5 Carolyn wants to use information from the company's marketing Web page during her sales presentation tomorrow. She won't have online access to the page during the presentation. To assure that she can access the Web page content during the presentation, how should you configure cache settings to check for updated page content on Carolyn's laptop?

A ○ Never

B ○ Every Visit to the Page

C ○ Automatically

D ○ Every Time You Start Internet Explorer

6 Joe complains that he does not see current information when he views the content of the company's Web page. You visit Joe's desk and confirm that he is not seeing the most recent updates. What is the most likely cause of the stale data that Joe is viewing?

A ○ The cache size on Joe's computer is too large.

B ○ The cache on Joe's computer has been moved.

C ○ The cache size is set to zero.

D ○ The cache setting to check for updated content is set to Never.

7 You bought a new laptop and want to retain the Internet Explorer cache information from your old computer. The old computer is running Windows 95, but the new one is running Windows 98. Which folder do you copy from your old computer to your new laptop?

A ○ The Cache folder

B ○ The Temporary Internet Files folder

C ○ The Profile folder

D ○ The General Settings folder

8 Joe wants to increase the size of the Internet Explorer cache on his Windows NT computer. The cache is on his C: drive, which is almost full. The D: drive has 100MB of space available. How do you move the cache to the D: drive?

A ○ Using Explorer, copy the Cache folder from the C: drive to the D: drive.

B ○ Within Internet Explorer, click the Move Folder button on the Internet Options Settings page. Indicate D: for the new location.

C ○ Using Explorer, copy the Temporary Internet Files folder from the C: drive to the D: drive.

D ○ Sorry. The cache won't function if it's not in the proper location in the C:\WINNT folder.

Answers

1 *A.* Increasing the cache size allows for more local Web page storage, which means that users access the Internet for Web pages less frequently. Answer B is incorrect because the cache is located in the Temporary Internet Files folder, not the cache folder. Answer C is not a good choice because it results in users viewing stale data. Answer D isn't correct because the users may be caching pages that are continually updated. *Review "How do I configure the cache?"*

2 *B.* The empty cache on the computer indicates the cache size is probably set to zero. Increasing the cache size allows the computer to store Web content locally, which increases the speed with which Web pages load. Answer A does not resolve the problem. Answer C does not speed access time. Answer D prevents caching altogether. *Review "How do I configure the cache?"*

3 *A and C.* Setting the cache size to zero prevents any caching, so access to content is always over the network. Answer C is also correct because by deleting the files in the cache, you remove any previously cached pages. The user must then retrieve all content from the Web to reestablish the cache. Answer B does not cause increased network access. Answer D results in using only cached pages, which decreases bandwidth usage. *Review "How do I configure the cache?" and "Caching and Performance."*

4 *D.* Clicking the Delete Files button removes all files and objects from the cache. Answer A would work, but it's not the quickest way to remove the files. Answer B results in an increased cache size. Answer C prevents future caching, but is not the best answer. *Review "How do I configure the cache?"*

5 *A.* By configuring the cache to never check for updated pages before Carolyn leaves the office, she can access the Web information via the previously cached page. Answers B, C, and D are not appropriate choices because Carolyn does not have online access. *Review "Caching and Performance."*

6 *D.* Because the cache never checks for updated content, Joe is viewing stale data. Answer A doesn't cause stale data. Answer B doesn't affect page updates. Answer C results in no caching at all. *Review "Caching and Performance."*

7 *B.* By default the cache stores in C:\WINDOWS\Temporary Internet Files. Answers A, C, and D are not correct because the cache is in the Temporary Internet Files folder. *Review "How do I configure the cache?"*

8 *B.* Because the cache is not in a folder named Cache, answer A is incorrect. Answer C is incorrect because the cache location changes from within Internet Explorer. Answer D is incorrect because it doesn't tell you how to relocate the cache. *Review "How do I configure the cache?"*

Part VII
Troubleshooting

The 5th Wave   By Rich Tennant

INTERNET ACCESS
.50¢ - Min.

In This Part...

Much as we'd like it to be otherwise, shooting troubles is part of the job, too. (After all, we've got to have something to justify all those beeping and ringing electronic gadgets hanging from our belts, right?) In Part VII, I discuss some of the troubleshooting scenarios that appear on the exam. Connectivity problems, deployment failures, and IE5 component failures are all covered in this part of the book. You'll also find information on modifying remote registries and dealing with IEAK wizard failure.

Chapter 21

Troubleshooting Network Connection Failures (It's Elementary, Watson!)

● ●

Exam Objectives

▶ Diagnose and resolve PPTP connectivity problems

▶ Diagnose and resolve Dial-Up Networking connectivity problems

▶ Diagnose and resolve proxy server connectivity problems

▶ Diagnose and resolve TCP/IP connectivity problems

● ●

*I*f you've already taken the Windows NT Server and Windows NT Server in the Enterprise exams, you may notice that much of the material you learned for those exams is useful in preparing for IEAK5. Well, dust off your TCP/IP manual as well! In this chapter, I review the basic troubleshooting tools used to investigate network connectivity failures.

For the exam, make sure that you're familiar with the following components of Microsoft TCP/IP networking:

    ✔ **WINS** — dynamic NetBIOS name resolution

    ✔ **DNS** — host name resolution

    ✔ **LMHOSTS** — cached file used for NetBIOS name resolution

    ✔ **HOSTS** — cached file used for host name resolution

Quick Assessment

IP Configuration Tools

1 To view the IP address and default gateway address on a Windows 95 or Windows 98 computer, use the _____ utility.

2 To display the IP configuration information for a Windows NT computer, use the _____ utility.

3 To view the WINS server configuration on your Windows NT computer, type _____ at the command prompt.

The PING Utility

4 The PING utility enables you to test _____ _____ between two computers.

5 The first address to test when troubleshooting with the PING utility is always the _____ address.

6 If PPTP fails after connecting through the ISP, you should check that the _____ _____ is correct for the VPN server.

The TRACERT Utility

7 The TRACERT utility is used to determine the _____ _____ between two network computers.

Using Network Monitor

8 To use Network Monitor to analyze traffic on a remote segment, install the Network Monitor utility from the _____ CD.

9 Before using Performance Monitor to monitor the Network Segment object, make sure the _____ _____ _____ is running on the target computer.

Using NSLOOKUP

10 Typing NSLOOKUP dummies.com will return the _____ _____ associated with this domain name.

Answers

1 *WINIPCFG.* See "Viewing IP configurations."

2 *IPCONFIG.* See "Viewing IP configurations."

3 *IPCONFIG/all.* Review "Viewing IP configurations."

4 *network connectivity.* See "Using PING."

5 *loopback.* See "Using PING."

6 *IP address.* See "Troubleshooting PPTP."

7 *hop count.* See "Using Trace Route."

8 *SMS.* Review "Using Network Monitor."

9 *Network Monitor Agent.* See "Using Network Monitor."

10 *IP address.* See "Using NSLOOKUP."

Troubleshooting 101: TCP/IP

If you have real world experience as a system administrator, you have experience with connectivity failure. Unfortunately, any network component is subject to failure and can defy your best efforts at fault tolerance and reliability. Troubleshooting these failures is increasingly difficult as the number of network devices between you and the destination host increases. Add a variety of network communication protocols to this tangle of devices and you have the potential for quite an internetworking traffic jam.

When your job is to unsnarl the traffic and identify the cause of the network traffic problem, remember to rely on standard investigative techniques:

- First, check the three C's. Make sure that all cables, cards, and cords are firmly seated. (I've wasted countless hours troubleshooting failures caused by loosely connected cables and network cards!)
- Test the local host first and gradually work outward toward the remote (or destination) host.
- Test connectivity to every point along the route to the destination host.
- Confirm the configuration settings on the local machine. The wrong gateway address or subnet mask is often the problem.
- Implement one change at a time when troubleshooting the problem.
- Document each change to a network device.

Fortunately, there are almost as many troubleshooting tools as there are network connectivity devices. On this exam, you're required to troubleshoot network connection failures by using the utilities described in the following sections.

Viewing IP configurations

If the IP configuration on your computer is incorrect, you may not be able to communicate with anyone. Remember, the IP configuration includes settings, such as IP address, default gateway, subnet mask, WINS server, and so on.

When troubleshooting a network connectivity problem, check the IP configuration of the computer to assure that all the settings are correct for your network. Depending on the operating system of the computer, use either the IPCONFIG or WINIPCFG tool to display the current IP configuration.

On Windows NT computers

On a Windows NT computer, type **IPCONFIG /all** at a command prompt. Figure 21-1 shows the resulting IP configuration display.

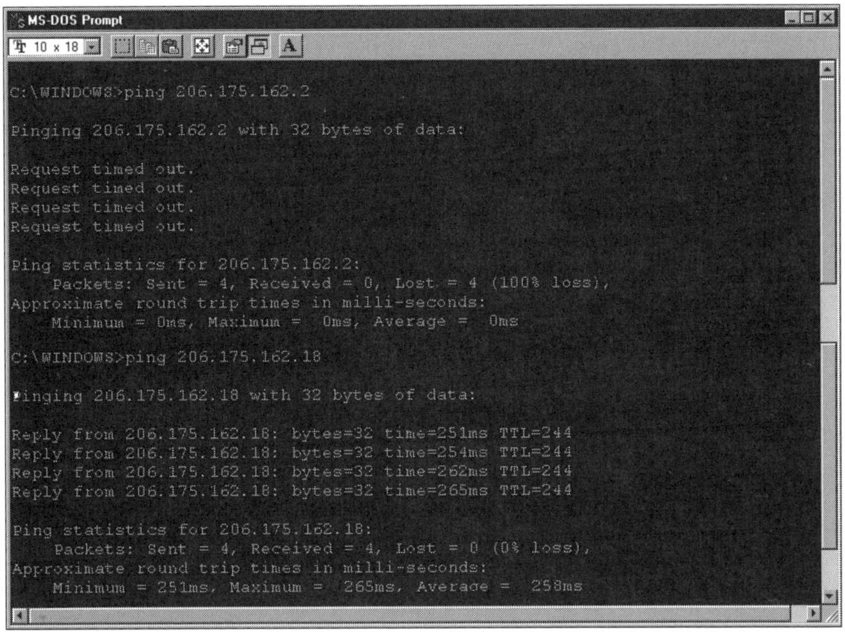

Figure 21-1:
IPCONFIG
/all on a
Windows
NT
computer.

```
C:\WINDOWS>ping 206.175.162.2

Pinging 206.175.162.2 with 32 bytes of data:

Request timed out.
Request timed out.
Request timed out.
Request timed out.

Ping statistics for 206.175.162.2:
    Packets: Sent = 4, Received = 0, Lost = 4 (100% loss),
Approximate round trip times in milli-seconds:
    Minimum = 0ms, Maximum =  0ms, Average =  0ms

C:\WINDOWS>ping 206.175.162.18

Pinging 206.175.162.18 with 32 bytes of data:

Reply from 206.175.162.18: bytes=32 time=251ms TTL=244
Reply from 206.175.162.18: bytes=32 time=254ms TTL=244
Reply from 206.175.162.18: bytes=32 time=262ms TTL=244
Reply from 206.175.162.18: bytes=32 time=265ms TTL=244

Ping statistics for 206.175.162.18:
    Packets: Sent = 4, Received = 4, Lost = 0 (0% loss),
Approximate round trip times in milli-seconds:
    Minimum = 251ms, Maximum =  265ms, Average =  258ms
```

Three command line switches control the information displayed with the IPCONFIG command, as shown in Table 21-1.

Table 21-1	IPCONFIG Switch Options
Option	*Displayed Information*
	Typing **IPCONFIG** with no switch causes only the IP address, subnet mask, and default gateway for each network adapter card installed in the computer to display.
/all	**IPCONFIG /all** shows all IP configuration data for all network adapter cards installed in the computer.
/renew [adapter]	The /renew switch is used when the computer is configured as a DHCP client. Typing **IPCONFIG /renew** causes the computer to renew all DHCP configuration settings. If more than one network adapter is installed, use the [adapter] parameter to specify which card is to renew its DHCP settings.
/release	**IPCONFIG /release** causes a DHCP client computer to release all its DHCP configuration settings. Again, use the [adapter] parameter as needed if there are multiple network cards installed.

Using the IPCONFIG utility, you can find out about the IP configuration of a particular computer. Lab 21-1 takes you through the process.

Lab 21-1   Using IPCONFIG to View IP Configuration

1. **On a Windows NT computer, go to a command prompt.**

2. **Type** IPCONFIG **and press the Enter key.**

   The IP address, default gateway, and subnet mask appear.

3. **Type** IPCONFIG /all **and press the Enter key.**

   All the IP configuration information for the computer appears.

On Windows 95/98 computers

On Windows 95 or Windows 98 computers, run **WINIPCFG /all** from the Start menu. Figure 21-2 shows the IP configuration on a Windows 95 computer.

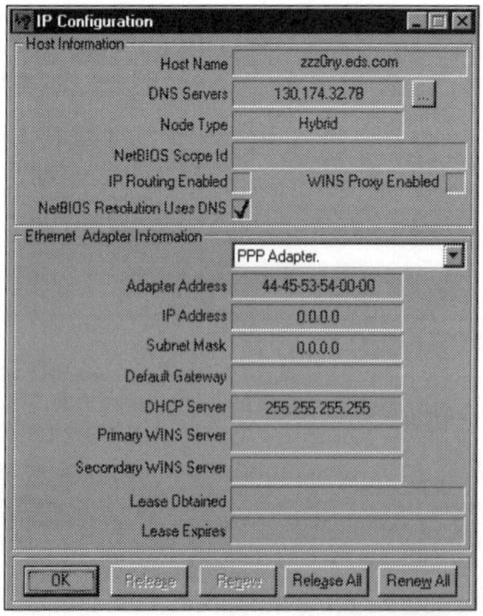

Figure 21-2: WINIPCFG /all on a Windows 95 computer.

The WINIPCFG utility has the following switch options when run from a command prompt or by choosing Start⇨Run, as shown in Table 21-2:

Table 21-2	WINIPCFG Switch Options
Option	*Displayed Information*
	WINIPCFG with no switch causes only the IP address, subnet mask, and default gateway to display. Click the More Info button (equivalent to /all switch) to show the remainder of the IP configuration information.

Option	Displayed Information
/all	**WINIPCFG /all** shows all IP configuration data.
/renew_all	The /renew_all switch is used when the computer is configured as a DHCP client. Typing **WINIPCFG /renew_all** causes the computer to renew all DHCP configuration settings for all network adapter cards.
/renew_[n]	The /renew_[n] switch is used when there is more than one network adapter card installed. This switch enables you to specify which network adapter card is to renew its DHCP settings.
/release_all	Causes a DHCP client computer to release all its DHCP configuration settings for all network adapter cards.
/release_[n]	The /release_[n] switch is used when there is more than one network adapter card installed. This switch enables you to specify which network adapter card is to release all its DHCP settings.

Expect to see a question that requires an administrator to check the IP configuration on a computer. You must know whether to use IPCONFIG or WINIPCFG and any appropriate switches. Lab 21-2 takes you through the steps of using the WINIPCFG utility.

Lab 21-2   Using WINIPCFG to View IP Configuration

1. **On a Windows 95 or Windows 98 computer, click the Start button.**

2. **Choose Run.**

3. **Type** WINIPCFG **in the dialog box.**

4. **Click OK.**

   The IP Configuration dialog box appears.

5. **Click the More Info button.**

   The remainder of the IP configuration appears.

6. **Click OK to close the dialog box after viewing the information.**

Using PING

The PING utility is undoubtedly the simplest and most useful troubleshooting tool for a TCP/IP network. You can use PING to determine whether a local or remote computer is available, whether there is network congestion, or whether there are name resolution problems on the network.

You can ping a destination computer by IP address or by hostname. The syntax for the PING utility is pretty foolproof:

```
Ping hostname
Ping IP address
```

If the destination host is reachable by using the IP address, but not the hostname, then the network has a name resolution problem.

You can save yourself a lot of time by learning to use PING effectively. To troubleshoot a network connectivity problem, follow these steps in sequence:

Lab 21-3   Troubleshooting TCP/IP Problems Using Ping

1. **Ping the loopback address (127.0.0.1).**

   The loopback address is a built-in testing address that the network adapter recognizes. If TCP/IP is configured correctly on the client, you get a reply to the ping.

   If you get a reply to the ping, move on to the next step. If you don't get a reply, reset the network adapter and try again. If you still don't get a reply, try a new network adapter card.

2. **Ping your IP address.**

   Again, if the TCP/IP configuration on your client computer is correct, you get a reply to the ping. If you get a reply, move on to Step 3. If not, check the TCP/IP configuration on the client.

3. **If you have successfully pinged the loopback address and your own address, ping the IP address of your default gateway.**

   If this ping is not successful, begin investigating problems on the local network segment. Try pinging the gateway from other hosts on the segment. If the ping works successfully, the near side of the router is properly configured.

4. **Next, ping the IP address of a destination host.**

   If you can successfully ping the address of the destination host, TCP/IP is working properly. If not, it's time to investigate other points of failure. Try to determine whether any intervening network devices are properly configured and active.

PING sends a series of packets from your computer to the destination computer. If the destination computer is available, it replies to each packet. If the destination computer is not reachable before a packet times out, PING returns a "request timed out" message. Figure 21-3 shows both a successful and an unsuccessful ping.

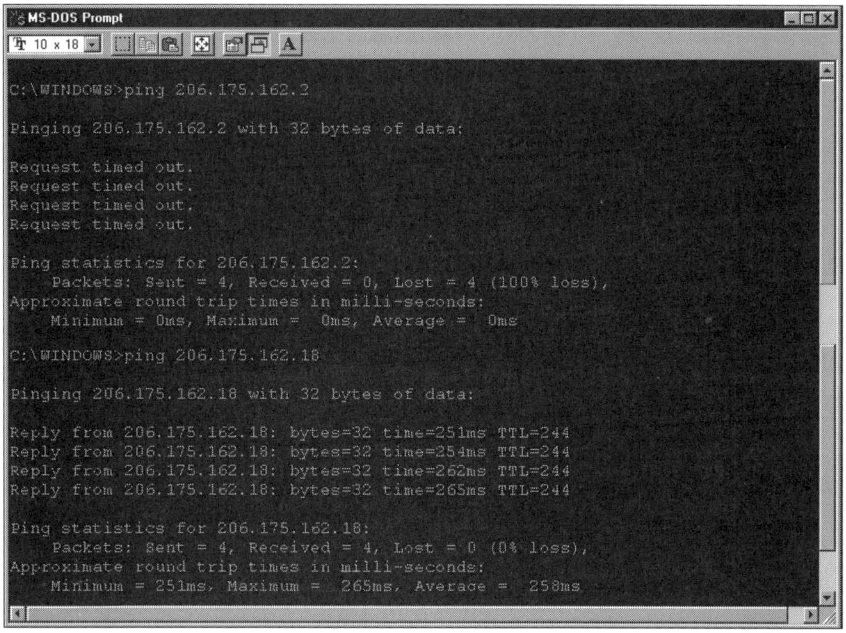

Figure 21-3:
Unsuccessful
and
successful
PING
attempts.

You can use the timing information provided in the PING reply string to determine whether there is congestion on the network. For example, if the response time between 2 computers is normally 20 milliseconds, but the current response time is 40 milliseconds, you're probably seeing an indication of heavy network traffic.

You can also alter the parameters of the PING command and its packets through a number of command line switches. The more common switches are shown in Table 21-3.

Table 21-3	PING Switch Options
Switch	*Result*
-a	Resolves the hostname of a given IP address.
-i *ttl*	Sets the Time to Live field to the value entered as *ttl*. Causes the packet to stay alive on the network longer.
-n *count*	*Count* determines the number of packets the PING utility sends. The default is 4.
-t	Continually pings the destination computer until you intervene.
-w *timeout*	*Timeout* specifies the timeout interval.

Using Trace Route

The TRACERT (Trace Route) utility does exactly what it suggests: It traces the route between your computer and a destination computer. This utility picks up where the PING utility leaves off in troubleshooting. After you determine that you can ping beyond the default gateway, use TRACERT to pinpoint the exact point of failure on the route to the destination computer.

TRACERT uses simple syntax:

```
tracert IP address
tracert hostname
```

Figure 21-4 shows the results of a TRACERT command.

As Figure 21-4 shows, the TRACERT utility returns the identity of each "hop" (router that it passes through) along the way. It also returns the amount of time required to reach each hop.

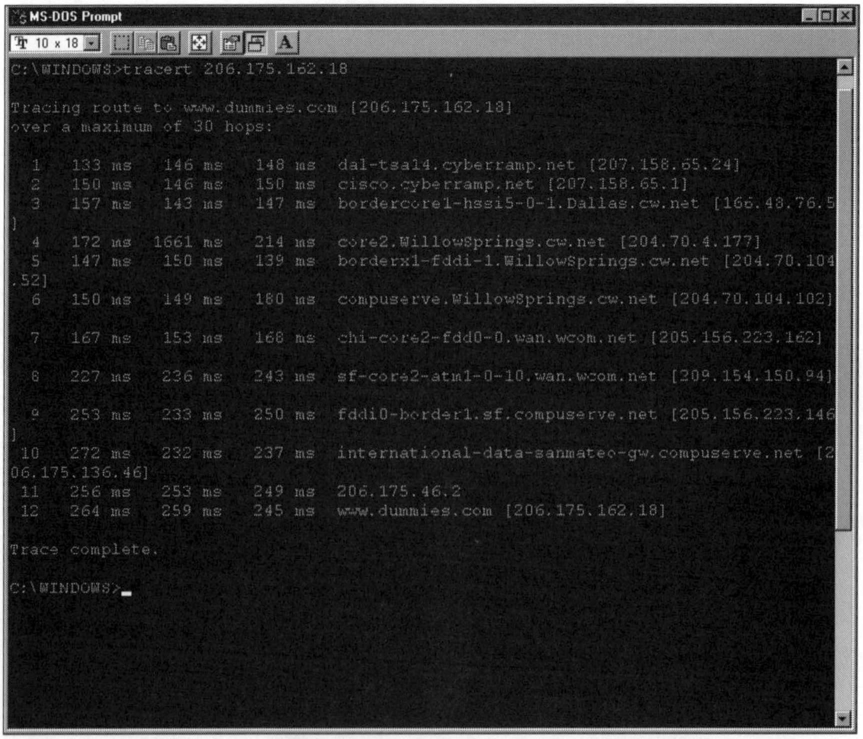

Figure 21-4:
Using
TRACERT to
locate a
point of
failure.

Using Network Monitor

Network Monitor is a powerful tool used to capture and analyze network packets. As a troubleshooting tool, it is useful for analyzing communication problems between two hosts or for identifying the source of a network broadcast storm. You can also use Network Monitor to tune and optimize a network.

Two versions of Network Monitor are available, and each ships with a different Microsoft product:

- ✔ **Windows NT Server 4.0 Network Monitor** is very simplistic. It only enables you to capture packets sent to or from the local computer running Network Monitor.

- ✔ **Microsoft Systems Management Server (SMS) Network Monitor** is more robust. This version enables you to capture packets from any devices on the network segment of the computer running Network Monitor. It's often used to capture and analyze packets on a remote segment.

Network Monitor consists of two components:

- ✔ **The Network Monitor application** runs on Windows NT, Windows 95, Windows 98, and Windows for Workgroups. Using the application component, you can capture, display, and save a series of packets. The Network Monitor application also presents statistics about traffic patterns on the network.

- ✔ **The Network Monitor Agent** runs on a computer that is capturing data. The captured data is sent to the computer running the Network Monitor application, where it is viewed or saved. Installing the Network Monitor Agent on a computer also creates the Network Segment object that you find in Performance Monitor.

    If the Network Monitor Agent isn't running on a computer, you can't monitor the Network Segment object in Performance Monitor.

Using NSLOOKUP

NSLOOKUP is a utility that enables you to resolve a domain name to an IP address or vice-versa. The syntax for NSLOOKUP is:

```
nslookup domain name
nslookup IP address
```

Think of NSLOOKUP as a telephone directory: You use a name to find a corresponding telephone number. With NSLOOKUP, you use a domain name to find a corresponding IP address. You can also use the IP address to locate the corresponding domain name.

The NSLOOKUP utility is available in Windows NT, but not in Windows 95 or Windows 98.

Troubleshooting Proxy Server Issues

Resolving a proxy server problem is a matter of either entering the correct proxy server name, or entering the correct TCP/IP port number in the proxy settings configuration of Internet Explorer 5 (see Figure 21-5). First, verify that you have entered the name of your proxy server correctly. (If your organization doesn't require a proxy server, leave this information blank.) Then verify that you've associated the correct port number for each service.

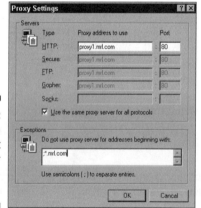

Figure 21-5: Entering the correct proxy server configuration.

Table 21-4 lists some of the most commonly used TCP/IP port numbers that you're likely to encounter on various exam questions. If you memorize these port numbers, it's likely that you can resolve some of the troubleshooting questions on the exam.

Table 21-4	Commonly Used Port Numbers
Service	*Port Number*
FTP (data)	20
FTP (control)	21
Telnet	23
SMTP	25
Gopher	70
HTTP	80
POP3	110
IMAP	143

If you've verified the proxy server name and the port number, yet still can't connect, troubleshoot for TCP/IP connectivity failures. Ping the proxy server by IP address and by name. Ping the destination address by name and by IP address. Refer to "Troubleshooting 101: TCP/IP" earlier in this chapter.

If the name or IP address of your organization's proxy server changes, you can alter the proxy configuration by using the IEAK Profile Manager, and then distribute the changed configuration to your users.

Troubleshooting Dial-Up Networking

For the exam, know how to configure Dial-Up Networking on the client computer. Know which components and services are needed and how to configure them.

The most frequently encountered problems with Dial-Up Networking are incorrect network settings:

- ✔ Make certain that TCP/IP is installed and is correctly configured for the dial-up connection.
- ✔ Be sure to select `Use default gateway on remote network` (see Figure 21-6).
- ✔ Enter DNS server addresses for the remote network.

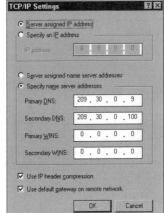

Figure 21-6:
Configuring
TCP/IP
settings for
Dial-Up
Networking.

Make only one change at a time when troubleshooting any connectivity problem.

Troubleshooting PPTP

The most frequently encountered problem when establishing a Virtual Private Network using PPTP is failure to connect to the VPN server attached to the private network. To troubleshoot a PPTP problem, remember that there are several steps involved in establishing the VPN, and troubleshoot from beginning to end:

- Make certain that the dial-up connection to the ISP was established. If you've used this connection successfully before, a failure at this stage is usually an incorrect ID or password for the dial-up connection, but can also be due to an unavailable authentication server at the ISP. If you've never used this connection successfully, troubleshoot your modem and network configurations.

- If the PPTP failure occurs after connecting through the ISP, check to make sure you've entered the correct IP address for the VPN server. If you are unsuccessful connecting using the server's name, try to connect using the IP address instead. Finally, check to make certain that the VPN server is online.

- Make certain to use the correct ID and password for the VPN server. This is a separate authentication step from authenticating when dialing in to the ISP. Although it's possible to configure the VPN connection to use the same ID and password for both the dial-up connection and the VPN server connection, the ID and password for these two connections are not necessarily the same. Check to make sure that the ID and password for the VPN server are correct.

Prep Test

1 Which utility can you use to test the network connectivity between two hosts? (Choose all that apply.)

A ❑ NSLOOKUP

B ❑ TRACERT

C ❑ Network Monitor

D ❑ PING

2 Sam works at a company that has two offices, Corporate and Sales. From his Windows NT Workstation at the Corporate office, Sam is troubleshooting a problem on a Windows NT server at the Sales office. Sam wants to use Performance Monitor to monitor network traffic at the Sales office. What should he do on the Windows NT Server to accomplish this?

A ○ Install Performance Monitor.

B ○ Run TRACERT.

C ○ Install Network Monitor Agent.

D ○ Install NT Workstation.

3 The NSLOOKUP utility is available on computers running which operating systems? (Choose all that apply.)

A ○ Windows 95

B ○ Windows for Workgroups

C ○ Windows 98

D ○ Windows NT

4 Jane and her coworkers are using Windows 98 computers. Jane cannot access the corporate Web site. You want to view the IP configuration on Jane's machine to make sure that the DNS server address is correct. How do you do this?

A ○ Go to a command prompt and type **IPCONFIG**.

B ○ Go to a command prompt and type **IPCONFIG /all**.

C ○ From the Start menu, choose Run. Then type **WINIPCFG**.

D ○ From the Start menu, choose Run. Then type **WINIPCFG /all**.

5 You installed Network Monitor from the SMS CD but are unable to capture network packets from your NT server. What is the most likely problem?

A ○ Network Monitor is not configured correctly.

B ○ Your network adapter is not on the HCL.

C ○ You can't ping the destination host.

D ○ The subnet mask is incorrect.

Troubleshooting Connections

6 Amy decides to test the loopback address of her NT Workstation. Which tools can she use to do this? (Choose all that apply.)

A ○ TRACERT
B ○ PING
C ○ NSLOOKUP
D ○ IPCONFIG /all

7 Cindy is unable to access the Web server at IP address 140.192.16.12. You used the ping utility at Cindy's workstation and did not get a reply from the server. Which utility should you use next?

A ○ PING /all
B ○ TRACERT
C ○ NSLOOKUP
D ○ Network Monitor

8 While troubleshooting a connection failure to a Web server named Talon, you successfully ping the server's IP address. You are not successful at pinging the server by name. Knowing this indicates a name resolution problem, you view the computer's IP configuration to check which of the following? (Choose all that apply.)

A ❑ DNS
B ❑ WINS
C ❑ LMHOSTS
D ❑ HOSTS

9 Jane is unable to connect to Internet Web sites. You check the proxy settings of her Internet Explorer 5 browser and find that the proxy server name is not entered. You enter the correct server name. Which port number should you enter?

A ○ 2020
B ○ 80
C ○ 21
D ○ 78

10 Tom is dialing in to the corporate network to access several Web pages. Although he connected and was able to log on to the network, he is unable to access any Web pages. Of the following choices, which is the most likely cause of this problem?

A ○ Use default gateway for remote network is not selected.
B ○ Port numbers for all proxy services are set to 80.
C ○ No DNS servers are configured for this dial-up connection.
D ○ Tom's network adapter is not listed on the HCL.

Answers

1 *B and C.* Both TRACERT and PING test the connectivity between two devices. NSLOOKUP is not a correct answer because it's used to resolve domain names. Network Monitor is not a correct answer because it's used to capture and analyze network packets. *Review "Using Trace Route" and "Using PING."*

2 *C.* The Network Monitor Agent must be running on the target computer so that Sam can capture information related to the Network Segment object. *See "Using Network Monitor."*

3 *D.* NSLOOKUP is available on Windows NT Server and Windows NT Workstation. NSLOOKUP is unavailable on Windows 95 or Windows 98. *Review "Using NSLOOKUP."*

4 *D.* WINIPCFG with the /all parameter returns all the IP configuration data for the Windows 98 computer. Without the /all parameter and without clicking the More Info button, only the IP address, default gateway, and subnet mask are visible. *See "Viewing IP configurations."*

5 *B.* Because the correct version of Network Monitor was loaded from the SMS CD, the network adapter is probably not supported. Answers C and D are incorrect because they describe connectivity failures. *See "Using Network Monitor."*

6 *B.* When troubleshooting the IP configuration on a computer, use PING to test the loopback address. Answer A is incorrect because it is senseless to trace a route to the local computer. Answer C is incorrect because NSLOOKUP is used to resolve a domain name. Answer D is incorrect because IPCONFIG /all only shows the IP configuration. *Review "Using PING."*

7 *B.* The TRACERT utility identifies the first point of failure. Answer A is incorrect because the /all parameter is not valid with PING. Answers C and D are incorrect because these utilities do not test connectivity between two devices. *See "Using Trace Route."*

8 *A and B.* DNS and WINS provide name resolution services. Answers C and D are incorrect because LMHOSTS and HOSTS file information doesn't appear in the IP configuration data. *Review "Viewing IP configurations."*

9 *B.* The correct port number for HTTP connectivity is port 80. *Review "Troubleshooting Proxy Server Issues."*

10 *C.* Because Tom was able to log on to the network, it's unlikely that he isn't already using the default gateway for the remote network, so A is not the correct answer. Answer B is not correct because it's acceptable for all proxy services to default to TCP port 80. D isn't correct because Tom is connecting via dial-up, not through the network adapter. *Review "Troubleshooting Proxy Server Issues."*

Chapter 22

Tweaking with Profile Manager

- -

Exam Objectives

▶ Using the IEAK Profile Manager to modify the Registry settings of a remote client computer

- -

*T*he Internet Administration Kit Profile Manager is a powerful tool. System administrators can use the Profile Manager to create and manage customized versions of Internet Explorer 5. While some of the settings that administrators can configure with the Profile Manager pertain to browser configuration, others relate to user and system settings. In this chapter, I show you how to use the Profile Manager to modify the Registry settings on a remote computer.

Quick Assessment

1 IE5 configuration parameters for a custom browser package are saved in _____ files created by the Customization wizard.

2 .ins files can be edited by using the _____ _____.

3 When you initially run the IEAK Customization wizard, the wizard generates _____ files for your customized browser package, as well as an Install.ins file that specifies the wizard parameters that you selected.

4 The _____ file also contains the Policies and Restrictions settings that you specified during Stage 5 of the Customization wizard.

5 After you create a custom browser package with the Customization wizard, you can create variations of the package by using _____ _____to edit the Install.ins file and save it with a new filename.

6 To change the configuration of an already deployed browser, you edit the .ins file with Profile Manager and save the new .ins file to an _____ _____ _____ or to an individual user's system.

7 You can add additional settings to the .ins file by importing any of the nine _____ that come with the Internet Explorer Administration Kit.

8 By enabling automatic configuration, you configure the browser to periodically check the _____ _____ for an updated .ins file.

9 If automatic configuration is not enabled, and an administrator needs to update a user's configuration, he can copy the .ins file to _____ _____ _____.

10 The settings and restrictions that are configured with Customization wizard and Profile Manager are applied to the _____ of the user's computer.

Answers

1 *.ins.* See "Understanding Profiles."

2 *Profile Manager.* See "Understanding Profiles."

3 *.cab or cabinet.* See "Understanding Profiles."

4 *Install.ins.* See "Understanding Profiles."

5 *Profile Manager.* See "Editing .ins Files."

6 *automatic configuration URL.* See "Editing .ins Files."

7 *templates or .adm.* See "Editing .ins Files"

8 *auto-config URL.* See "Troubleshooting with Profile Manager."

9 *the user's computer.* See "Troubleshooting with Profile Manager."

10 *Registry.* See "Troubleshooting with Profile Manager."

Understanding Profiles

Internet Explorer 5 profiles specify configuration parameters for the IE5 browser, the desktop, the user, and the system. These parameters are saved in .ins (instruction) files created by the Customization wizard or by editing an .ins file with the Profile Manager.

When you initially run the IEAK Customization wizard, the wizard generates cabinet files for your customized browser package, as well as an Install.ins file that specifies the wizard parameters that you selected. The Install.ins file also contains the Policies and Restrictions settings that you specified during Stage 5 of the Customization wizard.

You find the Install.ins file in the destination folder that you specified during Stage 1 of the Customization wizard. For example, when I ran the Customization wizard for the first time, I specified the following destination folder:

```
C:\builds\11231999
```

By default, the Customization wizard placed the Install.ins file in the following path:

```
C:\builds\11231999\INS\win32\EN\Install.ins
```

In Figure 22-1, I used the Notepad application to open the Install.ins file. The parameters that you see in this file are the instructions that specify the parameters for the custom browser package that you created with the Customization wizard. When a user installs the customized browser, the user's system obtains browser settings and Registry settings from this file.

Editing .ins Files

After you create a custom browser package with the Customization wizard, you can create variations of the package by using Profile Manager to edit the Install.ins file and save it with a new filename. Similarly, to change the configuration of an already deployed browser, you edit the .ins file with Profile Manager and save the new .ins file to an automatic configuration URL or to an individual user's system.

If you create only one version of the custom browser, you can leave the filename Install.ins. Giving the file a descriptive name, however, such as Ie5ver1.ins, is more useful because it identifies the version of the custom browser package.

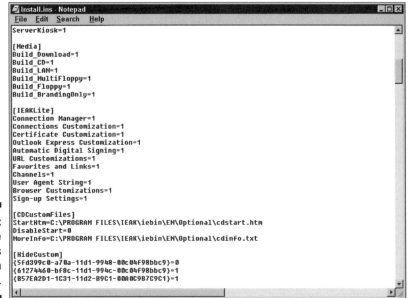

Figure 22-1:
Viewing the
Install.ins
file with
Notepad.

To edit the Install.ins file, click the Start button and choose Programs⇨
Microsoft IEAK⇨Profile Manager. Open the Install.ins file by choosing File⇨
Open and navigating to the destination folder to select the Install.ins file.

As shown in Figure 22-2, the Install.ins file contains the settings that I configured for my browser package when I ran the Customization wizard. To change
any of these settings, select a setting in the left pane of the Profile Manager.
You can alter the options and parameters that appear in the right pane.

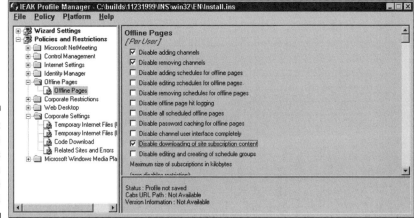

Figure 22-2:
Editing the
Install.ins
file with
Profile
Manager.

You can add additional settings to the .ins file by importing any of the nine policy templates (.adm files) that come with the Internet Explorer Administration Kit. Refer to Chapter 16 and Chapter 18 for more information on using policies and .adm files.

After making the desired changes, save the .ins file by choosing File⇔Save As. In the Save As dialog box, specify a new name for the .ins file and enter the URL for the .cab (cabinet) files. (New .cab files are only generated if the changes that you made to the .ins file require new .cab files.) (See Figure 22-3.)

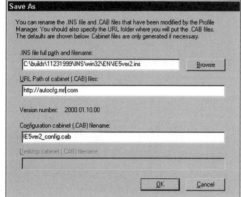

Figure 22-3:
Saving
modified
.ins and
.cab files.

Troubleshooting with Profile Manager

In the previous section, I explain how to change the settings and restrictions in an .ins file. This section explains how to troubleshoot a client computer by changing settings in the .ins file and how to roll the changed settings out to a client computer.

Suppose that an administrator in an organization with several remote locations creates and deploys a customized IE5 package to the Windows 98 computers in the organization. Joe User calls the help desk because he is unable to access the Internet from his Windows 98 system. After asking the standard troubleshooting questions, the administrator suspects that Joe needs a different proxy configuration for the IE5 browser.

The solution to the problem is to reconfigure the user's proxy server and then lock down this Registry setting so that the user can't alter it.

Assuming that the administrator didn't include an automatic configuration URL (see Chapter 16 for more information on automatic configuration) when he or she deployed the custom IE5 package, the administrator has two good options remaining to resolve this scenario:

✔ Edit the .ins file for the IE5 package and specify an automatic configuration URL. Then configure Joe's browser to access the .ins file from the automatic configuration URL when he restarts his computer.

✔ Edit the .ins file for the IE5 package. Copy the .ins file to Joe's system, configure his system to use the .ins file, and have him restart his system.

To save time during future troubleshooting, enabling an automatic configuration URL is the best choice. Using the Customization wizard, you can enable automatic configuration and specify an automatic configuration URL. By enabling automatic configuration, you configure the browser to periodically check the auto-config URL for an updated .ins file. The browser settings from the new .ins file are then applied to the browser to change its configuration. If automatic configuration is not enabled, choose option two and copy a new .ins file to Joe's system. (Chapter 16 gives detailed information on enabling automatic configuration.)

Lab 22-1 illustrates the steps that you would go through to solve the scenario described above.

Lab 22-1   Changing Registry Settings by Using Profile Manager

1. **From Profile Manager, open the Install.ins file of any package that you have created.**

2. **Under Wizard Settings in the left pane of Profile Manager, select Proxy Settings.**

3. **In the right pane, select the Enable Proxy Settings check box.**

4. **In the HTTP proxy address box, type** proxy1.mrl.com. **Type** 80 **in the Port box.**

5. **Near the bottom of the right pane, select the Use the Same Proxy Server for All Addresses check box.**

6. **In the left pane of Profile Manager, locate the Corporate Restrictions folder under Policies and Restrictions. Expand the folder by clicking the plus sign next to the folder icon. Select Connections Page.**

7. In the right pane of Profile Manager, select the Disable Changing Proxy Settings check box.

8. Choose File➪Save As.

9. In the Save As dialog box, enter a path and name the new file autoconf.ins. Enter a URL for the cabinet (.cab) files.

10. Copy the new autoconfig.ins file to the automatic configuration location that you specified in the Customization wizard.

11. Install the new package to a client computer and observe that the proxy settings have changed and that the proxy settings on the client cannot be modified.

12. Using the Registry Editor, view the following:

```
HKEY_CURRENT_USER\Software\Microsoft\Windows
         \CurrentVersion\Internet Settings
```

Verify that the proxy server parameter reads `proxy1.mrl.com:80`.

13. Close the Registry Editor without saving any changes.

Prep Test

1 Marcia is a corporate administrator for a large company with 2,500 Windows NT 4.0 and Windows 98 client computers. Help desk calls related to browser configurations are increasing steadily within the company. Marcia wants to restrict the users from changing some of the browser settings. What steps should she use to change the browser configuration for all users?

- A ❑ Use the Profile Manager to edit the .ins file of the existing deployed browser package.
- B ❑ Copy the .ins file to the auto-config URL.
- C ❑ Use the Customization wizard to create a new browser package with the new configuration.
- D ❑ Copy any resulting .cab files to the auto-config URL.

2 Jodi is a corporate administrator for a large company with 2,500 Windows NT 4.0 and Windows 98 client computers. One of her users, George, keeps experiencing problems with his Outlook Express settings. Jodi plans to use Profile Manager to restrict George from making future changes to his Outlook Express configuration. How can Jodi distribute the new .ins file to only George's computer?

- A ○ By copying the new .ins file to the auto-config URL.
- B ○ By copying the new .ins file to George's computer.
- C ○ By sending the new .ins file on a floppy disk.
- D ○ By copying the new .ins file to the auto-proxy URL.

3 Identify the types of files that are created by running the Customization wizard.

- A ❑ .adm
- B ❑ .ins
- C ❑ .cab
- D ❑ .pac

4 Which of the tools listed below can be used to create variations of an existing IE5 browser package?

- A ○ Customization wizard
- B ○ Registry
- C ○ Profile Manager
- D ○ Systems Policy Editor

5 (True/False). The Policies and Restrictions settings in a browser package are copied from the .adm policy templates that are installed with the IEAK.

- A ○ True
- B ○ False

Answers

1 *A, B, and D.* Marcia should first use the Profile Manager to edit the .ins file of the existing browser package that is currently deployed. After the changes are made, Marcia should copy the .ins file and any .cab files that resulted from the changed configuration to the auto-config URL for users to access. *Review "Troubleshooting with Profile Manager."*

2 *B.* If Jodi copies the new .ins file to George's computer, the browser will read the updates from the .ins file and apply them to the browser. Answer A is incorrect because the .ins file would be distributed to all users. Answer D is incorrect because the .ins file is distributed from the auto-config URL, not the auto-proxy URL. Answer C is incorrect because it's unnecessary for Jodi to send the file on a floppy disk. She can simply copy the file across the network. *Review "Troubleshooting with Profile Manager."*

3 *A and B.* The Customization wizard creates the Install.ins file and .cab, or cabinet, files. *Review "Editing .ins Files."*

4 *C.* The Customization wizard creates the initial browser package, but the Profile Manager is used to edit .ins files for existing browser packages. By saving .ins files with a new file name, administrators can create variations of the original package. *Review "Editing .ins Files."*

5 *A.* The .adm files are policy templates. The nine default templates are installed the first time that the Customization wizard is run. The settings and restrictions in these policy files make up the Policies and Restrictions settings in a custom browser package. *Review "Editing .ins Files."*

Chapter 23

Fixing Deployment Failures

● ●

Exam Objectives

▶ Identify failures during deployment of IE5

▶ Resolve deployment failures of IE5

● ●

*I*n a perfect world, all your Internet Explorer 5 deployments would be flaw-less! Your manager would be awed by your expertise, and you'd have little to do but spend your large paychecks.

Alas, the world isn't perfect. And occasionally a deployment doesn't go well. So in this chapter, I tell you how to identify the various reasons that an IE5 deployment fails, as well as how to fix it.

Quick Assessment

Finding the Needle in the Haystack

Trouble-shooting Setup

1 Whether downloading, using a flat installation, or using a single disk installation of an IE5 browser package, the Setup program must be able to access _____ files from the network.

2 The troubleshooting log file for the setup process is called _____ _____ _____ .

3 If you've run IE5 Setup on a computer previously, the setup routine renames the old log file to _____ _____ _____ .

4 The IE5 Setup routine checks for _____ _____ _____ _____ _____.

5 _____ _____ in Active Setup Log.txt help you decipher what the Setup program was doing when it failed, along with why the failure occurred.

6 The Active Setup Log.txt file is always located in _____.

7 By default, the Active Setup Log.txt file is located in the _____ folder on a Windows NT 4.0 computer.

Removing IE5

8 The _____ _____ file helps troubleshoot the failure of an IE5 uninstall process.

9 The Uninstall Log.txt file is always located in _____.

10 The Uninstall Log.txt file tracks the removal of IE5 files from the _____ and the _____.

Answers

1   *installation.* See "Finding the Needle in the Haystack."

2   *Active Setup Log.txt.* See "Troubleshooting Setup."

3   *Active Setup Log.bak.* See "Troubleshooting Setup."

4   *previous versions of Internet Explorer.* See "Troubleshooting Setup."

5   *Status codes.* See "Troubleshooting Setup."

6   *the %systemroot% folder.* See "Troubleshooting Setup."

7   *C:/WINNT.* See "Troubleshooting Setup."

8   *Uninstall Log.txt.* See "Removing IE5."

9   *the %systemroot% folder.* See "Removing IE5."

10   *computer, Registry.* See "Removing IE5."

Finding the Needle in the Haystack

Finding the cause of a deployment failure can be like looking for a needle in a haystack, particularly when using the download distribution method. If the installation files are distributed on removable media, such as a CD, network failures are not a problem issue. But when downloading, using a flat installation, or using a single-disk installation, the Setup program must be able to access installation files from the network. Chapter 22 details network troubleshooting steps.

IE5 deployments can fail for any number of other reasons, among which are:

- ✔ You lose network connectivity, which halts the download before it's finished.
- ✔ The operating system hangs and then the Setup program never finishes.
- ✔ Not all the installation files are copied to the distribution media.
- ✔ The deployment fails for reasons that you really don't understand.

Fortunately, Internet Explorer 5 includes log files to help you track the point of failure and resolve the deployment problem.

Troubleshooting Setup

Microsoft cleverly names the troubleshooting log file Active Setup Log.txt. The file is located in the c:\Windows folder for Windows 95/98 computers, and C:\WINNT folder for Windows NT 4.0 computers. (If you didn't install Windows into the default folder, the file will be in the folder where you installed Windows.)

Launching IE5 Setup immediately creates Active Setup Log.txt. If you've run IE5 Setup on the computer previously, the setup routine renames the old log file to Active Setup Log.bak. Active Setup Log.txt records every single step of the setup routine.

Figure 23-1 shows the log file from my own computer. Notice that the file begins with the date and time that the Setup program initiates. Look further and you see that Setup checks for previous versions of Internet Explorer, checks to see which operating system is installed, checks for previously downloaded files — and much, much more. Every step of the setup is recorded in the file, with the final entry being the date and time that setup ended.

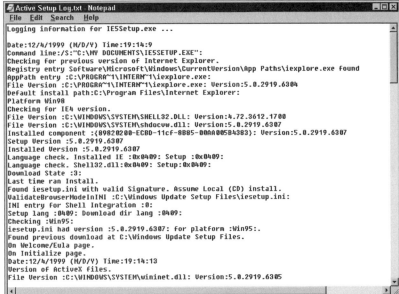

You may also notice in Figure 23-1 that several entries end with numbers surrounded by colons. For example, about halfway down the screen in Figure 23-1, you see the line:

```
Download State :3:
```

The colons, placed before and after the 3, signify that this is a status code. The status codes help you decipher what the Setup program was doing when it failed, along with why the failure occurred. Table 23-1 below is a list of Active Setup Log.txt codes.

Table 23-1	Active Setup Log.txt Error Codes
Error Code	*Description*
0	Initializing (making a temporary folder, checking disk space)
1	Dependency (checking for all dependencies)
2	Downloading (server is downloading files)
3	Copying (files are being copied from download folder to temporary install folder)
4	Retrying (Setup is restarting download because of a timeout error or other download error)

(continued)

Table 23-1 *(continued)*

Error Code	Description
5	Checking trust (checking permissions)
6	Extracting files
7	Setup program (an .inf or .exe file)
8	Finished (installation is finished)
9	Finished (files have finished downloading)
80100003	Files are missing from the download folder during installation
800bxxxx	An error code starting with 800b is a trust failure
800Cxxxx	An error code starting with 800C is a urlmon failure
800C005	File or server not found
800C00B	The connection timed out
8004004	The user canceled Setup

By looking at Table 23-1, you can see that the `Download State :3:` entry mentioned above means that Setup was copying files from the download folder to the temporary install folder. Similarly, a `:0:` code means that a process is initializing.

For the exam, know the location of the Active Setup Log.txt (`C:\WINNT` or the folder into which you installed Windows) file and the type of information in the file.

Figure 23-2 is another page of the setup log. Notice in this figure that several errors are recorded. Halfway down the screen you see the message: `The update to Windows is not completely installed on your computer. Are you sure you want to quit Setup?` Also, near the bottom of the file is a list of components that failed to install.

Obviously, the Active Setup Log.txt file provides great information for troubleshooting a deployment failure. You couldn't ask for a more precise tool!

```
Active Setup Log.txt - Notepad                                    _ □ X
File   Edit   Search   Help
File Version :C:\WINDOWS\SYSTEM\olepro32.dll: Version:5.0.4277.1
Run setup command. File:C:\WINDOWS\TEMP\IXP000.TMP\IESetup.inf: Section:MFCInstalled:
RunSetupCommand returned :0:
Queue components for the install engine:
QueueComponents took :0:
No_Integrated_Shell
Check for MFC files.
File Version :C:\WINDOWS\SYSTEM\mfc40.dll: Version:4.1.0.6140
File Version :C:\WINDOWS\SYSTEM\msvcrt40.dll: Version:4.10.0.6038
File Version :C:\WINDOWS\SYSTEM\olepro32.dll: Version:5.0.4277.1
Run setup command. File:C:\WINDOWS\TEMP\IXP000.TMP\IESetup.inf: Section:MFCInstalled:
RunSetupCommand returned :0:
Queue components for the install engine:
QueueComponents took :14:
MessageBox.
Title:Windows Update Setup:
Msg:The update to Windows is not completely installed on your computer. Are you sure you wan

Run setup command. File:C:\WINDOWS\TEMP\IXP000.TMP\IESetup.inf: Section:IE4Setup.Failure:
RunSetupCommand returned :0:
List of components failed to install:
Install failed:USP10:
Install failed:Frontpad:
Install failed:webpublish:
Install failed:WebFolders:
Install failed:Fontsup:
Install failed:IELPKAR:
Install failed:IELPKTH:
End of List of failed components.
Date:12/4/1999 (M/D/Y) Time:20:0:9
End of Logging.
```

Figure 23-2:
Examining
errors in the
Active
Setup
Log.txt file.

Removing IE5

Internet Explorer 5 also includes an uninstall log file called Uninstall Log.txt. As the name implies, this file helps troubleshoot the failure of an IE5 uninstall process.

The IE5 Uninstall Log.txt file is also located in the `systemroot` folder. It contains the same type of information as the setup log file, but instead tracks the removal of IE5 files from the computer and the Registry. If errors occur while removing IE5 files or Registry parameters during an uninstall, error messages are recorded in the Uninstall Log.txt file.

Prep Test

1 Roger is a corporate administrator and has created a custom IE5 browser package. While deploying the package, the installation failed on one Windows NT 4.0 computer. What should Roger do to determine the cause of the problem?

A ○ Roger should check the Active Setup Log.txt file.

B ○ Roger should check the Setup Log.txt file.

C ○ Roger should check the Install.txt file.

D ○ Roger should check for previous versions of Internet Explorer on the computer.

2 Roger is trying to uninstall IE5 so that he can install the Active Desktop for one of his users. He is unable to uninstall without receiving an error message. What log file should Roger check to find the cause of the problem?

A ○ Roger should check the Active Setup Log.txt file.

B ○ Roger should check the Setup Log.txt file.

C ○ Roger should check the Uninstall Log.txt file.

D ○ Roger should check the Install.txt file.

3 Roger is troubleshooting the deployment failure of an IE5 package on a Windows 98 computer. He has confirmed that the computer has network connectivity to the download site. He wants to know whether all the installation files were copied to the download site. What should Roger do to find out?

A ○ Roger should examine the download site and verify that each .cab file was copied.

B ○ Roger should verify that the .ins file was copied to the download site.

C ○ Roger should run the IEAK Customization wizard again.

D ○ Roger should open the Active Setup Log.txt file and examine the status codes.

4 Roger is troubleshooting the deployment failure of an IE5 package on a Windows NT 4.0 computer. He has confirmed that the computer has network connectivity to the download site. He wants to know which components of the custom package were not installed. What should Roger do to find out?

A ○ Roger should check the Setup Log.txt file in the `C:\WINNT` folder.

B ○ Roger should check the Setup Log.txt file in the `C:\WINNT\SYSTEM32` folder.

C ○ Roger should check the Active Setup Log.txt file in the `C:\WINNT` folder.

D ○ Roger should check the Active Setup Log.txt file in the `C:\WINNT\SYSTEM32` folder.

5 What information can be found in the Active Setup Log.txt file? (Choose all that apply.)

A ❑ A list of components that were not installed successfully.

B ❑ Error codes that indicate connection timeouts.

C ❑ Error codes that indicate a server could not be found.

D ❑ Status codes that indicate what stage of Setup was running when the installation failed.

E ❑ None of the above.

Answers

1 *A.* Active Setup Log.txt is the name of the log file that records each step of the installation process, so answers B and C are incorrect. Because the Setup program checks for previous versions of Internet Explorer automatically, answer D is incorrect. *Review "Troubleshooting Setup."*

2 *C.* Because Uninstall Log.txt is the correct name of the uninstall log file, answers A, B, and D are incorrect. *Review "Removing IE5."*

3 *D.* The status codes help you decipher what the Setup program was doing when it failed, along with why the failure occurred. Error code 80100003 indicates that files are missing from the download folder during installation. *Review "Troubleshooting Setup."*

4 *C.* The Active Setup Log.txt file is located in the `C:\WINNT` folder by default. Along with status codes and other information, the file contains a list of components that were not successfully installed. *Review "Troubleshooting Setup."*

5 *A, B, C, and D.* The Active Setup Log.txt file contains a list of components not installed successfully, error codes that indicate connection timeouts, error codes that indicate a server could not be found, and status codes that signify the stages of the setup routine. *Review "Troubleshooting Setup."*

Fixing Deployment Failures

Chapter 24

Resolving IEAK Customization Wizard Problems

* *

Exam Objectives

▶ Diagnose IEAK wizard problems
▶ Resolve IEAK wizard problems

$\mathbf{D}$on't expect to see many problems when you're running the IEAK Customization wizard. The IEAK is simple and easy to use. The hardest part is planning for the information to provide on each screen.

You occasionally run into a minor misstep with the wizard on this yellow brick road, and you have to search for the Oz . . . I mean *cause* (yellow brick road, wizard, Oz . . . I just had to do that!). The most common problems arise from network connectivity issues and customization codes. This chapter tells you how to diagnose a problem, should you have one, and how to resolve it to successfully run the wizard.

Quick Assessment

Custom-
ization
Code Errors

1 You cannot run the IEAK wizard without a _____ _____.

2 You cannot run both the _____ _____ and _____ _____simultaneously on the same computer.

Network
Connection
Errors

3 When package downloads are interrupted by network failures, _____ _____ detects the failure and picks up where it left off before the error occurred.

4 If you haven't run the Customization wizard once before, then you can't disable _____.

Custom-
ization
Errors

5 The Feature Selection screen of the IEAK _____ _____ enables administrators to indicate the features that they want to customize in the IE5 package.

6 Not all customization options are available for all _____ or for all _____.

7 If _____ install is selected as the installation option, the wizard does not show all the customization screens because the user will not be presented with those options.

8 Custom IE5 browser packages are supported for the following UNIX operating systems: _____ and _____.

9 In regard to the IEAK, Windows NT 3.51 is considered a _____ operating system because it runs the _____ version of the browser.

10 Custom IE5 packages must be created on a computer running a _____ _____ _____ _____ and running Internet Explorer 5.

Answers

1 *customization code.* See "Customization Code Errors."

2 *Customization wizard, Profile Manager.* See "Customization Code Errors."

3 *Active Setup.* See "Network Connection Errors."

4 *AVS (Automatic Version Synchronization).* See "Network Connection Errors."

5 *Customization wizard.* See "Customization Errors."

6 *roles, platforms.* See "Customization Errors."

7 *silent.* See "Customization Errors."

8 *Solaris 2.5.1, Solaris 2.6.* See "Customization Errors."

9 *16-bit, 16-bit.* See "Customization Errors."

10 *Windows 32-bit operating system.* See "Customization Errors."

Customization Code Errors

First and foremost, remember that you cannot run the IEAK wizard without a customization code. The wizard simply doesn't work without the code. You can go through the wizard screens, but none of the information will be saved — no package is created.

Enter the code correctly. I once inadvertently entered the wrong code and encountered the error message shown in Figure 24-1. (All right, I did it more than once!)

Figure 24-1:
Use the
correct
custom-
ization code.

After you enter the code correctly and successfully run the wizard, notice that when you next launch the wizard your code is retained.

Remember that you cannot run both the IEAK Customization wizard and the IEAK Profile Manager simultaneously on the same computer. If you try, you'll see an error message that instructs you to close one of the two IEAK programs.

Be sure that you select the appropriate licensing agreement for your role. If you select the Service Provider role or the Content Developer role, then you can't see as many customization options as with the Corporate Administrator role. This isn't an error; it's simply a matchup of role to licensing agreement. If you need the Corporate Administrator options, go back and fill out the appropriate licensing agreement.

Network Connection Errors

You probably encounter network connection errors most often. But fortunately, Microsoft has blessed us with Active Setup. When package downloads are interrupted by network failures, Active Setup detects the failure and picks up where it left off before the error occurred. What a time-saver!

You may encounter network connection errors in a couple of areas while using the wizard:

- ✔ **During Stage 2 when you reach the Microsoft Download Site screen.** If you don't have network connectivity when you reach this screen, you won't see the list of available sites for file downloads. If you have repeated problems downloading from one site, switch to another site. (It all sounds so obvious, but I did promise to warn you about the pitfalls and potholes.)

- ✔ **At the Automatic Version Synchronization (AVS) screen.** Here's a real Catch-22: If you haven't run the wizard once before, then you can't disable AVS. And if AVS isn't disabled, the wizard is going to attempt to connect to the Microsoft download site to compare file versions. So be certain that you've got an Internet connection on the workstation from which you're running the wizard for the first time.

AVS can't be disabled the first time you run the Customization wizard.

Customization Errors

Customization errors are normally the result of poor planning or of a misconfigured Internet Explorer 5 installation on the administrator's workstation.

The most common error encountered is that of not seeing the desired customization screens while running the wizard. The most common causes of this scenario are:

- ✔ **Selecting the wrong role:** Not all customization options are available for all roles. For example, the ISP role includes the option to customize a sign-up server, while the corporate administrator role does not. Similarly, the corporate administrator role includes the option of creating packages for UNIX clients, but the ISP role does not. The corporate administrator role is the most feature-rich role of the three available roles.

- ✔ **Selecting the wrong operating system:** Not all customization features are available on all the supported operating systems. For example, the Windows Update Setup wizard is not available for browsers running on UNIX client computers. Similarly, many of the security features available for the 32-bit operating systems are not available for the 16-bit and UNIX operating systems.

Custom IE5 browser packages are supported for the following UNIX operating systems: Solaris 2.5.1 and Solaris 2.6.

Although custom IE5 packages run on 16-bit, 32-bit, and UNIX platforms, the custom packages must be created on a computer running a Windows 32-bit operating system and running Internet Explorer 5.

In regard to the IEAK, Windows 3.51 is considered a 16-bit operating system. The IEAK runs the 16-bit browser version instead of the 32-bit version.

✔ **Not installing the component on the build computer:** If you're not seeing the customization options that you expect during the wizard, you may not have the component installed (or properly customized) on your workstation. For example, if you try to customize the Windows Desktop Update but don't see the appropriate screens, make sure that you installed the Windows Desktop Update on the build computer.

Your custom package is based on the Internet Explorer 5 installation on the computer on which the wizard is run (the build computer).

✔ **Not specifying the feature on the Feature Selection screen during Stage 1 of the Customization wizard:** Perhaps you skipped or excluded the component during an earlier stage of the wizard. The Feature Selection screen (Figure 24-2) of the IEAK Customization wizard enables administrators to indicate the features that they want to customize in the IE5 package. Only the screens for selected features appear in the wizard. If you don't see a screen that you were expecting to see in the wizard, go back to the Feature Selection screen and make sure that the feature is selected.

✔ **Selecting the wrong installation option:** If silent install is selected as the installation option, the wizard does not show all the customization screens because the user doesn't make choices during the installation.

Figure 24-2:
Selecting features to appear in the Customization wizard.

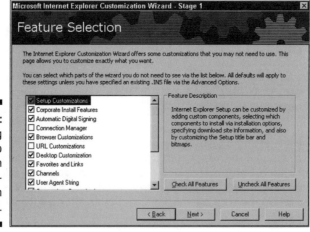

If users install a new customized IE5 browser and then complain that they can't use the Active Desktop, it's not due to an error in the customized package. Only users who had Active Desktop installed under Internet Explorer version 4.0 are able to use the Active Desktop. To correct this scenario, uninstall IE5, reinstall IE4 and Active Desktop, and then reinstall IE5 once again. For those users who are currently running Windows 98 and Windows 2000 as their operating system, Active Desktop is included in the operating system.

Prep Test

1 Sharon is a corporate administrator creating a custom IE5 package. She is running the IEAK Customization wizard for the first time. When she gets to the screen labeled Automatic Version Synchronization, she gets an error message. What could be causing the problem? (Choose all that apply.)

A ❑ Sharon is not running the IEAK on a 32-bit operating system.

B ❑ Sharon is not connected to the Internet.

C ❑ Sharon has never run the Automatic Version Synchronization before, and AVS is currently disabled.

D ❑ Sharon did not select AVS on the Feature Selection screen.

2 Sharon has successfully created and deployed a custom package to upgrade employees from IE4 to IE5. Several users have called to complain that they cannot use the Active Desktop, yet others in their department are able to. What could be causing this problem for the users who can't use the Active Desktop? (Choose all that apply.)

A ❑ These users were not using the Active Desktop with their IE4 installation.

B ❑ These users are using UNIX computers.

C ❑ These users are using 16-bit versions of Windows.

D ❑ These users are not using IE4 compatibility mode.

3 James is a corporate administrator using the IEAK to create a custom browser package for employees at XYZ, Inc. The custom package will be distributed to Windows 95, Windows 98, and Windows NT 4.0 client computers. While running the Customization wizard, James is unable to view all the customization screens for Outlook Express. What could be causing the problem? (Choose all that apply.)

A ❑ Outlook Express is not installed on James's build computer.

B ❑ James did not select Outlook Express on the Feature Selection screen of the wizard.

C ❑ James chose the silent installation option.

D ❑ James is using a UNIX computer as his build computer.

4 Carol is the administrator at an ISP and is creating a custom IE5 package for distribution to ISP customers. She is unable to view the sign-up screen in the Customization wizard. Using the Back button in the wizard, Carol goes backward through the screens and verifies that she chose the ISP role. What else could be preventing Carol from viewing the sign-up screens in the wizard?

A ○ Carol did not install a sign-up server prior to running the wizard.

B ○ Carol did not install the sign-up option on her build computer prior to running the wizard.

C ○ Carol did not select the sign-up feature on the Feature Selection screen of the wizard.

D ○ Carol did not select the silent installation option.

5 Maria is a corporate administrator for a large corporation. She is creating a custom IE5 browser package for Windows 98, Windows NT 3.51, and Windows NT 4.0 computers. Maria runs the Customization wizard in the corporate administrator role and selects the Windows 9x/NT 4.0 platform option. Will Maria's completed package run on the NT 3.51 clients?

A ○ Yes. NT 3.51 is a 32-bit operating system and the package will run on the NT 3.51 clients.

B ○ No. NT 3.51 is a 32-bit operating system but the package will not run on the NT 3.51 clients.

Answers

Wizard Problems

1 *B and C.* If Sharon isn't connected to the Internet at this point in the Customization wizard, and if she has never used AVS to synchronize files against those available from the Microsoft Web site, then she will be unable to proceed past the AVS screen. Sharon must enable AVS and connect to the Internet so that she can complete the wizard. Answer A is incorrect because the IEAK only runs on 32-bit operating systems, and Sharon has successfully installed and begun to use the wizard. Answer D is incorrect because Sharon is not required to select AVS on the Feature Selection screen, which appears in a subsequent stage of the AVS screen in the wizard. *Review "Network Connection Errors."*

2 *A, B, and C.* Active Desktop is only available on 32-bit Windows operating systems. In order to run the Active Desktop in IE5, Active Desktop must have been installed and running in IE4 prior to upgrading to IE5. Answer D is incorrect because compatibility mode doesn't enable users to use Active Desktop. *Review "Customization Errors."*

3 *A and B.* To be presented with all the Outlook Express customization screens, Outlook Express must be installed on the build computer. In addition, James must select Outlook Express on the Feature Selection screen of the wizard. The feature selection screen is where James indicates which customization screens he wants to view while running the Customization wizard. Answer C is incorrect because choosing the silent installation option wouldn't prevent James from seeing the Outlook Express customization screens. Answer D is incorrect because James can't run the IEAK on a build computer at all. *Review "Customization Errors."*

4 *C.* If Carol has verified that she is using the ISP role, then the most likely reason for not seeing the sign-up screens is that she didn't select it on the Feature Selection screen. Although a sign-up server is required for the sign-up feature to work once the browser is deployed, it isn't necessary to install the server prior to running the wizard. The URL for the sign-up page must be specified during the wizard, but the URL doesn't have to exist prior to running the wizard. *Review "Customization Errors."*

5 *B.* Although Windows NT 3.51 is a 32-bit operating system, Windows NT 3.51 runs the 16-bit version of the browser. Maria must run the Customization wizard again and select the Windows 3.11/WFW/NT 3.51 platform option. *Review "Customization Errors."*

Chapter 25

Dealing with Outlook Express and NetMeeting Failures

● ●

Exam Objectives

▶ Diagnose and resolve connection failures of Outlook Express

▶ Diagnose and resolve connection failures of NetMeeting

● ●

*1*n this chapter, I help you figure out how to resolve and correct application configuration problems. (For assistance with troubleshooting other connectivity failures, see Chapter 22.)

Outlook Express and NetMeeting connection failures are usually a result of

✔ Network failure

✔ Name resolution failure

✔ Incorrectly configured applications

Fortunately, the Internet Explorer Administration Kit can help you minimize configuration issues by letting you preconfigure application settings before you distribute a browser package to your organization. But you should still prepare to troubleshoot Outlook Express and NetMeeting failures if they arise.

Quick Assessment

Diagnose and Resolve Connection Failures of Outlook Express

1 A _____ is a set of rules that define how data is transferred on a network.

2 The default port for the POP3 protocol is _____.

3 _____ is a messaging protocol that enables Internet users to remotely connect to an outgoing mail server to send messages.

4 The default port number for SMTP is _____.

5 The _____ contains a list of commands exchanged with your incoming (or POP3) mail server.

6 _____ contains commands exchanged with NNTP news servers.

Diagnose and Resolve Connection Failures of NetMeeting

7 If you cannot access a directory server, try placing the NetMeeting call using the _____ _____ of the remote computer.

8 Unless you have _____ _____ installed on your computer, you won't be able to send video to other callers.

9 The _____ _____ _____ adjusts audio settings for better reception.

10 To send and receive audio simultaneously, the system must have a _____ _____ card installed and enabled.

Answers

1 *protocol.* See "Messaging Protocols."

2 *110.* See "Messaging Protocols."

3 *SMTP.* See "Messaging Protocols."

4 *25.* See "Messaging Protocols."

5 *POP3.log.* See "Using Outlook Express Logs."

6 *INETNEWS.log.* See "Using Outlook Express Logs."

7 *IP address.* See "Directory Server Errors."

8 *video camera.* See "Tuning Audio and Video."

9 *Audio Tuning Wizard.* See "Tuning Audio and Video."

10 *full-duplex sound.* See "Tuning Audio and Video."

Troubleshooting Outlook Express

When troubleshooting Outlook Express failures, determine the type of issue you're dealing with by using a systematic approach. You can achieve quick results by answering the following questions:

- ✔ **Is the problem currently occurring on more than one computer in the organization?** If yes, troubleshoot for network or name resolution failures (see Chapter 22).

- ✔ **Is the problem occurring on a single workstation?** If yes, troubleshoot the configuration settings for Outlook Express.

Verifying Outlook Express settings

Begin troubleshooting by checking to make sure that the Outlook Express configuration hasn't been altered. That may seem obvious, but many times it's a step that's overlooked and quite often this turns out to be the problem. Follow the steps in Lab 25-1 to check this configuration.

| Lab 25-1 | Viewing the Outlook Express Configuration |

1. **To verify the Outlook Express configuration, you must first make sure that Outlook Express is the default e-mail program.**

   From IE5, choose Tools⇨Internet Options; then click the Programs tab. Verify that Outlook Express appears in the E-Mail drop-down box (see Figure 25-1).

   Aside from an incorrect mailbox name and password, incorrect server names are the most common Outlook Express configuration error.

2. **Confirm that the user's e-mail account and e-mail server are configured correctly.**

   Figure 25-2 shows the Servers tab of an e-mail server Properties dialog box. (To view an account's properties, choose Tools⇨Accounts. In the Accounts dialog box, select the correct mail account and click the Properties button. In the Properties dialog box, select the Servers tab to view server properties.) Verify that both the incoming and outgoing mail server names are correct. Ensure that the user's account name and password are correct.

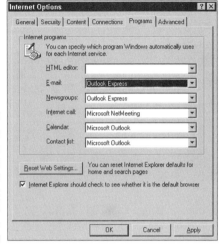

Figure 25-1:
Using
Outlook
Express as
the default
e-mail
program.

Know the difference between a POP3 server and an SMTP server. Also,
know the IP port numbers for POP3 and SMTP.

Figure 25-2:
Confirming
the account
ID and
server are
correct.

**3. Click the Advanced tab of the e-mail server Properties dialog box and
verify that the port numbers are configured correctly.**

In addition, you must know whether or not these servers require a
secure connection (see Figure 25-3).

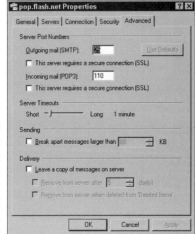

Figure 25-3:
Viewing the
Advanced
properties
for Outlook
Express.

You typically find configuration errors on one of the screens (refer to Figures 25-2 and 25-3). In Lab 25-2, I take you through the steps of verifying Outlook Express settings to make certain that the application is properly configured.

Lab 25-2   Verifying an Outlook Express Configuration

1. **Start the Outlook Express application.**

2. **Choose Tools⇨Accounts.**

3. **Click the Mail tab and then select the mail account that you want to verify. Click the Properties button.**

4. **In the Properties dialog box, click the Servers tab.**

    Under Server Information, verify that the mail server names are typed correctly in both the Incoming mail and Outgoing mail text boxes.

    Under Incoming Mail Server, verify that the user has typed the correct account name (or user ID) and password for the mail server.

5. **Click the Advanced tab.**

    Verify that the correct port numbers are entered for both POP3 and SMTP. Use the defaults unless your organization or ISP has specified different port numbers.

    If your organization or ISP requires a secure connection to either the incoming or the outgoing mail server, select the check box labeled `This server requires a secure connection (SSL)`.

6. **Click OK to close the Properties dialog box.**

7. **Click Close to exit the Internet Accounts dialog box.**

Messaging protocols

A *protocol* is a set of rules that defines how data is transferred on a network. Some protocols, such as POP3 and SMTP, deal specifically with transferring e-mail messages on the network. The protocols defined below are the messaging protocols you should know for the exam.

✔ **POP3 (Post Office Protocol 3)** is a messaging protocol that enables Internet users to remotely connect to a mail server for their incoming messages. The default port is 110.

✔ **SMTP (Simple Mail Transport Protocol)** is a messaging protocol that enables Internet users to remotely connect to an outgoing mail server to send messages. The default port is 25.

✔ **NNTP (Network News Transfer Protocol)** is a messaging protocol that is used to post and retrieve messages from a news server. The default port is 119.

✔ **IMAP (Internet Message Access Protocol)** is a messaging protocol that is used to remotely access public folders on a mail server. Internet Explorer 5 is IMAP version 4 (IMAP4) compliant. The default port is 143.

Using Outlook Express logs

If you can't resolve the problem by verifying Outlook Express configuration settings, you can use the Outlook Express log files to troubleshoot the problem. Outlook Express tracks all commands exchanged with a server in one of several log files:

✔ Mail

✔ News

✔ IMAP

✔ HTTP

Lab 25-3 takes you through the steps of turning on the mail log files.

Lab 25-3   Enabling the Mail Log Files

1. **After starting Outlook Express, choose Tools⇨Options.**

2. **Click the Maintenance tab.**

   Locate the troubleshooting section near the bottom of the tab.

3. **Select the check box labeled** Mail option to enable logging.

4. **Click OK to close the Options dialog box.**

By default, the log files are named:

- POP3.log
- SMTP.log
- INETNEWS.log
- IMAP.log

The log files are stored deep within the *%systemroot%* folder on the computer. The easiest way to find them is to search your computer for files ending with the .log extension.

The POP3.log file (see Figure 25-4) contains a list of commands exchanged with your incoming (or POP3) mail server. The SMTP.log file contains commands exchanged with the outgoing (SMTP) mail server. Similarly, INETNEWS.log contains commands exchanged with NNTP news servers, and IMAP.log contains commands exchanged with IMAP directory servers.

```
Pop3.log - Notepad                                                    _ □ ×
File   Edit   Search   Help

Outlook Express 5.00.2919.6600
POP3 Log started at 12/14/1999 05:14:56
POP3: 05:14:56 [rx] +OK QPOP (version 2.53-DSMSv1.6-19991018) at nessie starting.
POP3: 05:14:56 [tx] USER mloughry
POP3: 05:14:56 [rx] +OK Password required for mloughry.
POP3: 05:14:56 [tx] PASS ********
POP3: 05:14:56 [rx] +OK mloughry has 0 messages (0 octets).
POP3: 05:14:56 [tx] STAT
POP3: 05:14:57 [rx] +OK 0 0
POP3: 05:14:57 [tx] QUIT
POP3: 05:14:57 [rx] +OK Pop server at nessie signing off.
POP3: 05:16:10 [rx] +OK QPOP (version 2.53-DSMSv1.6-19991018) at yeti starting.
POP3: 05:16:10 [tx] USER mloughry
POP3: 05:16:10 [rx] +OK Password required for mloughry.
POP3: 05:16:10 [tx] PASS ********
POP3: 05:16:10 [rx] +OK mloughry has 1 message (1201 octets).
POP3: 05:16:10 [tx] STAT
POP3: 05:16:11 [rx] +OK 1 1201
POP3: 05:16:11 [tx] LIST
POP3: 05:16:11 [rx] +OK 1 messages (1201 octets)
POP3: 05:16:11 [rx] 1 1201
POP3: 05:16:11 [rx] .
POP3: 05:16:12 [tx] RETR 1
POP3: 05:16:12 [rx] +OK 1201 octets
POP3: 05:16:12 [tx] DELE 1
POP3: 05:16:12 [rx] +OK Message 1 has been deleted.
POP3: 05:16:12 [tx] QUIT
POP3: 05:16:12 [rx] +OK Pop server at yeti signing off.
```

Figure 25-4: Viewing the POP3.log file for trouble-shooting Outlook Express.

For the exam, know how to enable the troubleshooting logs, as I explain in Lab 25-3.

After you finish troubleshooting Outlook Express, disable the logging feature on the user's computer. Log files can grow very large (very quickly) because they record every command sent to and received from the server. You don't want to consume the user's hard drive with logged information!

Troubleshooting NetMeeting

NetMeeting is a more complex application than Outlook Express and has additional categories (such as audio and video) to troubleshoot. Usually, however, network connection failures and incorrectly configured settings are the primary causes of problems with NetMeeting. You can ask the same basic questions when troubleshooting NetMeeting as when you're troubleshooting Outlook Express (or most any other application):

🖝 **Is the problem currently occurring on more than one computer in the organization?** If yes, troubleshoot for network or name resolution failures (see Chapter 22).

🖝 **Is the problem occurring on a single workstation?** If yes, troubleshoot the configuration settings for NetMeeting.

After you determine that a problem is occurring on a single workstation, begin by checking the system's hardware. Ensure that all audio and video devices are connected and configured properly. If the hardware functions correctly and the problem persists, proceed to troubleshooting the NetMeeting configuration on the client computer. The following section explains this procedure.

Directory server errors

The first configuration error that is likely to occur when users start NetMeeting is the inability to connect to the specified directory server. Often, this occurs because of network failures. (Read Chapter 22 for information on troubleshooting connection failures.) But sometimes the directory server has changed, or a user has selected the wrong directory server.

Figure 25-5 shows the error message displayed when the specified directory server can't be found. As you can see, it's a very descriptive message that outlines the troubleshooting steps to follow:

🖝 Check for network connectivity.

🖝 Confirm the spelling of the server name.

🖝 Change to a different directory server.

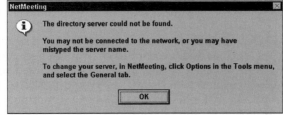

Figure 25-5:
Trouble-
shooting a
directory
server
access
problem.

Once network failures and spelling failures are ruled out, follow the steps in the error message in Figure 25-5 to change to a different directory server.

If you cannot access a directory server, try placing the NetMeeting using the IP address of the remote computer.

Tuning audio and video

After connecting to a NetMeeting call, audio and video problems occasionally arise. Use the audio tuning wizard to adjust audio settings for better reception. Lab 25-4 details the steps in running the audio tuning wizard.

Lab 25-4 Using the Audio Tuning Wizard

1. **Start the audio tuning wizard in NetMeeting by choosing Tools⇨ Audio Tuning Wizard. Click Next on the first page of the wizard to begin tuning settings.**

2. **The second screen of the wizard presents the installed audio devices on the machine. Select the correct device from the Recording drop-down menu, then from the Playback drop-down menu. Click Next to advance to the next wizard screen.**

3. **The third screen of the wizard lets you test the volume of speakers or headphones. Click the Test button near the bottom of the wizard screen; then use the Volume slide bar to select a comfortable volume. Once you've tuned the volume, click Next to advance to the next wizard screen.**

4. **The fourth screen allows you to adjust the recording volume of the microphone. Read the script displayed in the center of the wizard screen. The wizard automatically adjusts the recording volume as you read. Click Next to advance to the next screen.**

5. **The final screen appears, informing you that you've reached the end of the audio tuning wizard. Click Finish to end the wizard.**

Sometimes NetMeeting users find that they cannot send and receive audio at the same time. This is like being on a speaker phone. When one person in the room is speaking, you cannot hear audio from the other caller and vice versa. To send and receive audio simultaneously, the system must have a full-duplex sound card installed and enabled. Follow the steps in Lab 25-5 to enable full-duplex audio.

Lab 25-5   Enabling Full-Duplex Audio

1. **In NetMeeting, choose Tools⇨Options.**

2. **In the Options dialog box, select the Audio tab.**

3. **Check the box next to** Enable full-duplex audio so you can speak while receiving audio. **Click OK to close the Options dialog box.**

The most common video problem encountered during NetMeeting is very easy to resolve. Users often complain that the video doesn't begin sending when a call begins. Sending video as the call begins is a configurable setting. If you don't enable this setting, a caller must press the Start button to begin sending video, then the Stop button to stop sending. To enable automatic video sending, follow the steps in Lab 25-6 below.

Lab 25-6   Sending Video Automatically

1. **In NetMeeting, select Tools⇨Options.**

2. **In the Options dialog box, select the Video tab.**

3. **On the Video tab, check the box next to** Automatically send video at the start of each call. **Click OK to close the Options dialog box.**

Prep Test

1 Dennis is a corporate administrator at a company with Windows 98 and Windows NT 4.0 client computers. One of the company employees is unable to access e-mail messages. While troubleshooting the problem, Dennis can see no obvious reason that the Outlook Express application isn't working. What should Dennis do next?

A ○ Dennis should reinstall Outlook Express.

B ○ Dennis should turn on the mail logging files.

C ○ Dennis should run the Outlook Express tuning wizard.

D ○ Dennis should build a new mail server.

2 Jerry is troubleshooting a user's NetMeeting problem. When the user begins a NetMeeting call, the camera does not send video to the other caller. What should Jerry check first?

A ○ Jerry should check to make sure the camera is connected.

B ○ Jerry should make sure the user is connected to a directory server.

C ○ Jerry should verify that a full-duplex card is installed.

D ○ Jerry should verify that Automatically send video at the start of each call is enabled.

3 David is trying to establish a NetMeeting call with a coworker. He is unable to connect to the corporate directory server. Is there any way that David can establish the call without access to the directory server?

A ○ Yes. If David knows the IP address of the computer he is trying to call, he can dial the computer using the IP address.

B ○ No. Without access to the directory server, David will be unable to place NetMeeting calls.

4 (True/False) Unless you have a video camera installed on your computer, you won't be able to send and receive video.

A ○ True

B ○ False

5 Dennis is a corporate administrator and has created and deployed a custom IE5 browser package with NetMeeting and Outlook Express included. Dennis receives a call from a NetMeeting user who is unable to distinctly hear NetMeeting calls. What should Dennis instruct the user to do to resolve this problem?

A ❏ Dennis should tell the user to make sure his speakers are properly connected.

B ❏ Dennis should tell the user to change to a different directory server.

C ❏ Dennis should tell the user to run the Audio Tuning wizard.

D ❏ Dennis should turn on the log files to locate the NetMeeting problem.

6 Dennis is a corporate administrator and has created and deployed a custom IE5 browser package with NetMeeting and Outlook Express included. Dennis receives a problem call from a NetMeeting user who is unable to access a directory server. In what order should Dennis perform the following troubleshooting steps?

1. Check network connectivity.
2. Check connections for speakers and cameras.
3. Verify the name of the directory server.

A ○ 1, 2, 3

B ○ 3, 2, 1

C ○ 2, 1, 3

D ○ 3, 1, 2

Answers

1 *B.* Dennis should turn on the mail logging files. Outlook Express tracks all commands exchanged with a server in one of four log files: POP3, NNTP, IMAP, and HTTP. Reinstalling Outlook Express and building a new mail server will not resolve the issue if there is a configuration problem on the client computer. Answer C is incorrect because there is no Outlook Express tuning wizard. *Review "Using Outlook Express Logs."*

2 *A.* Jerry should check to make sure that the camera is connected. Although answer D is also correct, Jerry should first make sure that the camera is properly installed. Checking for a directory server connection is not helpful after the call is in progress, because the caller has already connected. Answer C is incorrect because full-duplex pertains to sound cards, not video cards. *Review "Troubleshooting NetMeeting."*

3 *A. Yes.* If David knows the IP address of the computer he is trying to call, he can dial the computer using the IP address. The directory server keeps an up-to-date list of user names and corresponding IP addresses. But if David can obtain his coworker's IP address, he can place the call by "dialing" the IP address. *Review "Directory Server Errors."*

4 *B. False.* Without a video camera, you cannot send video to other callers, but you can still receive video sent by other callers. *See "Troubleshooting NetMeeting."*

5 *A and C.* Dennis should tell the user to make sure that his speakers are properly connected. Dennis should tell the user to run the Audio Tuning wizard. Unless the user first makes certain the speakers are connected properly, running the Audio Tuning wizard may not help. Changing the directory server will not improve the audio reception, nor will turning on log files. *Review "Tuning Audio and Video."*

6 *D. 3, 1, 2.* Because the problem is connecting to a directory server, Dennis should first verify the name of the directory server, then make sure the computer has network connectivity. Checking speaker and camera connections will not help in accessing a directory server, so this would be the last step Dennis should take in this scenario. If the problem involved audio/video reception problems, the correct order of steps would be that in Answer C. *Review "Troubleshooting NetMeeting."*

Part VIII
The Part of Tens

The 5th Wave   By Rich Tennant

"As a candidate for network administrator, how well versed are you in remote connectivity protocols?"

In This Part...

No *For Dummies* book is complete without a Part of Tens! The Part of Tens contains lists, tips, and resources that help you with the exam or with the material covered in the book. We group these items into lists of ten because . . . well, uh . . . because we just do it that way! Anyway, in this Part of Tens you'll find ten tips to help you succeed on the IEAK exam, and ten on-line resources that enhance your understanding of the IEAK.

Chapter 26

Ten Tips for Exam Success

Set a Goal, Set a Schedule

Schedule a date for your exam, and then create a study schedule. You can remain motivated to study more easily when you have an exam date on the calendar.

Know Your Body Clock

Study during your own prime-time hours. If you're a morning person, then mornings may be the best time for you to study. I'm a night person and study best during the evening hours. Forty-five minutes is the longest amount of time I study before taking a break. Any longer than that and I have trouble concentrating. After a 15-minute break, I hit the books for another 45 minutes.

Read the TOC of Each Chapter

Reading the TOC, or table of contents, before beginning a new chapter fixes the topics and their relationships in your mind. It helps you to avoid wondering "Why am I reading this?" while you're reading the text.

Review the Exam Objectives

Always review the exam objectives of a chapter. You may find it easier to digest the information when it's clearly associated with an objective.

Take Notes Effectively

Don't spend a lot of time writing out lengthy study notes. Instead, highlight relevant information in the text as you read the chapter. When you finish the chapter, go back and reread the highlighted passages. Finally, jot down words and brief phrases to trigger recall of the information you just read. When you can read an exam objective and construct an answer based on these brief notes, you know that you're ready for the exam.

Take Practice Exams

Don't take a practice exam until you feel that you're ready for the exam. If you miss an answer, go back and study that section of the chapter again. Then review the exam question so that the answer makes sense to you. Memorizing the answer to a question does little good unless you understand the concepts behind that answer.

Visit the Test Center Before Taking the Exam

The testing environment is important. Ask about seat numbering so that when you call to schedule the exam you can ask for the best seat. Don't take the seat next to the printer! Sitting next to people waiting for their results to print out is very distracting. Also, avoid the seat closest to the door.

Find a Study Partner

Study with a partner so that you can stay on a preset study schedule. Set the same exam dates so that you and your partner can push each other to stick to the schedule.

Develop Acronyms and Word Games

If you're having trouble remembering a lengthy list of items, make up an acronym from the first letter of each item in the list. If that doesn't work, create a rhyme or a silly sentence by using the words in the list. When you enter the exam room, write this memory jogger on the scratch paper immediately so that you have it handy to refresh your memory.

Review, Review, Review

After reading through all the chapters, schedule at least two review sessions. During the first review, reread highlighted text and jot down brief notes. During the second review, read the exam objectives and construct answers from your notes. Finally, read the exam objectives and answer the questions without using notes.

Chapter 27

Ten Online Resources

In This Chapter

▶ Utilizing the Microsoft Web site

▶ Surfing other online resources

*M*ost of the good information about the Internet Explorer Administration Kit is available from the Microsoft Web site. But you have to jump around a bit to find some of it. The ten online resources listed in this chapter will be most helpful to you in preparing for the exam.

IEAK Home Page

http://www.microsoft.com/windows/ieak/

The IEAK Home Page is the starting point for downloading the IEAK. This page provides great analysis of all the features of IE5 and the IEAK.

Corporate Deployment Guide

http://www.microsoft.com/windows/ieak/en/deploy/Corp/

The Corporate Deployment Guide provides comprehensive, screen-by-screen explanations and information on using the IEAK in the corporate administrator role.

Internet Service Provider Deployment Guide

```
http://www.microsoft.com/windows/ieak/en/deploy/ISP/
```

Similar to the Corporate Deployment Guide, this document provides screen-by-screen information from the ISP perspective.

Courtesy Licenses

```
http://www.microsoft.com/Windows/ieak/en/licensing
    /courtesy/
```

If you're like me, you sometimes find that Microsoft's licensing requirements are incomprehensible! This URL takes you to a Web page where Microsoft has provided courtesy copies of the IEAK licensing agreements, which make it much easier for you to determine what licenses you need. The site is also quite helpful when you're trying to determine which role you should choose and how you should report distributed copies of IE5.

Microsoft Seminar Online

```
http://www.microsoft.com/Seminar/1033
/19990916TQN1017AB2/Portal.htm
```

This site features an online seminar on using the Internet Explorer Administration Kit. The seminar, entitled "How to Deploy Internet Explorer 5 Using the Internet Explorer Administration Kit (IEAK)," is a great tool for use at the beginning of your studies.

Self-Study Course

```
http://www.microsoft.com/TechNet/IEAK/training
/c1400.asp
```

At this site, you find a self-study course called "Deploying and Customizing MS Internet Explorer 5 Using the Internet Explorer Administration Kit." Although the course is entry level, the site is a good starting point for your studies.

Internet Explorer Administration Kit Discussion Group

```
http://www.internexis.com/mcp/discnav.htm
```

A discussion group for topics dealing with the Internet Explorer Administration Kit.

Windows NT Magazine

```
http://www.winntmag.com/
```

Windows NT Magazine has published several good articles about using the IEAK. You can find copies of past articles on this Web site. Among the relevant articles are "Automatic Configuration," by Douglas Toombs and "The Guide to Internet Explorer Security Zones," by Mark Joseph Edwards.

Microsoft Windows Update

```
http://windowsupdate.microsoft.com/
```

Check the Windows Update site frequently for information about current security patches and bug fixes. The site posts critical downloads, recommended downloads, and fun-to-have downloads.

MCP Magazine

```
http://www.mcpmag.com/
```

MCP Magazine is a gold mine of information about Microsoft Certification exams. Check its index of past articles for information on the IEAK exam.

Part IX

Appendixes

"We take network security very seriously here."

In this part . . .

The appendix chapters are some extras that we saved for the end of the book. Here you'll find instructions for using the CD that accompanies the book, a practice exam, and some planning tools that help you with the exam and with IEAK projects. Enjoy!

Appendix A

Practice Exam

- -

Practice Exam Rules

▶ You have 75 minutes to complete this exam

▶ You must get 30 correct to pass

▶ You have a total of 40 questions

- -

*T*ry to answer the questions in this test as if you were taking the actual MCSE exam. Avoid looking back through the book for answers. You can review the correct answers and explanations at the end of this chapter.

1 Tom plans to install Internet Explorer 5.0 on his Windows NT Workstation 4.0 computer. He currently uses Internet Explorer 3 and Netscape Navigator. What would be the result of the installation? (Choose two.)

A ❑ Netscape Navigator is replaced.

B ❑ Netscape Navigator is not replaced.

C ❑ Netscape Navigator could be replaced.

D ❑ Internet Explorer 3 is replaced.

E ❑ Internet Explorer 3 is not replaced.

F ❑ Internet Explorer 3 could be replaced.

2 Mike wants to deploy Internet Explorer 5.0 by using a custom package he created with the IEAK. He plans to utilize the hands-free installation option. Which of the following roles allow for this option?

A ○ Corporate Administrator

B ○ Service Provider

C ○ Content Provider/Developer

D ○ All of the above

3 Marci wants to use only one administrative utility to manage system settings, including Internet Explorer 5.0 settings. She supports 75 Windows NT Workstation 4.0 and 5 Windows NT servers. Which of the following provides Marci with this ability?

A ○ Use the Windows NT System Policy Editor to create a CONFIG.POL file.
B ○ Run the IEAK Customization wizard each time a system change is required.
C ○ Use Logon Scripts.
D ○ Import policy files into the IEAK Profile Manager.

4 John wants to deploy Internet Explorer 5.0 and many other custom components by using the IEAK. He's concerned that the package is extremely large for the download media method. What's the maximum number of custom components supported by the IEAK Active Setup?

A ○ 5
B ○ 8
C ○ 10
D ○ 15
E ○ 20

5 George plans to deploy a customized package of Internet Explorer 5.0. He wants to add new Favorites to already existing browsers. How should Jim perform this synchronization?

A ○ Use the Internet Explorer Customization wizard to update the auto-config file.
B ○ Use User Manager for Domains to update the customization database.
C ○ Use customized logon scripts.
D ○ Use Profile Manager to update the auto-config file.

6 Mike is the MIS director for ABC, Inc. Corporate management has advised him that all e-mail leaving the company needs an identification disclaimer. Mike has yet to deploy Outlook Express 5.0. What can Mike do to plan for this request?

A ○ Use a separator file in the Customization wizard.
B ○ Use a signature file in the Customization wizard.
C ○ Use a banner page in the Profile Manager.
D ○ Use a signature file in the Profile Manager.

7 Ryan wants to deploy Internet Explorer 5.0 via a custom package created by using the IEAK. He plans to use the CD-ROM media installation method. Ryan is going to enable his users to install this custom package without his supervision. Which of the following features of the CD-ROM installation method makes Ryan's administration of this deployment simplified?

A ○ Silent Install

B ○ Hands-Free Install

C ○ AVS

D ○ Autorun

E ○ All of the Above

8 Rob wants to deploy a custom package of Internet Explorer 5.0 and other custom components to 250 Windows NT Workstation 4.0 computers. His company requires that users have online audio and video conferences. All users must have the same settings on their desktops due to constant turnover.

Required Result:

All workstations need to use the same mail application.

Optional Results:

All workstations need to participate in audio and video conferencing on the Internet and intranet.

All workstations need to use the same ILS Server.

Proposed Solution:

Create a custom package by using the Customization wizard. Include Outlook Express and NetMeeting in the custom package. Configure the workstations to use the same DNS server.

A ○ The proposed solution produces the required result and both optional results.

B ○ The proposed solution produces the required result and one of the optional results.

C ○ The proposed solution produces the required result and none of the optional results.

D ○ The proposed solution does not produce the required result.

9 Larry plans to deploy a custom package of Internet Explorer 5.0 by using the silent install option to ensure that no user intervention occurs. He wants to use the single floppy disk installation method. Which of the following describes Larry's choices? (Choose two.)

A ❑ A maximum of five download sites can be specified with the silent install.

B ❑ Only one download site can be specified with the silent install.

C ❑ The single floppy disk method cannot be used with the silent install.

D ❑ AVS is not available.

10 Jennifer has already deployed Internet Explorer 5.0 and other custom components by using the IEAK. She needs to modify this deployment, but did not specify and update server. Which of the following is the most appropriate method to perform the update?

A ○ Batch File.

B ○ Have users update their own settings.

C ○ Create and deploy a new custom package.

D ○ Logon Scripts.

11 Michelle works at an Internet Service Provider. She is going to create and deploy a custom package of Internet Explorer 5.0 for ISP customers. What installation method is only available for Internet Service Providers?

A ○ Download

B ○ Single-disk branding

C ○ Multiple floppy disks

D ○ Single floppy disk

12 Tom uses the Corporate Administrator role to set up a custom package of Internet Explorer by using the IEAK. The installation needs to be as easy as possible. What installation method is appropriate in this scenario?

A ○ Single floppy disk

B ○ Multiple floppy disks

C ○ Single-disk branding

D ○ CD-ROM

13 Wayne wants to create and deploy a custom package of Internet Explorer 5.0 by using the Customization wizard. Many of the users he supports share the same computer. Which of the following gives Windows users and Internet Explorer 5.0 users the ability to keep individual preferences and desktop settings?

A ○ User Agent String

B ○ System Policies

C ○ User Profiles

D ○ Computer Profiles

14 Jim plans to create and deploy Internet Explorer 5.0 and many other custom components in his custom package. Which of the following IEAK roles requires Jim to report Internet Explorer 5.0 distribution counts?

A ○ Service Provider

B ○ Content Provider/Developer

C ○ Corporate Administrator

D ○ None of the Above

15 Warren wants to create and deploy a custom package of Internet Explorer 5.0 by using the IEAK Customization wizard. He chooses to install Internet Explorer, Web Folders, NetMeeting, FrontPage Express, Outlook Express, and a few other custom components. When he reaches the Automatic Version Synchronization (AVS) option of the Customization wizard, he sees red X's next to each component. What should Warren do?

A ○ Enable Automatic Version Synchronization.

B ○ Synchronize.

C ○ Close the Customization wizard and then run it again.

D ○ Do nothing; the component is currently updating.

16 James wants to deploy Internet Explorer 5.0 to the 25 users that he supports. James's company currently runs a peer-to-peer network. He wishes to deploy the custom package across the network. What method of installation would James most likely use in this environment?

A ○ Flat

B ○ Download

C ○ Single floppy disk

D ○ Single-disk branding

17 You work for a Web site development company. You constantly download source code from other Internet Web partners. Which of the following security settings allow files to be downloaded without any problems? (Choose all that apply.)

A ❑ Low security on the Internet zone

B ❑ Medium-low security on the Internet zone

C ❑ Medium security on the Internet zone

D ❑ High security on the Internet

18 Which of the following files should you use to build custom Internet Setup files?

A ○ CUSTOM.INS

B ○ SETUP.INS

C ○ INSTALL.INS

D ○ CONFIG.INS

19 Mark wants to free up as much hard drive space as possible. What can Mark do when creating a custom package within the Customization wizard to free up as much space as possible?

A ○ Set Internet Explorer 5.0 to be the only browser on the system.

B ○ Disable saving uninstall information.

C ○ Enable saving uninstall information.

D ○ Set Internet Explorer 5.0 to be the default browser.

20 John makes routine purchases online. He receives messages asking him to submit these requests after processing the request. Security settings have not been modified. How should Internet Explorer 5.0 security be configured on John's machine?

A ○ These sites should be removed from the Restricted Sites zone.

B ○ Add these sites to the Trusted Sites zone, using the default settings.

C ○ Add these sites to the Trusted Sites zone, but the default settings should be changed.

D ○ Add these sites to the Local Intranet zone, using the default settings.

21 Brad wants to use the IEAK Profile Manager to create and modify an Internet Setup file. His intent is to change Internet Explorer 5.0 at regular intervals. What should he do to accomplish this task?

A ○ Modify an existing logon script to download the .INS file.

B ○ Advise all Windows NT Workstation clients to reinstall Internet Explorer 5.0 by using the .INS file when prompted.

C ○ Create a batch file to download the .INS file.

D ○ Instruct the Windows NT Workstation clients to download the .INS file and then synchronize.

22 Tristan wants to deploy Internet Explorer 5.0 by using the IEAK Customization wizard. The auto-config file will be selected as part of the custom package created by the IEAK. By default, when will Internet Explorer 5.0 updates take place on network workstations?

A ○ Daily

B ○ Weekly

C ○ Automatically

D ○ At startup

23 AI accesses the Web site www.datek.com daily. He wants to view the most updated daily version of the page when visiting the site. What Temporary Internet Files setting should he set to accomplish this need?

A ○ **Change** `Check for new versions of stored pages` to `Never`.

B ○ **Change** `Check for new versions of stored pages` to `Automatically`.

C ○ **Change** `Check for new versions of stored pages` to `Every time you start Internet Explorer`.

D ○ **Change** `Check for new versions of stored pages` to `Every visit to the page`.

24 Joe wants the Local Intranet zone and the Trusted Sites zone to be prompted to download signed ActiveX controls. He doesn't, however, want the Internet zone or the Restricted Sites zone to download signed ActiveX controls. What security settings should be applied? (Choose two.)

A ❑ Leave the Internet zone and the Restricted Sites zone at their default settings.

B ❑ Leave the Local Intranet zone and the Trusted Sites zone at their default settings.

C ❑ Customize the Trusted Sites zone security.

D ❑ Set the Internet zone to High.

25 Art, your corporate administrator, determines that the class B IP addresses of 125.192.x.x and 126.192.x.x should be included within the Restricted Sites zone. What restriction should he place in the Restricted Sites zone?

A ○ `*://*.*.*.*`

B ○ `*://125-126.192.x.x`

C ○ `http://125.192.*.*;126.192.*.*`

D ○ `*://125-126.192.*.*`

E ○ `*://255.255.0.0`

26 Bryan uses Internet Explorer 5.0 exclusively. He notices that all the Web sites he accesses don't refresh unless he does it manually with the Refresh button. What should he do to fix the problem?

A ○ Start and restart IE5 more often.

B ○ Change his cache settings.

C ○ Synchronize more often.

D ○ Delete Temporary Internet Files.

27 Junior wants his departmental users to download files from any network location. He does not, however, want users to access Web pages that contain unsigned content. He also wants the logon process to be automated.

> **Required Result:**
> Prevent users from downloading ActiveX and Java controls from untrustworthy sites.
> **Optional Results:**
> Allow file downloads for all sites.
> Require users to automatically logon only in the Intranet zone.
> **Proposed Solution:**
> Change the Internet zone to Low security.

A ○ The proposed solution produces the required result and both optional results.

B ○ The proposed solution produces the required result and one of the optional results.

C ○ The proposed solution produces the required result and none of the optional results.

D ○ The proposed solution does not produce the required result.

28 Malcolm is having difficulty accessing the Web site www.obscure.com. The Web appears to not be functional. What's the problem?

A ○ Browsing the site has been disabled in Content Advisor.

B ○ The proxy server blocks many aspects of the site.

C ○ The site is included in the Restricted Sites zone.

D ○ The site is written poorly.

29 Which of the following security zones is the least utilized with Internet Explorer 5.0?

A ○ My Computer

B ○ Trusted Sites

C ○ Restricted Sites

D ○ Internet

E ○ Local Intranet

30 Which of the following gives Internet Explorer 5.0 the ability to install snap-ins?

A ○ Enable Install on Demand

B ○ Active Desktop

C ○ Windows Desktop Update

D ○ IEAK

31 Mike works for an Internet Service Provider. Paul's ISP doesn't want to gather information about new customers at sign-up. He does, however, want to provide an interface for connection setup. What installation option would work best for Paul's needs?

A ○ Server-based sign-up using the Internet Connection wizard
B ○ Server-based sign-up using full-screen kiosk mode
C ○ Serverless sign-up
D ○ No sign-up

32 Chris works for an Internet Service Provider. He wants to make the installation as easy as possible for ISP customers. He chooses to use the single floppy disk media selection type. Which of the following must also be included during the creation of the custom package when using the Internet Explorer Customization wizard?

A ○ Flat media site
B ○ Multiple floppy disks
C ○ Download site
D ○ A CD-ROM
F ○ Single-disk branding

33 Mark wants to deploy Internet Explorer 5.0 by using a custom package created with the IEAK. His users are going to use Netscape Navigator and Internet Explorer 5.0. The users complain when using IE5 many of the sites they use with Netscape are asking them to download custom components so the sites will function properly. What is the cause of this problem?

A ○ Internet Explorer 5.0 does not import proxy server settings from Netscape.
B ○ Internet Explorer 5.0 does not import plug-ins from Netscape.
C ○ Internet Explorer 5.0 does not import cookies from Netscape.
D ○ Internet Explorer 5.0 does not import security settings from Netscape.

34 Jeff wants to deploy Internet Explorer 5.0 by using the IEAK Customization wizard. Users ask that Internet Explorer 3.0 settings be available with Internet Explorer 5.0.

> **Required Result:**
> Internet Explorer 5.0 must import cookies and Favorites from IE3.
> **Optional Results:**
> Proxy server settings must be imported.
> Plug-ins must be imported.
> **Proposed solution:**
> Use the flat method to install the custom package of Internet Explorer 5.0.

A ○ The proposed solution produces the required result and both optional results.

B ○ The proposed solution produces the required result and one of the optional results.

C ○ The proposed solution produces the required result and none of the optional results.

D ○ The proposed solution does not produce the required result.

35 Jerry plans to make significant changes to Internet Explorer 5.0 after deployment. Most of the users he supports are on his LAN. Which of the following enables Jerry to easily modify Internet Explorer 5.0 browsers with the least amount of administration? (Choose the best answer.)

A ○ Logon Scripts

B ○ IEAK Customization wizard

C ○ User Profiles

D ○ IEAK Profile Manager

36 The Temporary Internet Files folder is taking up significant disk space on the Windows NT Workstation 4.0 that Lyle uses. What can he do to optimize the use of the disk space taken up by Temporary Internet Files?

A ○ Delete the Temporary Internet Files manually.

B ○ Delete the Temporary Internet Files and Clear History manually.

C ○ Set Temporary Internet Files to use a lower disk space percentage.

D ○ Change the location of Temporary Internet Files.

37 Cindy needs to access the LA office. She obtains permission to dial-up remotely by using the office's RAS server. She cannot, however, communicate with the rest of the WAN when connected. What's the problem?

A ○ She needs to use WINS.

B ○ She needs to use the default gateway on the remote network.

C ○ She needs to enable IP forwarding.

D ○ She needs to specify a DNS server addresses.

38 Melissa, Steve, and Susan are trying to connect to their e-mail server. The e-mail server has an IP address of 125.2.125.125. Melissa's IP Address is 75.1.1.50, her Subnet Mask is 255.255.255.0, and her Default Gateway is 75.1.1.10. Steve's IP Address is 75.1.1.51, his Subnet Mask is 255.255.255.0, and his Default Gateway is 75.10.1.10. Susan's IP Address is 148.10.1.52, her Subnet Mask is 255.255.0.0, and her Default Gateway is 148.10.125.125. Melissa and Susan have no problem connecting, but Steve cannot connect. What's the problem?

A ○ Steve has an invalid IP address.
B ○ Steve has an invalid default gateway.
C ○ The e-mail server has an invalid IP address.
D ○ Steve has an invalid subnet mask.

39 Outlook Express is unable to authenticate your request to log on to your mail server. Your SMTP server name is `mail.email.net`. Your POP3 server name is `mail.email.net`. You manually enter your e-mail username and password at each logon. Your Outlook Express configuration is as follows:

SMTP Server: `mail.email.net`
POP3 Server: `mail.email.net`
What is the most likely problem?

A ○ Invalid SMTP server host name
B ○ Invalid POP3 server host name
C ○ Invalid password
D ○ Network congestion

40 Jay wants to deploy a custom package of Internet Explorer 5.0. He's concerned that installation errors may occur when deploying the package. Which of the following files gives Jay troubleshooting information so he can determine errors that occur during the setup of Internet Explorer 5.0?

A ○ Setup Log.txt
B ○ Install Log.txt
C ○ Active Install Log.txt
D ○ Active Setup Log.txt

Answers

1 *B, D.* Any newer version of Internet Explorer replaces a previous version. For example, Internet Explorer 3.0 and Internet Explorer 5.0 cannot coexist on the same system. Internet Explorer 5.0 does not replace Netscape Navigator.

2 *A.* Only the Corporate Administrator has the ability to customize a package of Internet Explorer without user feedback (hands-free installation). The Service Provider role and the Content Provider/Developer role don't allow for this configuration.

3 *D.* The IEAK Profile Manager allows policy files to be imported, which enables additional management of other computer settings besides IE5 settings. The System Policy Editor can be used for the same thing, but the administrator must create .POL files instead of .INS files. A is incorrect because Windows NT by default uses a policy file called NTCONFIG.POL, not CONFIG.POL. Windows 9.*x* clients use CONFIG.POL. Logon scripts require the use of an .INS file, which likely increases management. Answer B isn't a good solution.

4 *C.* The maximum number of custom components that can be added in the Internet Explorer Active Setup is ten.

5 *D.* To modify existing installations of Internet Explorer, run the Profile Manager, open the .INS file you wish to update, and make the appropriate changes. If the auto-config setting is specified in an existing IE5 browser, no additional steps are necessary. Answer A isn't the best solution after a deployment. Answer C would work with this situation, but requires more administration and configuration than using the Profile Manager. Answer B isn't even close.

6 *B.* Signature files are useful for adding a name, address, phone number, return e-mail (even though they just got one from you), and other information to an e-mail sent by a user. The Customization wizard is the best utility to use because the package has yet to be deployed. Therefore, answer B is correct. A separator file and banner page are used with Windows NT and NetWare printing, respectively.

7 *E.* All of the above make an installation of IE5 simplified. The silent install lets administrators make all the custom choices of the package and doesn't allow users to see what's occurring during the installation. The hands-free install, which can be used instead of the silent install, enables administrators to make all the custom choices of the package, but does allow users to see what's occurring during the installation. AVS (Automatic Version Synchronization) checks for latest version information so that the package is up-to-date upon deployment. The Autorun feature is used with CD-ROM custom packages. When a user inserts the CD-ROM, the Autorun program automatically launches the setup.

8 *B.* Outlook Express 5.0 achieves the required result. NetMeeting achieves the first required result. To achieve the second optional result, the custom package needs to have the same LDAP server or ILS server. Therefore, the correct answer is B.

9 *B, C.* The silent install enables corporate administrators to specify only one download site. The single floppy disk method is only available with ISPs. Thus, the silent install method isn't available with the single floppy disk method. AVS is always an option with any role or method.

10 *D.* Creating a custom logon script that downloads an .INS file to the registry of each computer is the best way to modify a previous deployment. Therefore, answer D is correct. Enabling users to update their own settings can result in a lot of unnecessary administration. Creating and deploying a new custom package can cause complaints and require reconfiguration due to the new deployment. Batch files are used with setup files to produce certain results.

11 *D.* The single floppy disk installation method is only available for ISPs. The disk contains enough files to continue the remaining portion of the installation after connecting to the ISPs installation (download) server. Single-disk branding is used to customize an existing installation of Internet Explorer. Multiple floppy disks is available with the Content Provider/Developer, but not the Corporate Administrator role.

12 *D.* The CD-ROM installation method is the appropriate method because of its Autorun support. The single floppy disk installation method is only available for ISPs. Multiple floppy disks is only available to ISPs and Content Provider/Developers. Single-disk branding is used to customize an existing installation of Internet Explorer.

13 *C.* User profiles enable several users to use the same computer and have customizable desktop settings, including Internet Explorer 5.0. These settings are stored within a directory that is specific to each user. The user profile file with Windows NT Workstation 4.0 is called NTUSER.DAT. Hardware or computer profiles are specific to the machine, not the user. A user agent string allows Web sites to track what browsers are accessing the Web site. The system policy editor is used to apply restrictions to the machine by using system policy files.

14 *A.* Microsoft only requires Internet Service Providers (ISPs) to report the amount of browsers distributed.

15 *B.* Three possible symbols can display during the AVS option: Red, Yellow, and Green. Red represents that a component is not downloaded for the Customization wizard to use unless you synchronize. Yellow means that the component isn't updated or that AVS is disabled during this phase of the Customization wizard. Green represents that the latest version of the component is synchronized and downloaded.

16 *A.* The flat install is used for Local Area Networks. Therefore, A is the correct answer. The single floppy disk installation method is only available for ISPs. Single-disk branding is used to customize an existing installation of Internet Explorer. The download method is used primarily in Client/Server environments.

17 *A, B, C.* Five security settings exist: Low, Medium-low, Medium, High, and Custom. All, with the exception of High, allow for file downloads.

18 *C.* The Customization wizard creates the Internet Setup file INSTALL.INS. INSTALL.INS can then be used as a template in creating other .INS files.

19 *B.* Internet Explorer 5.0 backs up uninstall information by default. You must select to disable saving uninstall information, which saves hard drive space.

20 *B.* Adding the URL to the Trusted Sites zone prevents these messages from occurring. The Trusted Sites zone doesn't prompt downloading signed ActiveX controls by default. Therefore, answer B is correct.

21 *A.* Logon scripts are used to download Internet Setup (.INS) files to the registry of each computer. Therefore, answer A is correct. Batch files are used with setup files to produce certain results. Reinstalling is not a good option, and no such procedure to download the .INS file and synchronize exists.

22 *D.* The update interval, if left blank, causes an update to process each time Internet Explorer starts. This setting can later be modified in the IE Profile Manager or manually.

23 *D.* Internet Explorer 5.0 stores frequently visited pages in the Temporary Internet Files directory. Upon revisiting the page, IE accesses the downloaded HTML file from the hard drive, rather than requesting it from the Web site. This speeds up access. Newer versions of the page, however, may not be refreshed. You can modify this setting by going to the Internet Options dialog box, clicking the General tab and the Settings button. Then select the Check for newer versions of stored pages option. In this example, every time Internet Explorer starts would be sufficient. Therefore, D is the correct answer.

24 *C, D.* Low security enables without prompts the downloading of signed ActiveX controls. Medium-low and Medium prompt to download signed ActiveX controls. High security disables the downloading of signed ActiveX controls. The Trusted Sites zone, therefore, doesn't need to be modified, and the Internet zone needs to be given High security. Answers C and D are correct.

25 *D.* The best answer is D. Become familiar with the restriction wildcards that can be placed within zone security.

26 *B.* Changing cache settings to a more frequent refresh rate fixes this problem. Starting and restarting IE5 isn't the answer because Bryan only gets an updated page if he does it manually. Starting and restarting IE5 is actually a cache setting that Bryan can implement. Synchronizing is a feature of subscriptions, which isn't mentioned in this case. Deleting Temporary Internet Files is a one-time fix to the problem, which will occur later if the Temporary Internet Files setting is not modified.

27 *A.* The Internet zone with its default security of Medium allows for file downloads, prevents users from downloading ActiveX and Java controls from unsigned sources, and requires users to automatically logon only in the Intranet zone. By changing the Internet zone to Low security, users are now given the choice via prompts to download unsigned content. Therefore, the required result is not met and answer D is the correct answer.

28 *C.* The Restricted Sites zone enforces High security by default, which may cause the site to not be fully functional. Answer A would completely block the site from being accessed. Answers B and D are invalid conclusions.

29 *A.* The My Computer zone is the least utilized security zone with Internet Explorer. The My Computer zone manages security for files on the local machine and can only be configured from the IEAK Customization wizard and the IEAK Profile Manager. The My Computer zone should be used for specific requirement purposes on local files only.

30 *A.* Enable Install on Demand allows Web sites to install applications so they can be properly viewed.

31 *C.* The `Server-based sign-up using the Internet Connection wizard` installation option is used to exchange information with the setup screens of Internet Explorer, enabling ISPs to gather information about customers to be placed in their database. This installation option also allows connection settings to be implemented. The `Server-based sign-up using full-screen kiosk mode` installation option is similar to the `Server-based sign-up using the Internet Connection wizard` installation option, but doesn't show toolbars during the setup. The `Serverless sign-up` installation option doesn't require a sign-up server and prompts the IEAK user to fill in the connection settings. The `No sign-up` installation option enables users to make their own connections to the Internet. No automated connection procedures are implemented during the install of IE5. Only IE5 is installed.

32 *C.* You must configure an installation server when using the single disk floppy media selection, because all necessary configuration files cannot fit on one floppy disk. Therefore, the Download option is the correct answer.

33 *B.* Internet Explorer 5.0 doesn't import plug-ins and security settings from Netscape. But security settings aren't the problem because the sites were usable with Netscape. Cookies and proxy server settings are imported by IE5 from Netscape.

34 *B.* The installation method has nothing to do with the end result. Internet Explorer 5.0 automatically imports proxy server settings, cookies, and Favorites from Internet Explorer 3.0. IE5 does not, however, import plug-ins. Plug-ins must be reinstalled. Therefore, the correct answer is B.

35 *D.* To easily modify existing installations of Internet Explorer 5.0, run the Internet Explorer Profile Manager. Activating the Profile Manager applies to local or remote users, depending upon the distribution server. Logon scripts also enable Jerry to modify IE5 settings, but they require additional administration compared to Profile Manager. The Customization wizard, in general, is used to deploy IE5. User Profiles store a user's customized desktop settings.

36 *C.* In the General tab of the Internet Options dialog box, click the Settings button. This option enables you to set Internet Explorer to use a lower disk space percentage for Temporary Internet Files. Answers A and B only delete the space used for a period of time. Answer D does nothing in this example.

37 *B.* The problem is a result of not using the default gateway of the remote network. To enable this, select modify the TCP/IP settings of the Connection in Dial-up networking properties.

38 *B.* Steve's IP address and subnet mask are consistent with Melissa's, but his default gateway address is different. Therefore, answer B is correct. The e-mail server's IP address isn't the problem because Melissa and Susan have no problem connecting.

39 *C.* Because the SMTP server and the POP3 server configuration are correct, answers A and B are incorrect. Answer D is also an unlikely answer. Answer C, however, is a problem that does occur during the authentication process.

40 *D.* The Active Setup Log.txt file is useful in determining the cause of setup problems that occur during the Active Setup installation of Internet Explorer 5.0. Answer A is used with the setup of Windows computers. Answers B and C are fictitious log files.

Appendix B

About the CD

*O*n the CD-ROM you can find:

- ✔ The QuickLearn game, a fun way to study for the test
- ✔ Practice and Self-Assessment tests, to make sure you are ready for the real thing
- ✔ Practice test demos from Transcender, QuickCert, and Super Software

System Requirements

Make sure that your computer meets the minimum system requirements listed below. If your computer doesn't match up to most of these requirements, you may have problems using the contents of the CD.

- ✔ A PC with a 486 or faster processor.
- ✔ Microsoft Windows 95 or later.
- ✔ At least 16 MB of total RAM installed on your computer. For best performance, we recommend at least 32 MB of RAM installed.
- ✔ A CD-ROM drive — double-speed (2x) or faster.
- ✔ A sound card for PCs.
- ✔ A monitor capable of displaying at least 256 colors or grayscale.
- ✔ A modem with a speed of at least 14,400 bps.

Important Note: To play the QuickLearn game, you must have a 166 or faster computer running Windows 95 or 98 with SVGA graphics. You must also have Microsoft DirectX 5.0 or later installed. If you do not have DirectX, you can install it from the CD. Just run D:\Directx\dxinstall.exe. Unfortunately, DirectX 5.0 does not run on Windows NT 4.0, so you cannot play the QuickLearn Game on a Windows NT 4.0 or earlier machine.

Using the CD with Microsoft Windows

To install the items from the CD to your hard drive, follow these steps.

1. **Insert the CD into your computer's CD-ROM drive.**

2. **Click Start⇨Run.**

3. **In the dialog box that appears, type** D:\IDG.EXE.

   Replace *D* with the proper drive letter if your CD-ROM drive uses a different letter. (If you don't know the letter, see how your CD-ROM drive is listed under My Computer.)

4. **Click OK.**

   A license agreement window appears.

5. **Read through the license agreement, nod your head, and then click the Accept button if you want to use the CD — after you click Accept, you'll never be bothered by the License Agreement window again.**

   The CD interface Welcome screen appears. The interface is a little program that shows you what's on the CD and coordinates installing the programs and running the demos. The interface basically enables you to click a button or two to make things happen.

6. **Click anywhere on the Welcome screen to enter the interface.**

   Now you are getting to the action. This next screen lists categories for the software on the CD.

7. **To view the items within a category, just click the category's name.**

   A list of programs in the category appears.

8. **For more information about a program, click the program's name.**

   Be sure to read the information that appears. Sometimes a program has its own system requirements or requires you to do a few tricks on your computer before you can install or run the program, and this screen tells you what you might need to do, if necessary.

9. **If you don't want to install the program, click the Back button to return to the previous screen.**

   You can always return to the previous screen by clicking the Back button. This feature allows you to browse the different categories and products and decide what you want to install.

10. **To install a program, click the appropriate Install button.**

    The CD interface drops to the background while the CD installs the program you chose.

11. **To install other items, repeat Steps 7–10.**

12. **When you've finished installing programs, click the Quit button to close the interface.**

    You can eject the CD now. Carefully place it back in the plastic jacket of the book for safekeeping.

In order to run some of the programs on this *MCSE Internet Explorer 5 For Dummies* CD-ROM, you may need to keep the CD inside your CD-ROM drive. This is a Good Thing. Otherwise, the installed program would have required you to install a very large chunk of the program to your hard drive, which may have kept you from installing other software.

What You'll Find

Shareware programs are fully functional, free trial versions of copyrighted programs. If you like particular programs, register with their authors for a nominal fee and receive licenses, enhanced versions, and technical support. Freeware programs are free, copyrighted games, applications, and utilities. You can copy them to as many PCs as you like — free — but they have no technical support. GNU software is governed by its own license, which is included inside the folder of the GNU software. There are no restrictions on distribution of this software. See the GNU license for more details. Trial, demo, or evaluation versions are usually limited either by time or functionality (such as being unable to save projects).

Here's a summary of the software on this CD.

Dummies test prep tools

This CD contains questions related to MCSE Internet Explorer 5 For Dummies. Most of the questions are Internet Explorer Administration Kit topics that you can expect to be on the test. We've also included some questions on other networking topics that may or not be on the current test or covered in the book, but that you will need to perform your job.

QuickLearn game

The QuickLearn Game is the *For Dummies* way of making studying for the Certification exam fun. Well, okay, less painful. OutPost is a DirectX, high-resolution, fast-paced arcade game.

Answer questions to defuse dimensional disrupters and save the universe from a rift in space-time. (The questions come from the same set of questions that the Self-Assessment and Practice Test use, but isn't this way more fun?) Missing a few questions on the real exam almost never results in a rip in the fabric of the universe, so just think how easy it'll be when you get there!

Please note: QUIKLERN.EXE on the CD is just a self-extractor, to simplify the process of copying the game files to your computer. It will not create any shortcuts on your computer's desktop or Start menu.

Note: Don't forget, you need to have DirectX 5.0 or later installed to play the QuickLearn game; and it does not run on Windows NT 4.0.

Practice test

The Practice test is designed to help you get comfortable with the certification testing situation and pinpoint your strengths and weaknesses on the topic. You can accept the default setting of **XX** questions in **XX** minutes, or you can customize the settings. You can choose the number of questions, the amount of time, and even decide which objectives you want to focus on.

After you answer the questions, the Practice test gives you plenty of feedback. You can find out which questions you answered correctly and incorrectly and get statistics on how you did, broken down by objective. Then you can review the questions — all of them, all the ones you missed, all the ones you marked, or a combination of the ones you marked and the ones you missed.

Self-Assessment test

The Self-Assessment test is designed to simulate the actual certification testing situation. You must answer **XX** questions in **XX** minutes. After you answer all the questions, you find out your score and whether you pass or fail — but that's all the feedback you get. If you can pass the Self-Assessment test regularly, you're ready to tackle the real thing.

Links Page

I've also created a Links Page, a handy starting place for accessing the huge amounts of information on the Internet about the certification tests. You can find the page at D:\Links.htm.

Screen saver

A spiffy little screen saver that the Dummies team created. Maybe, like sleeping with the book under your pillow, this can help you learn subliminally! Screen shots of test questions will fill your screen, so when your computer is not doing anything else, it can still be quizzing you! And if you'd like to visit the *Certification For Dummies* Web site, all you have to do is press the space bar while the screen saver is running — your default browser will be launched and send you there! (You might want to keep this in mind if you're the kind of person who hits the space bar to get rid of your screen saver. . . .)

Commercial demos

QuickCert Exam Simulator, from Specialized Solutions

This package from Specialized Solutions offers QuickCert practice tests for several Certification exams. Run the QuickCert Demo to choose the practice test you want to work on. For more information about QuickCert, visit the Specialized Solutions Web site at www.specializedsolutions.com.

Transcender Demo Sampler, from Transcender Corporation

Transcender's demo tests are some of the most popular practice tests available. The Certification Sampler offers demos of many of the exams that Transcender offers.

MCSEprep IE 5, from Super Software

This demo, designed to help you prepare for the Microsoft IE 5 exam, gives you another 20 practice questions. Get lots more by ordering the software. Learn more by visiting the Web site, www.mcseprep.com.

If You've Got Problems (Of the CD Kind)

I tried my best to compile programs that work on most computers with the minimum system requirements. Alas, your computer may differ, and some programs may not work properly for some reason.

The two likeliest problems are that you don't have enough memory (RAM) for the programs you want to use, or you have other programs running that are affecting installation or running of a program. If you get error messages such as Not enough memory or Setup cannot continue, try one or more of these methods and then try using the software again:

- ✔ **Turn off any anti-virus software that you have on your computer.** Installers sometimes mimic virus activity and may make your computer incorrectly believe that it is being infected by a virus.

- ✔ **Close all running programs.** The more programs you're running, the less memory is available to other programs. Installers also typically update files and programs; if you keep other programs running, installation may not work properly.

✔ **In Windows, close the CD interface and run demos or installations directly from Windows Explorer.** The interface itself can tie up system memory, or even conflict with certain kinds of interactive demos. Use Windows Explorer to browse the files on the CD and launch installers or demos.

✔ **Have your local computer store add more RAM to your computer.** This is, admittedly, a drastic and somewhat expensive step. However, adding more memory can really help the speed of your computer and enable more programs to run at the same time.

If you still have trouble installing the items from the CD, please call the IDG Books Worldwide Customer Service telephone number: 800-762-2974 (outside the U.S.: 317-572-3342).

Appendix C

Planning Worksheet
for IEAK Customization Wizard

● ●

*P*lanning is a critical step to creating a customized Internet Explorer 5 deployment. The Internet Explorer Administration Kit (IEAK) gathers a great deal of information while generating your customized configuration. Use this planning worksheet to gather and record all the information for running the IEAK Customization Wizard.

Stage 1: Gathering Information

Company Name:

Customization Code:

Role: (circle one)

   Content Provider/Developer   Service Provider   Corporate Administrator

---

Select a platform to create: (circle one)

   Windows 9x/NT 4.0   Windows 3.11/WFW/NT 3.51   UNIX

Destination folder:

Path of .INS file to import settings from:

Component Download folder:

Target Language:

Media Selection:

   ❏ Download   ❏ Multiple floppy disks

   ❏ CD-ROM   ❏ Single floppy disk

   ❏ Flat   ❏ Single disk branding

Feature Selection:

❑ Setup Customizations	❑ Favorites and Links
❑ Corporate Install Features	❑ Channels
❑ Automatic Digital Signing	❑ User Agent String
❑ Connection Manager	❑ Connections Customization
❑ Browser Customizations	❑ Certificate Customization
❑ URL Customizations	❑ Security Zones and Content Ratings
❑ Desktop Customization	❑ Programs Customization
❑ Outlook Express Customization	❑ Policies and Restrictions

Stage 2: Specifying Setup Parameters

Download Site

Components and versions to download:

Custom components to add:

❑ Component:

❑ Location:

❑ Command:

❑ Parameter:

❑ GUID:

❑ Description:

Stage 3: Customizing Setup

CD Autorun Customizations

❑ Title bar text:

❑ Custom background bitmap location:

❑ Standard text color:

❑ Highlight text color:

❑ Button style: Standard beveled buttons / 3D bitmap buttons /
    Custom button bitmap

More CD Options

❑ More information text file:

❑ Use kiosk mode start page?

❑ Kiosk mode start page HTML file:

Customize Setup

❑ Setup wizard title bar text:

❑ Left Setup wizard bitmap path (first page):

❑ Top Banner Setup wizard path (all pages except first):

❑ Custom Components Installation Title:

Silent Install

○ Interactive Install

○ Hands-free Install

○ Completely Silent Install

Installation Options

❑ Option:

❑ Description:

❑ Components to install:

Component Download

❑ Remove the Windows Update option from the Tools menu

❑ Use the default URL for the Windows Update

❑ Use a custom add-on URL and menu text

  ❑ Menu text for Add-on Component URL:

  ❑ URL of Add-on Component page:

❑ Download components from Microsoft after install?

Installation Directory

    ○ Allow the user to choose the installation directory

    ○ Install in the specified folder within the Windows Folder

    ○ Install in the specified folder within the Program Files folder

    ○ Specify the full path of a custom folder:

Corporate Install Options

    ❏ Disable Custom installation option?

    ❏ Disable saving uninstall information?

    ❏ Disable Internet Explorer Compatibility Mode?

    ❏ Internet Explorer is set as the default browser

    ❏ Internet Explorer is not set as the default browser

    ❏ User Choice

Advanced Installation Options

    ❏ Optimize for web download?

    ❏ Show Custom Components Options screen for:

Connection Manager Customization

    ❏ Path of custom profile:

Windows Desktop Update

Do you want to integrate the Windows Desktop Update in your custom package?   Y   N

Digital Signatures

❑ Company Name on certificate:

❑ Software Publishing Certificates (.SPC) file:

❑ Private Key (.PVK) file:

❑ Description text:

❑ More information URL:

Stage 4: Customizing the Browser

Browser Title

❑ Title Bar Text:

❑ Toolbar background bitmap:

Browser Toolbar Buttons

❑ Delete existing toolbar buttons?

❑ Toolbar caption

❑ Toolbar action (script or executable)

❑ Toolbar color icon

❑ Toolbar grayscale icon

❑ Show on toolbar by default?

Animated Logo

○ Path of small (22x2) custom animated bitmap:

○ Path of large (38x38) custom animated bitmap:

Static Logo

○ Path of small (22x22) custom logo bitmap:

○ Path of large (38x38) custom logo bitmap:

Important URLs

❑ Home page URL:

❑ Search bar URL:

❑ Online support page URL:

Favorites and Links

❑ Favorites to include:

❑ Links to include:

Channels

❏ Channels to add:

❏ Channel categories:

Welcome Page

○ Display default Microsoft Internet Explorer 5 welcome page

○ Do not display a welcome page

○ Use a custom welcome page (specify URL):

Active Desktop

○ Do not customize the Active Desktop

○ Import the current Active Desktop components

○ Path of custom desktop wallpaper file:

Desktop Toolbars

○ Do not customize Desktop Toolbars

○ Import the current Desktop Toolbar settings

Folder Webviews

❏ Path of My Computer custom HTML file:

❏ Path of Control Panel custom HTML file:

User Agent String

❏ Custom string to be appended to user agent string:

Connection Settings

○ Do not customize Connection Settings

○ Import the current Connection Settings

○ Delete existing Connection Settings, if present

Security

❏ Certification Authorities

○ Do not customize Certification Authorities

○ Import current Certification Authorities

❏ Authenticode Security

○ Do not customize Authenticode Security

○ Import current Authenticode Security information

Security Settings

❑ Security Zones

○ Do not customize security zones

○ Import the current security zones settings

❑ Content Ratings

○ Do not customize Content Ratings

○ Import the current Content Ratings settings

Stage 5: Customizing Components

Programs

○ Do not customize Program Settings

○ Import the current Program Settings

Outlook Express Accounts

❑ Incoming mail server:

❑ POP3 or IMAP?

❑ Outgoing mail (SMTP) server:

❑ Internet news (NNTP) server:

❑ Make server names read only?

❑ Disable access to accounts

Outlook Express Custom Content

❏ InfoPane URL:

❏ Local file: ❏ HTML path:

                       ❏ Image path:

❏ Custom welcome message HTML path:

❏ Sender:

❏ Reply-to:

Outlook Express Custom Settings

❏ Make Outlook Express the default program for: ❏ Mail   ❏ News

❏ Specify newsgroups:

❏ Service Name for additional mail accounts:

❏ Service URL for additional mail accounts:

❏ Turn on Junk Mail Filtering?

Outlook Express View Settings

Basic:	❏ Folder bar	❏ Outlook bar	❏ Folder list
	❏ Status bar	❏ Contacts	❏ Tip of the day

Toolbar:	❏ Show toolbar
	❏ Show text on toolbar buttons

Preview pane: ❏ Show preview pane

⭘ Below messages   ⭘ Beside messages

❏ Show preview pane header

Outlook Express Compose Settings

⭘ Append a signature to each message:

⭘ Use a different signature for news messages:

❏ For mail messages, make HTML message composition the default

❏ For news messages, make HTML message composition the default

---

Address Book Directory Service

❏ Service Name:

❏ Server Name:

❏ Logon using SPA?

❏ Service Web Site:

❏ Search Base:

❏ Service Bitmap:

❏ Search Timeout:

❏ Maximum number of matches to return:

❏ Check names against this server when sending mail?

Index

J

K

L

• N •

• M •

• O •

• P •

IDG Books Worldwide, Inc., End-User License Agreement

READ THIS. You should carefully read these terms and conditions before opening the software packet(s) included with this book ("Book"). This is a license agreement ("Agreement") between you and IDG Books Worldwide, Inc. ("IDGB"). By opening the accompanying software packet(s), you acknowledge that you have read and accept the following terms and conditions. If you do not agree and do not want to be bound by such terms and conditions, promptly return the Book and the unopened software packet(s) to the place you obtained them for a full refund.

1. **License Grant.** IDGB grants to you (either an individual or entity) a nonexclusive license to use one copy of the enclosed software program(s) (collectively, the "Software") solely for your own personal or business purposes on a single computer (whether a standard computer or a workstation component of a multiuser network). The Software is in use on a computer when it is loaded into temporary memory (RAM) or installed into permanent memory (hard disk, CD-ROM, or other storage device). IDGB reserves all rights not expressly granted herein.

2. **Ownership.** IDGB is the owner of all right, title, and interest, including copyright, in and to the compilation of the Software recorded on the disk(s) or CD-ROM ("Software Media"). Copyright to the individual programs recorded on the Software Media is owned by the author or other authorized copyright owner of each program. Ownership of the Software and all proprietary rights relating thereto remain with IDGB and its licensers.

3. **Restrictions on Use and Transfer.**

    (a) You may only (i) make one copy of the Software for backup or archival purposes, or (ii) transfer the Software to a single hard disk, provided that you keep the original for backup or archival purposes. You may not (i) rent or lease the Software, (ii) copy or reproduce the Software through a LAN or other network system or through any computer subscriber system or bulletin-board system, or (iii) modify, adapt, or create derivative works based on the Software.

    (b) You may not reverse engineer, decompile, or disassemble the Software. You may transfer the Software and user documentation on a permanent basis, provided that the transferee agrees to accept the terms and conditions of this Agreement and you retain no copies. If the Software is an update or has been updated, any transfer must include the most recent update and all prior versions.

4. **Restrictions on Use of Individual Programs.** You must follow the individual requirements and restrictions detailed for each individual program in Appendix B of this Book. These limitations are also contained in the individual license agreements recorded on the Software Media. These limitations may include a requirement that after using the program for a specified period of time, the user must pay a registration fee or discontinue use. By opening the Software packet(s), you will be agreeing to abide by the licenses and restrictions for these individual programs that are detailed in Appendix B and on the Software Media. None of the material on this Software Media or listed in this Book may ever be redistributed, in original or modified form, for commercial purposes.

5. **Limited Warranty.**

   (a) IDGB warrants that the Software and Software Media are free from defects in materials and workmanship under normal use for a period of sixty (60) days from the date of purchase of this Book. If IDGB receives notification within the warranty period of defects in materials or workmanship, IDGB will replace the defective Software Media.

   (b) IDGB AND THE AUTHOR OF THE BOOK DISCLAIM ALL OTHER WARRANTIES, EXPRESS OR IMPLIED, INCLUDING WITHOUT LIMITATION IMPLIED WARRANTIES OF MERCHANTABILITY AND FITNESS FOR A PARTICULAR PURPOSE, WITH RESPECT TO THE SOFTWARE, THE PROGRAMS, THE SOURCE CODE CONTAINED THEREIN, AND/OR THE TECHNIQUES DESCRIBED IN THIS BOOK. IDGB DOES NOT WARRANT THAT THE FUNCTIONS CONTAINED IN THE SOFTWARE WILL MEET YOUR REQUIRE-MENTS OR THAT THE OPERATION OF THE SOFTWARE WILL BE ERROR FREE.

   (c) This limited warranty gives you specific legal rights, and you may have other rights that vary from jurisdiction to jurisdiction.

6. **Remedies.**

   (a) IDGB's entire liability and your exclusive remedy for defects in materials and workmanship shall be limited to replacement of the Software Media, which may be returned to IDGB with a copy of your receipt at the following address: Software Media Fulfillment Department, Attn.: *MCSE Internet Explorer 5 For Dummies,* IDG Books Worldwide, Inc., 10475 Crosspoint Boulevard, Indianapolis, IN 46256, or call 800-762-2974. Please allow three to four weeks for delivery. This Limited Warranty is void if failure of the Software Media has resulted from accident, abuse, or misapplication. Any replacement Software Media will be warranted for the remainder of the original warranty period or thirty (30) days, whichever is longer.

   (b) In no event shall IDGB or the author be liable for any damages whatsoever (including without limitation damages for loss of business profits, business interruption, loss of business information, or any other pecuniary loss) arising from the use of or inability to use the Book or the Software, even if IDGB has been advised of the possibility of such damages.

   (c) Because some jurisdictions do not allow the exclusion or limitation of liability for consequential or incidental damages, the above limitation or exclusion may not apply to you.

7. **U.S. Government Restricted Rights.** Use, duplication, or disclosure of the Software by the U.S. Government is subject to restrictions stated in paragraph (c)(1)(ii) of the Rights in Technical Data and Computer Software clause of DFARS 252.227-7013, and in subparagraphs (a) through (d) of the Commercial Computer–Restricted Rights clause at FAR 52.227-19, and in similar clauses in the NASA FAR supplement, when applicable.

8. **General.** This Agreement constitutes the entire understanding of the parties and revokes and supersedes all prior agreements, oral or written, between them and may not be modified or amended except in a writing signed by both parties hereto that specifically refers to this Agreement. This Agreement shall take precedence over any other documents that may be in conflict herewith. If any one or more provisions contained in this Agreement are held by any court or tribunal to be invalid, illegal, or otherwise unenforceable, each and every other provision shall remain in full force and effect.

Installation Instructions

To install the items from the CD to your hard drive, follow these steps.

1. **Insert the CD into your computer's CD-ROM drive.**

2. **Click Start⇨Run**

3. **In the dialog box that appears, type** D:\IDG.EXE.

   Replace D with the proper drive letter if your CD-ROM drive uses a different letter. (If you don't know the letter, see how your CD-ROM drive is listed under My Computer.)

4. **Click OK.**

   A license agreement window appears.

5. **Read through the license agreement, nod your head, and then click the Accept button if you want to use the CD — after you click Accept, you'll never be bothered by the License Agreement window again.**

   The CD interface Welcome screen appears. The interface is a little program that shows you what's on the CD and coordinates installing the programs and running the demos. The interface basically enables you to click a button or two to make things happen.

6. **Click anywhere on the Welcome screen to enter the interface.**

   Now you are getting to the action. This next screen lists categories for the software on the CD.

7. **To view the items within a category, just click the category's name.**

   A list of programs in the category appears.

8. **For more information about a program, click the program's name.**

   Be sure to read the information that appears. Sometimes a program has its own system requirements or requires you to do a few tricks on your computer before you can install or run the program, and this screen tells you what you might need to do, if necessary.

9. **To install a program, click the appropriate Install button.**

   The CD interface drops to the background while the CD installs the program you chose.